WHAT MATTERS IN P

Change, values and lea
turbulent time

Auke van Dijk, Frank Hoogewoning
and Maurice Punch

First published in Great Britain in 2015 by

Policy Press
University of Bristol
1-9 Old Park Hill
Bristol
BS2 8BB
UK
t: +44 (0)117 954 5940
pp-info@bristol.ac.uk
www.policypress.co.uk

North America office:
Policy Press
c/o The University of Chicago Press
1427 East 60th Street
Chicago, IL 60637, USA
t: +1 773 702 7700
f: +1 773-702-9756
sales@press.uchicago.edu
www.press.uchicago.edu

British Library Cataloguing in Publication Data
A catalogue record for this book is available from the British Library

Library of Congress Cataloging-in-Publication Data
A catalog record for this book has been requested

ISBN 978-1-4473-2692-2 paperback
ISBN 978-1-4473-2691-5 hardcover
ISBN 978-1-4473-2695-3 ePub
ISBN 978-1-4473-2696-0 Kindle

Cover design by Hayes Design
Front cover image: www.alamy.com
Printed and bound in Great Britain by CMP, Poole
Policy Press uses environmentally responsible print partners

Contents

Acknowledgements   v
Abbreviations   vii
Foreword: a crisis in public policing   xi
Preface   xiii

one	**Policing in perilous times: change and leadership**	**1**
	What matters?	1
	System change and leadership	4
	Policing in the Netherlands	6
	Policing in the UK	9
	Drivers of change	10
	Inhibitions to change	16
	Leadership in policing	19
	Matters of concern	23

two	**Police systems, perspectives and contested paradigms**	**29**
	Police systems	29
	Brodeur: low and high policing, militarised policing	32
	Policing paradigms	38
	British policing: paradigm shift	45
	The Netherlands: paradigm lost	51
	Contested paradigms and fuzzy rhetoric	60
	Centralisation and regression to the mean	64
	Conclusion	66

three	**Sea of troubles: the nature of policing**	**69**
	The nature of policing	69
	Police organisation	76
	Police occupational culture	79
	Deviance, corruption and the 'enemy within'	84
	Accountability	87
	Conclusion	91

four	**When matters become 'really real': commanding operations**	**95**
	Major incidents and leadership	97
	'Command and control' in British policing	121
	'Command and control' in Dutch policing	125
	Conclusion	128

five	**Leadership and leadership development**	**133**
	Exploring leadership	133
	Implications for police leadership	140
	Developing police leaders	144
	Making it to the top in England and Wales	151
	Making it to the top in the Netherlands	156
	Leadership development: necessary ingredients	168
	Conclusion	174

six	**Towards a comprehensive paradigm**	**177**
	Beyond cutting crime	177
	Symbolic value of policing	180
	Reflective practitioners and honest policing	181
	Comprehensive paradigm	183
	Conclusion	185

Appendix	**187**
Part One: Two cases of why COP falls short of its promise: London and Seattle	188
Part Two: Netherlands, Amsterdam: agora, safe haven for confrontational thinking	197

References	201
Index	219

Acknowledgements

In February 2013, we visited the UK and would like to thank the following for their willingness to meet with us and share their ideas, which was most valuable: Professor Ben Bowling (King's College London); Professor Robert Reiner, Dr Janet Foster, Dr Jennifer Brown (London School of Economics); Julian Dixon (Inspector, British Transport Police); Geoffrey Markham (former Assistant Chief Constable, Essex Police); Stan Gilmour (Detective Superintendent, Thames Valley Police); and Professor Peter Neyroud (Visiting Fellow Nuffield College, Oxford; Resident Scholar at the Institute of Criminology, Cambridge; former Chief Constable of Thames Valley Police and previously Chief Executive Officer of the former National Police Improvement Agency). In particular, we are grateful to Peter Neyroud for his hospitality at Nuffield College and for his illuminating presentation and discussion on leadership, change, knowledge and professionalisation in British policing.

We also drew on the expertise of a number of colleagues through visits, Skype and phone calls on one or more occasions, and much appreciate the useful information and insights from Professor Michael Useem and Preston Cline (Center for Leadership and Change Management, Wharton School, University of Pennsylvania); Professor Steve Savage (University of Portsmouth); Professor Philip Stenning (Griffith University); Professor Andrew Goldsmith (Flinders University); Ralph Crawshaw (former Chief Superintendent, Essex Police); Dr Jonathan Crego (Critical Simulations Ltd, Hydra Foundation and University of Liverpool); Warwick Jones and Vicki Herrington (Australian Institute of Police Management); Dr Steve Tong (Canterbury Christ Church University); Professor Peter Manning (Northeastern University); Professor David Bayley (State University of New York, Albany); Professor Paul Rock (London School of Economics); Dennis Weeks (Metropolitan Police Federation); Caroline Geradts (National Police, Amsterdam Unit); Pierre van Steen (Commissioner, National Police, Amsterdam Unit); Nick Hogeveen (photographer, National Police, Amsterdam Unit); Chris Noble (Chief Superintendent, Police Service of Northern Ireland); and Richie Adams (Chief Inspector, Police Scotland).

Our gratitude also extends to those who commented critically and valuably on the draft text – Ben Bowling, Jennifer Brown, Robert Reiner, Peter Manning, Clifford Shearing and Bernard Welten – and for the thoroughness of the three anonymous reviewers. We also much appreciate the amicable professionalism of the team at Policy Press. Finally, we would especially like to thank our partners, Connie, Christa and Corry, and other family members for their support and encouragement while writing this book.

Auke van Dijk, Frank Hoogewoning and Maurice Punch
Baarn/Leiderdorp/Amstelveen, January 2015

Abbreviations

United Kingdom

We use 'UK' when referring to the society comprising England, Wales, Northern Ireland and Scotland, and 'British' – with excuses for any offence – for the police forces of England, Wales, Northern Ireland and Scotland. Much of our material on British policing relates to England and Wales and we shall indicate when that is not the case. There are, in fact, three separate police systems, so there is no single UK model, but they do have some common roots and features, and people frequently refer to the 'British policing model'. In recent years, all three systems have been subject to substantial change. For example, the Association of Chief Police Officers (ACPO, England and Wales) has been abolished and the Council of Chief Officers, which was the central part of ACPO, has become the National Police Chiefs Council (NPCC) (Parker Report, 2014). ACPO was formally a limited company, with considerable influence but rather unclear accountability, and comprised nearly 300 members including all chief officers and some other police related personnel. Policing in Northern Ireland, which was always closer to the 'colonial' model of policing within a separate administrative and judicial framework, is conducted by a single force, has become closer to policing in England and Wales in recent years (with chief officers attending ACPO, although not in a formal capacity), and follows much of the legislation passed in England and Wales. There are sometimes amendments to that legislation and to governance to fit the specific circumstances of Northern Ireland. Scotland has always had its own distinct judicial system and had an Association of Chief Police Officers Scotland (ACPOS) until 2013, when it formed a single, national force with one Chief Constable. For clarification, 'chief officers' refer in most British forces to Assistant Chief Constable (ACC), Deputy Chief Constable (DCC) and Chief Constable (CC). London's Metropolitan Police Service (MPS or colloquially 'the Met') uses different terms for chief officers while the chief is known as 'Commissioner'. The other ranks are constable, sergeant, inspector, chief inspector, superintendent and chief superintendent.

ACC   Assistant Chief Constable
ACPO   Association of Chief Police Officers (England and Wales) (until 2015)

ACPOS	Association of Chief Police Officers Scotland (until the founding of Police Scotland in 2013)
BPM	British policing model
CC	Chief Constable
COBRA	Cabinet Office Briefing Room A (government's crisis facility for multi-agency consultation and coordination)
DCC	Deputy Chief Constable
HMIC	Her Majesty's Inspectorate of Constabulary
HPDS	High Potential Development Scheme
IPCC	Independent Police Complaints Commission
IRA	Irish Republican Army
LSE	London School of Economics
MACP	Military aid to the civil power
MI5	Security service
MODACE	Management of disasters and civil emergencies
MOPAC	Mayor's Office for Police and Crime (London)
MPS	Metropolitan Police Service (London)
NCA	National Crime Agency (since 2013)
NPCC	National Police Chiefs Council
NPIA	National Police Improvement Agency (until 2011)
PCC	Police and Crime Commissioner (since 2012)
PNAC	Police National Assessment Centre
PSI	Policy Studies Institute
PSNI	Police Service of Northern Ireland (since 2001)
PS	Police Scotland (since 2013, officially 'Police Service of Scotland')
RIC	Royal Irish Constabulary (1836-1922)
RUC	Royal Ulster Constabulary (1922-2001)
SAS	Special Air Services Regiment (referred to with certain other military units as 'Special Forces')
SCC	Strategic Command Course
SOCA	Serious Organised Crime Agency (2006-13)
SYP	South Yorkshire Police
WYP	West Yorkshire Police

Netherlands

'The Netherlands' is the formal name for the Dutch state, although 'Holland' is often used as a synonym; this is incorrect. The police ranks (with rough British equivalents) are *agent* (constable), *hoofdagent* (senior constable), *brigadier* (sergeant), *inspecteur* (inspector), *hoofdinspecteur* (chief inspector), *commissaris* (superintendent and chief superintendent), and *hoofdcommissaris* (chief commissioner). The latter is a rank so there may have been more than one *hoofdcommissaris* in a force but only one who was *Korpschef* (Chief of Police). There is now only one *Korpschef* in the country, referred to as 'First Chief Commissioner of Police'.

AIVD	General Intelligence and Security Service (*Algemene Inlichtingen- en Veiligheidsdienst*)
CCPC	Council of Chief Police Commissioners (*Raad van Hoofdcommissarissen*) (until the founding of the National Police in 2013)
DPA	Dutch Police Academy (*Politie Academie*) (since 2004)
KLPD	National Police Services Agency (*Korps Landelijke Politiediensten*) (this was a central services and investigatory agency alongside the 25 regional forces since 1993)
LE	Since 2013 the 11th 'unit' – National Unit (*Landelijke Eenheid*) within the NP – which has absorbed the former KLPD
LSOP	Central Selection and Training Institute for the Police (*Landelijk Selectie en Opleidingsinstituut Politie*) (1992–2004)
ME	Mobile Unit (*Mobiele Eenheid*) (public order unit)
NP	National Police (*Nationale Politie*) (since 2013)
NPA	Netherlands Police Academy (*Nederlandse Politie Academie*) (only for senior officer training, until 1994)[1]
SGBO	Staff Large-scale and Special Operations (*Staf Grootschalig en Bijzonder Optreden*)
SPL	School for Police Leadership (*School voor Politie Leiderschap*)
WGPL	Working Group on Police Leadership (*Werkgroep Operationeel Leiderschap Nationale Politie: Werkgroep Welten*)

Other

CCTV	Closed circuit television
CEO	Chief Executive Officer
COP	Community-oriented policing (usually 'community policing')
CRS	*Compagnies républicaines de sécurité*
EU	European Union
FBI	Federal Bureau of Investigation

ICT	Information and Communication Technology
MBA	Master in Business Administration
NIJ	National Institute of Justice (US)
NGO	Non-governmental organisation
NOP	Neighbourhood-oriented policing (usually 'neighbourhood policing')
NPM	New Public Management
NYPD	New York City Police Department
POP	Problem-oriented policing
RCMP	Royal Canadian Mounted Police
SWAT	Special Weapons and Tactics
UN	United Nations
WTO	World Trade Organization
WWI	World War One
WWII	World War Two

Foreword: a crisis in public policing

Crime has gone down, yet the police are in crisis. The police forces of two states studied in this book – the UK and the Netherlands – have been going through their most convulsive changes since the 1960s. The Dutch system, after decades of devolved forces, has been centralised into a single national force. In the UK, Scotland has adopted the Dutch or Nordic model of a single force, and England and Wales has decentralised and imposed a radical change in democratic oversight. All the changes have a common driver in the perception that public policing needs to be reformed to meet future challenges and to respond to past and present problems. The very fact that crime has gone down across the developed world has allowed a political stock take of the investment in policing and a reassessment of its relative contribution against other public services at a time of deep austerity. Cybercrime, people trafficking and organised crime have presented challenges to public policing to which the 20th-century model cannot respond effectively. Bounded by geography, public policing has struggled to find ways to tackle crimes without boundaries. Meanwhile, police legitimacy in their core mission has been under pressure. On the one hand, the very deterrence-based strategies – particularly stop and search – that were deployed to reduce crime in public places have created a gulf between police and young people and minority communities. On the other, there have been failures to tackle domestic violence and the sexual exploitation of children. Hence this study of police leadership is timely and insightful.

The Netherlands and the UK have shared a common approach to many policing issues for several decades. Both have sought to develop a consent-based, community-focused model. Both have wrestled with the need to balance local control of priorities with national strategic requirements within a unitary state. Both have been edging towards a more professional framework for education and ways of enhancing the contribution of research and knowledge into practice. Neither has yet been wholly successful. This book is a product of the type of partnership between academic and practitioner that is critical to that ambition. Professor Punch has long been one of the most articulate and insightful commentators on the interface between police science and police practice. Auke van Dijk and Frank Hoogewoning bring their personal experience from the field and their involvement in the reform programme to create the new Dutch National Police. The authors are, thus, well placed to shed light on the paths that police leadership needs to take to build a 21st century public policing to meet the crisis that is currently engulfing the profession.

Peter Neyroud, Institute of Criminology, University of Cambridge, UK

Preface

We write from our diverse backgrounds and roles – having shared a long involvement in research, education and change regarding policing – with considerable concern about the future of public policing. The context in which we write is the reorganisation in 2013 of the Dutch police from a decentralised system with 25 regional forces and a national unit – the National Police Services Agency (*Korps Landelijke Politiediensten*, KLPD) – into a single National Police (*Nationale Politie*) with 10 regional 'units' and one national unit based on the former KLPD. In the wake of that system change, two of us, Auke van Dijk and Frank Hoogewoning, were involved in implementing an assignment from the Chief of the National Police, Gerard Bouman, initially to Bernard Welten, then Head of the School for Police Leadership (SPL), to shape a leadership programme for senior officers to replace the existing courses given at the Dutch Police Academy.[2] Bernard Welten was previously Police Chief of the Regional Police of Amsterdam-Amstelland – now the Amsterdam Police Unit in the new national structure – and chaired the Working Group on Police Leadership (WGPL) that was implementing the assignment from the Chief of the National Police. The WGPL produced a final report (Final Report TOLNP, 2013) to complete the research phase into, as well as the design of, a new leadership programme. This SPL leadership project involved a range of people, from within and without the police, who functioned in the WGPL and, along with van Dijk and Hoogewoning, the members included Professor Bob Hoogenboom (LSE and Nyenrode Business University); Astrid van Gerwen, Jan Nap and Marjanne Rauh of the Dutch Police Academy; Caroline Geradts (National Police, Amsterdam Unit); and Jaco van Hoorn (National Police, Zeeland-West Brabant Unit).

Auke van Dijk and Frank Hoogewoning are policy advisers for strategy and development within the Amsterdam Police Unit of the National Police. Maurice Punch is an academic with a background in police research and education in the UK, US, the Netherlands and other countries and has an advisory role in their specific project. The three of us were involved in helping to deliver a new leadership programme for senior officers. As a part of this process, we examined in some detail developments in the UK, primarily in England and Wales but also Scotland, concerning police leadership and training and also the professionalisation of policing. During and prior to the project, we had many wide-ranging discussions on these themes, which then stimulated us to write this book. We do so independently from that project so that our book cannot be taken as reflecting in any way the official views on the system change in progress. Maurice took the lead in the final writing, but our combined effort drew on diverse policy documents already written by Auke and Frank, or by them with others, and including a joint publication and conference paper by the three of us (van Dijk et al, 2012, 2013). There was throughout a collective shaping of the text on structure, style and content. Yet at the same time as focusing on that delineated project, the three of us are acutely aware that the major institutional changes in the two societies we look at – the Netherlands and the UK, while also touching on other societies including the US – are altering the historic structure and governance systems and, implicitly, the policing 'paradigm' of recent decades. Clearly, these system changes have a potentially huge impact on police leadership and leadership training and have, therefore, to be borne constantly in mind when mulling over 'what matters' in policing.

Notes

[1] The former Netherlands Police Academy – known as the NPA (*Nederlandse Politie Academie*) – was the training institute specifically and exclusively for senior officers; there were separate training 'schools' for the lower ranks. We shall refer to the Dutch Police Academy for the contemporary, broadly tasked institute that opened in 2004.

[2] Other than its name suggests, and unlike police 'academies' in some other countries, the DPA has the broad task of coordinating all selection, training, management development and research for the Dutch police.

ONE

Policing in perilous times: change and leadership

'Some people ask why we are reforming the police. For me, the reason is simple. We need them to be the tough, *no-nonsense crime-fighters* they signed up to become ... the test of the effectiveness of the police, the *sole objective* against which they will be judged ... is their *success in cutting crime*.' (British Home Secretary Theresa May in 2011, quoted in Millie [2013, p 147]; emphasis added)

What matters?

Policing is at a perilous turning-point and its future remains opaque and uncertain. By 'policing' is meant primarily, but not exclusively, the activities of the public police: and it is the public police, and all that it stands for, that is at stake at this time.[1] It has been subject to waves of change for several decades, but the pace of change is accelerating. For police chiefs, it must at times seem like frantic gaming, tackling unforeseen hazards while predators await any slip. Except that the 'game', and its consequences, are real. Those choices taken under persistent pressure from multiple stakeholders will help determine how the next generation of police will function. This is plainly of profound significance because the police organisation is a unique agency with exceptional powers. Indeed, how it functions in a democracy is of vital importance in the relationship of police to the state and the state to its citizens (Manning, 2010). This in turn has implications for the sort of society we live in and how people are treated by the prime and powerful agents of the criminal justice system. Their conduct can influence whether or not people feel they are living in a just society where the police can be trusted (Lerner, 1980; Cook, 2001; Tyler and Huo, 2002).

In essence, there is widespread and major restructuring with shifting criminal justice landscapes. Within that there is (variously) centralisation and economies of scale; new agencies within and without the police accompanied by a degree of fragmentation; a narrowing of the police mandate with a dominant focus on crime reduction;

and a punitive paradigm of justice and incarceration. These have been accompanied by austerity measures yet with relentless pressure for results; intense public and media scrutiny; and alterations in the technology of policing and in the composition of the workforce. Above all, there have been significant developments in accountability embedded in new governance structures. There was, for example, the reform of the police in Northern Ireland, and the founding of the National Police Scotland, which is viewed as the 'most radical change in the history of policing in Scotland in over 100 years' (Fyfe, 2014, p 504); and in England and Wales there has been a stream of measures including the most fundamental reform of governance in over 50 years with the introduction of elected Police and Crime Commissioners (PCCs) in 2012 with ostensibly considerable powers over chief constables (Neyroud Report, 2011; House of Commons, 2013). The Dutch police has become a national force altering the local structure of governance, with roots stretching back some 200 years, and other police systems are undergoing debate, scrutiny and restructuring. These include forces in Eastern Europe, New Zealand, Canada, the US and Scandinavia (Halstrom, 2013).[2] Reform and debate in the US has been overshadowed by the turbulence and societal reactions to the deaths of Afro-American men from police actions during 2014 with President Obama launching a task force on policing in the 21st century (Wolfgang, 2014). In general, the very architecture of policing – and of criminal justice – is changing.

Profound concern is expressed in this book that these changes have the danger of taking policing backwards. Policing in many ways has developed positively in recent decades to be a responsive, caring and multi-faceted agency geared to the needs of diverse groups and its constituent communities. However, the cool wind of neo-liberal ideology and harsh policies threaten to distort that considerable achievement by resorting to a one-sided and misguided insistence on crime reduction, as if policing can be reduced to a one-factor mandate. This can be viewed as destructive of the many positive developments in policing in recent decades while blatantly ignoring the accumulated academic evidence about the nature of crime control and the limited role that police can play in it (Reiner, 2013). For policing is complex and engages in many tasks; it is clearly crucial to law enforcement and to tackling crime, security and safety, but it also carries out, and always has carried out, diverse functions and duties, including responding to the range of problems that citizens approach the police with in search of aid and solutions. The earliest research dwelt on these 'social' and 'peace-keeping' tasks (Bittner, 1967, 1970) while subsequent work has consistently revealed that policing is a 'secret social service' (Punch, 1979b). Also, by the intrinsically sensitive nature of its work, policing raises fundamental issues around justice, rights, abuse of power, privacy, equity, diversity and integrity. As a consequence, it is of prime importance that it is an accountable agency under the democratic rule of law that provides a service to citizens and communities (Manning, 2010). This in turn implies attention to values and to grappling with the dilemmas and choices that accompany policing. In this perspective leadership is complex and demanding, requiring a palette of skills, including the flexibility to shift from the everyday to emergency mode, the ability to lead with authority and the willingness to engage with values and to embrace accountability.

The danger is of a deliberate misunderstanding of the police role; an undermining of its multiple functions by an insistence on one overriding goal and the denigration of social tasks; resort to the false 'force versus service' dichotomy; and a demeaning, top-down, hectoring approach to professionals who carry immense responsibilities. The destructive reductionism of seeing policing as a simple and taken-for-granted matter and of viewing substantial system change as a purely instrumental affair with its reliance on ostensibly value-free management practices from the world of private business, is inimical to the virtues of sound policing. For the latter, there is the accumulated body of knowledge in the 50-odd years of our discipline but especially from work conducted in the past 10 years, including Bayley (2006a), Reiner (2007, 2010), Bowling (2008), Brodeur (2010), Manning (2010), Neyroud Report (2011), Neyroud (2013), Stevens Report (2013), Brown (2014) and other publications and reports from the US, the UK, the Netherlands and elsewhere. In contrast to the issues and evidence raised in this material, you can see in much political discourse the studied neglect of values and the broader functions of the police as well as of the crucial matters of accountability and governance.

Allied to this is the insistence that somehow knowledge driving police practice should be focused predominantly on 'what works?', as if 'scientific' research will produce universally applicable guidelines based on irrefutable evidence. This 'what works?' approach in the sense of evidence-based experimental work has undoubtedly produced valuable material that has enhanced policing practice in a range of areas (Sherman, 2013). It is the leitmotif of this book, however, that 'what works?' should always be superseded by the vital and essential question for any true profession, 'what matters?' (Loader, 2014). Throughout this work, the authors will dwell on many aspects of policing, police leadership and police development, and will offer a comprehensive paradigm to bridge the 'force' and 'service' divide, whereby some politicians focus exclusively on the former while dismissing the latter. This is true of Theresa May's statement above, in which she also asserted that police are not 'social workers'. They may not be social workers as such, but they do perform social tasks and Home Secretary May, in responding to the perennial public concern about crime and safety, is simply erasing that feature of policing and deriding that social role. In contrast, underpinning our choice of subjects, selection of sources and highlighting of themes, there is that insistent demand for reflection on issues, values and choices in the light of 'what matters?'.

System change and leadership

Given these considerations, along with the broad range of police functions and often sensitive nature of police work, it is patently obvious that, more than ever, policing requires clear direction and sound leadership. This is not only because police leaders have to cope with the acute dilemmas and resilient issues that continually confront them, but also, more importantly, because the manner in which that leadership is practically exercised will itself influence the future of policing. This leads to the question as to what police leadership should look like given these complex circumstances. The reorganisation of the Dutch police in 2013, for example, gave rise to a fair number of issues, but a key one was 'what type of leadership is required in the new and challenging situation?'. However, that question of how to refresh leadership development for senior officers cannot be answered without looking at the broader context in which the police organisation has to operate, how this context is changing, and what future developments can be expected. And subsequently, what are the implications gleaned from this for police leadership? Some of these institutional changes may be specific to a particular society, while others may be more generic in nature. On a general level, it appears that constant change and near permanent reorganisation have become a characteristic afflicting many police systems and forces. Developments in recent decades within the UK among its three policing components certainly provide a clear example of that trend. To gain a better understanding of which aspects of the context are specific and which are part of a broader process of restructuring and change, a comparative perspective is adopted to look primarily at police in the Netherlands and in the UK.

The US forms a continual background reference, as it has often led the way in police innovations, saw the beginnings of police research in the 1960s and has produced a rich wealth of scholars, research initiatives, journals and publications. Often, as evidenced by the pioneering work of August Vollmer and O.W. Wilson, US policing has led in change, management and technology and has also produced much of our conceptual vocabulary on policing (Manning, 2010, pp 86-7). There is, however, no US police 'system', and much research focuses disproportionately on patrol work in large cities and in areas of high crime. Moreover, US criminal justice has become disproportionally focused on young, poor males from minority communities with deleterious societal consequences. Taking a comparative perspective, and emphasising diversity in policing and justice systems within various societies, reveals both alternative police practices and fresh conceptual lenses to the US. This further implies that generalising about US policing and applying insights from research there to other societies need to be tempered with caution.

The focus on the UK and the Netherlands in particular is interesting for a number of reasons. First, both policing systems are facing major structural changes, including substantial reform of their educational programmes (Neyroud, 2011; Final Report TOLNP, 2013).The Stevens Report, *Policing for a better Britain* (2013, p 13), for example, states that the British police service faces 'huge changes ahead' and has been 'subject to a radical reform programme instigated by the Government' including the setting up of the new College of Policing. This refers primarily to England and Wales, but some changes will also affect the Police Service of Northern Ireland (PSNI) and Police Scotland. Second, both police systems have produced a range of reports and publications focusing on mission, strategy, operations and leadership that represent a substantial body of thinking about the nature of police work, the police profession and the future direction for policing. The book touches on these throughout. And third, both police agencies have clearly different backgrounds but at the same time seem to struggle with comparable issues. And, although the Dutch police is recognisably 'continental' in its history and structure, it has in recent decades operated closer to the Anglo-Saxon 'consent' paradigm exemplified in the 'British policing model' (derived from 'Peel's Principles' and 'policing by consent', dealt with in Chapter Two) than many other foreign forces. If one is interested in 'lessons to be learnt', it seems sensible to look at police systems that display some resemblance yet at the same time come from a widely different background.[3]

Policing in the Netherlands

The Dutch police system is undergoing the most significant reorganisation in its recent history. To understand the dimensions of this requires some sense of the historic development of the 'French-Continental' model of police – which shaped the Dutch system – and that of the alternative, 'Anglo-Saxon', model. The latter, deriving from the Metropolitan Police in London in the 1820s and other forces, was based on one form of policing under one ministry, which was not armed or militarily trained, and which outside of London was rooted in local control. This model was exported in various forms to the US and what later became known as 'Commonwealth' countries that had been part of the British Empire. We return to this later in Chapter Two when examining the diversity of policing systems.

Modern Dutch democracy dates back some 200 years and was constructed following the French Occupation (1795-1813). Indeed, the Dutch police from its inception in the early 19th century after that occupation continued to reflect strongly the French-Continental model, with diverse forces under several ministries and with local policing coming mostly under direct civil and judicial control (Fijnaut, 2007). This remained the pattern and was maintained, for example, even in the immediate post-war period when there was a necessary restructuring following the German Occupation (1940-45). In that post-war era, there was a large number (148) of municipal forces – *gemeentepolitie* – in cities of a specific size. In the smaller cities and countryside there was the National Police Force (*Rijkspolitie*) – which was divided into 17 regional units and which also performed a number of national tasks.[4] There was too the long-standing Gendarmerie (*Marechaussee*), founded in 1814, for certain duties within the military as well as a variety of policing functions.[5] Hence, there were three sorts of police and 165 forces (counting the 17 *Rijkspolitie* units as 'forces') that ranged in size in the *gemeentepolitie* from around 30 to 3,500 personnel. Three ministries had authority over policing – Justice, Interior and Defence. This system was highly fragmented for such a relatively small society. There was a post-war population of about 8 million, growing to around 17 million now, and a small geographic size. There was, moreover, from the earliest days – and related to that institutional fragmentation – continuous debate and infighting between the ministries about powers, responsibilities and funding and between the separate forces with the ministries about the central-local dimension and among themselves about territory, tasks and coordination. This pattern of a 'war between the police' is fairly typical of multi-agency systems (Brodeur, 2010, p 11). Structurally, this meant in the Netherlands a high level of segregation and duplication – with the three police systems having separate training establishments – while everyone complained that this made change difficult. This was roundly acknowledged as an inexplicably complex matrix of agencies, powers, accountability and governmental control lacking institutional coherence, yet it remained intact into the early 1990s.

Furthermore, of considerable significance for the topic of leadership in Dutch policing is that from the development of democratic government in the late 1840s the Police Law had explicitly stated that the police chief was 'subordinate' to the official authorities appointed by the government and its ministers. This has long been interpreted that the chief is meant to play a rather subservient role. Indeed, when the influential politician Thorbecke was shaping the foundations of Dutch parliamentary democracy in 1848, he pronounced, 'We desire a police of which as little as possible is seen and as little as possible is said' (Meershoek, 2004, p 9). Up to the 1960s, mayors were still firmly reminding police chiefs that policy was their preserve and the chief's function was not to reflect on it but merely to implement it (Zwart, 2004). From the 1970s onwards, however, there emerged, as will be made clear in Chapter Two, a new dynamic of police chiefs pushing for more autonomy and voice. At times they achieved advances only to feel periodic regression. For example, after much debate and planning there was in 1993/94 a substantial reorganisation into 25 regional forces and one central agency through a merging of the *Rijkspolitie* and *gemeentepolitie* into one police system while the *Marechaussee* was not affected by this. Yet the law accompanying this again contained the clause about subordination to the authorities. This was galling to the forward-thinking, media-conscious and at times outspoken chiefs: one of them caustically remarked 'that text in the Law is a political signal: get back in your kennel' (Boin et al, 2003, p 100). Indeed, some contemporary politicians are once more baldly stating that a police chief's only task is to enforce the law fully and not interpret it. Hence a constant thread in Dutch policing has been a fear among politicians of having a 'too independent' police matched by an equally strong police concern of becoming a 'state' police with central direction and low professional freedom for senior officers. This remains highly relevant today.

Running through this near 200 years of developments in policing is a persistent pattern of central steering, but with a high measure of local control, which has been a prominent feature of Dutch society since the emergence of the Dutch Republic in the 16th century (Rietbergen,

2011). It also meant that ministers could long counter critical questions about a specific police matter by calling it a local responsibility and asserting that the minister had no legal authority to intervene (van der Vijver, 2009). And a constant brake on reform in the post-war period was the entrenched position of the mayors, formally responsible for local policing, battling tooth and nail to retain 'their' police forces. It is remarkable, then, that the largest and most far-reaching reform of Dutch policing in nearly two centuries, the formation of a National Police in the period 2010-13, was completed fairly rapidly and decisively (Cornelisse, 2013). This is indicative of a move to the right politically, with a strong focus on crime and security; of a desire by government and the influential Public Prosecution Service to sort out the unwieldy police system with its persistent localism and not always responsive chiefs; and of adopting new-style decision making by cutting through the traditional culture of consultation and consensus that was now clearly viewed as cumbersome, unsatisfactory and time consuming.

This reform was top-down and geared to central control with power wielded by one ministry, which was renamed the Ministry of Security and Justice in 2010, to convey its broader mandate. As a result of this government determination to reform firmly and swiftly, there has been since 2013, for the very first time outside of the German Occupation, a National Police (*Nationale Politie*), which forms a single police force for the entire country with a single chief, the 'First Chief Commissioner' answering directly to one ministry (Security and Justice) in The Hague. There are also 11 'unit' chiefs (10 regional and one central). In terms of the implementation process, this restructuring will involve a massive reorganisation in the next few years. All of the employees will have to be reassigned within what is formally a new organisation.[6] Indeed, with some 64,000 personnel, the National Police has become the largest employer in the country, larger than the Dutch armed forces. This unusually swift policy process in the Netherlands can be analysed in policy terms as drawing on a 'window of opportunity' when a constellation of personalities, interests and proposals combine and foster rapid change (Terpstra and Fyfe, 2014). There was dissatisfaction with the structure of police governance and with police performance; divisiveness at the top of the police; a political shift to the right; a belief in the advantages of centralisation regarding increased coordination, efficiency and effectiveness; and influential 'policy entrepreneurs' arose within government and the Prosecution Service.

Policing in the UK

Since the end of the 20th century, policing in the UK has faced unprecedented change, and this already after three decades of persistent pressure to reform and restructure (Henry and Smith, 2007; Reiner, 2010; Neyroud, 2013). In Northern Ireland, the Royal Ulster Constabulary (RUC) was disbanded following the transformation process after the Good Friday Agreement (1998) had formally ended the 'Troubles' after 30 years of conflict.[7] Following the recommendations of the Patten Report (1999) on police reform, the Police Service of Northern Ireland (PSNI) was founded to replace the RUC and to accord more closely to policing in the rest of the UK. This ended a form of neo-colonial policing in the Province with roots in the early 19th century. There has also been the founding of Police Scotland with one Chief Constable instead of the Association of Chief Police Officers Scotland (ACPOS) and a Scottish Police Board replacing the local police boards. In England and Wales, there has been the introduction of Police and Crime Commissioners. The candidates could stand with a political affiliation, which threatened to compromise the impartiality of police chiefs, there were doubts about the quality of some candidates and the electoral turnout in 2012 was meagre (around 15%), which rather undermined the promise of enhancing local 'democratic' oversight in policing. Furthermore, the new, wide-ranging and multi-tasked College of Policing in England and Wales has the mandate to become an overarching institute regarding the 'professionalisation' of policing and as a research-based foundation for operational policing (College of Policing, 2013). There are no plans for a similar College of Policing in Scotland. Two symbols of the radical change taking place are that Bramshill Police Staff College, which has long played a vital role in the education of generations of officers from home and abroad, and New Scotland Yard, the iconic headquarters of the Metropolitan Police and constant backdrop for TV reports, were both put up for sale in 2014.

These system changes are clearly historic and far reaching. They have also been accompanied in the UK by downsizing and changes to employment conditions so that less will have to do more, but differently, and with an increasing sense of insecurity (Winsor Review, 2013; HMIC, 2014). In England and Wales, this has fostered an adversarial relationship between the government and disgruntled officers – some 30,000 took part in a protest march in 2012 – and an especially abrasive relationship between the Home Secretary and the Police Federation (a trade union in all but name). There has too been a number of damaging scandals and affairs: one source referred to 2012 as an *annus horribilis* for the police, with the service coming under near unprecedented media and oversight scrutiny (Brunger, 2013). Yet 2014 brought a fresh scandal in the Metropolitan Police, which again raised the spectre of grave institutional failings in policing. The accusations concerned questionable practices in certain cases, some historical, including by undercover officers from a covert unit involved in the deep infiltration of diverse activist movements accompanied by manipulating evidence; officers not cooperating fully with a public inquiry; and also corruption in the high-profile Stephen Lawrence case (Ellison Report, 2014).[8] Accompanying this persistent critical spotlight on policing generally are indications of low morale and officers leaving the service early (Anon, 2013; *Guardian*, 2014).[9] Indeed, morale was said to be at 'an all-time low', according to the President of ACPO, Sir Hugh Orde (Reiner, 2013, p 171). This profound concern is also the tenor of the Stevens Report on *Policing for a better Britain* (2013), which is the product of an Independent Police Commission set up by the Opposition Labour Party (meaning that some do not see it as independent). It was chaired by Lord Stevens, a former Met Commissioner and it mentions an 'uncertain future', 'radical reform' and 'tumultuous change' that will require hard choices to be made; in response to a perceived loss of direction, it claims to provide a vision of better policing. It also contains survey data that confirm the presence of low morale among officers along with anxiety and demotivation; and it is accompanied by an impressive and wide-ranging collection of papers on policing from British and foreign academics and practitioners (Brown, 2014).

There is, then, a deep sense of unease if not crisis in policing, especially in England and Wales, with scandals, unrest, demoralisation and officers resigning early in their career. There was a reform agenda that began to be shaped early in the last decade by a police elite calling for change and for a Royal Commission on the police as the last one was in 1964 (Blair, 2005). The Stevens Commission represents the latest and most explicit formulation of what the reformists would have liked to have seen in a Royal Commission 50 years on. But the Cameron-led Conservative–Liberal Democrat government is in a hurry to further reform policing. It desires a police service that costs less yet performs better and is judged by the single, overriding goal of reducing crime.

Drivers of change

Permeating this work is the insistent realisation that in many Western societies police systems are facing multiple and demanding challenges that may have serious consequences for those societies. For the socio-political environment in which police function is increasingly unstable and unpredictable. Police systems face fundamental structural change, while some are confronted with stringent economies and considerable downsizing in the face of the economic crisis that took hold in 2008. What has been driving change in recent decades, and is still driving change, has importance for the future of policing and for the multiple and shifting demands placed on police leaders (Bayley and Shearing, 2001; Shearing and Johnston, 2003; Savage, 2007a). Behind that impetus for change has been at the macro level the geo-political impact of globalisation; deregulation of financial markets; removal of borders and ease of travel; demographics and patterns of migration; and the rise of new economies with substantial shifts in labour markets. There has too been the creation of an embryonic 'super-state', with the EU encompassing some 30 countries (when the latest newcomers have joined). Underpinning much of this has been the neo-liberal ideology based on free markets; 'small' government; shareholder value for companies with bottom-line management having major consequences for employment conditions and labour relations; and a reshaping of the welfare state. From this intricate context, ten main drivers can be discerned impinging on system and organisational change in police services.

First, there has been a general socio-political move to the right in recent decades, with an accompanying discourse around crime, fear of crime, migration, security/safety, organised crime and terrorism (Garland, 2001; Loader and Walker, 2007). Particularly in the US and the UK, these themes have become a staple of political and media debate and have strongly influenced the electorate (Tonry, 2004; Reiner, 2007). Encapsulated in this shift are punitive views calling for tougher sentencing and more severe prison regimes. With regard to the latter, the US has a massive penal system, with executions, 'super-max' prisons and long sentences often without remission or possibility of parole (Shalev, 2009). The tough police response to this punitive mood emerged with 'zero tolerance' enforcement in New York and other US cities in the 1990s, with this style of policing being exported to many societies, including even the progressive Netherlands (van Swaaningen, 2000, 2004; Punch, 2007).

Second, and to a degree in relation to the previous point, there is a tendency towards tighter central control. Increasingly governments and ministers in both societies under consideration have become exasperated by not being able to expect a uniform response from 'their' police force (unlike many Continental colleagues). In the UK, there were until 2013 over 50 forces while there were five modes of governance within the three systems,[10] and there were 25 regional forces in the Netherlands. In the former, each one was ostensibly independent and in the latter most acted as if they were independent. In turning to centralisation, the Dutch have gone the whole hog, with one force for the entire country under one chief who reports to one minister. This reverses some 200 years of localism based on dual civil and judicial control and with a corresponding dual ministerial control. The Minister of Security and Justice is now both the chief's political boss and the 'force manager'; in the regional system after 1993/94 the 'force manager' was the mayor of the largest local authority in the region. That is no longer the case for the 10 regional 'units' of the National Police, but the mayor still retains authority over local policing.

Third, a key driver has been the rise and pre-eminence of New Public Management (NPM). And what is understood as NPM has also gone through several phases in the UK, since in the 1980s the Conservative governments of Margaret Thatcher launched a sustained assault on public services that later included the police. There was no respite under the Labour governments of Tony Blair; the Home Office and other agencies, including the Cabinet Office, Audit Commission and the Treasury, harassed the police organisation mercilessly to alter its structure, culture, performance style and mode of accountability. This 'maelstrom' of reform, maintaining that public services should be run on the managerial lines of private corporations, also represented a substantial shift to the central direction of policing with a bewildering battery of 'performance indicators' (Leishman et al, 2000; Gilmour, 2006). This focusing on performance, quantitative results and rewards/sanctions, has fostered a more interventionist political style of top-down pressure from central government on public services including the police. 'Hitting the numbers' became linked to electoral performance as governments promised to reform and to achieve improved results in policing, with crime control becoming the central indicator of success. In England and Wales, moreover, it became plain that the Blair Labour administration was keen to have police chiefs who did what they were told; and, faced with some, in its eyes, 'recalcitrant' chiefs, it brought in legislation to enable the government to remove them. There is no doubt but that the reform was being driven from the centre, effectively from Downing Street itself, that the government was exerting increasing control and that the main focus was on crime control and on achieving results while having to be mindful of 'value for money' within budgets (Williamson, 2008). The key words were effectiveness, efficiency and results, with police chasing multiple targets, and this mirrored both NPM and the 'zero tolerance' movement in the US. Since 2010, the Conservative-Liberal Democrat government has been pursuing NPM values and practices with even more vigour, along with increased austerity in public services funding. These NPM-related demands also strongly influenced Dutch policing for a time (Vlek et al, 2004; Punch, 2007; van Dijk et al, 2010), and, while that impetus seemed to have ebbed away, it has come back strongly in some of the rhetoric espoused within the new National Police.

Partly related to the ideas of NPM, economies of scale became an issue as the multiplicity of forces, with much duplication of effort and expense and with wide variation in establishments, called out for restructuring, especially as private companies had long been downsizing headquarters and paring overheads. In that climate, it was increasingly difficult in the Netherlands to justify 25 regional forces with 25 separate headquarters and with establishments unevenly stretching from 600 to 6,000 personnel. Hence, there has been a move to one central headquarters in The Hague, 10 regional units and one national unit, with numbers per unit ranging from 3,000 to 7,000, promising a more sensible distribution of resources along with potentially considerable savings. The discrepancy in force sizes is great in the UK, with London's Metropolitan Police having nearly 50,000 personnel (with some 32,000 officers and 17,000 other staff), while some provincial forces only have around 1,000 officers. In fact, England and Wales policing was on the verge of a wave of force mergers in 2005, but the plans were shelved for political reasons. Almost certainly, economies of scale will return to the agenda. Indeed, influential figures have been calling for some time for larger regional forces through amalgamations and the formation of a number of national agencies (Blair, 2003, 2005). This is reiterated in the Stevens Report (2013), which pulls back from calling for a national police, which is not electorally attractive to the main political parties with an election looming in 2015, although the Scottish Police went national in 2013.

Fourth, there has been a movement to open up policing to people with managerial and other skills through lateral entry and to alter the dominant police culture by appointing civilians to high positions. This has happened with the Chief of the Royal Canadian Mounted Police and in the UK at chief officer level but until now in non-operational functions. However, since 2014, recruitment has a 'fast track' possibility of becoming an inspector within three years and 'direct entry' at the level of superintendent. The Conservative–Liberal Democrat government has also put an elected civilian 'watchdog', the Police and Crime Commissioner, in nearly every force in England and

Wales. This is not without considerable controversy, and the Stevens Report (2013), with others, sees it as a seriously flawed initiative that should be abandoned.

Fifth, NPM brought with it the novel idea for many officers that members of the public were their 'customers'. Where this was taken seriously, there were 'service delivery standards' shaped through broad inter-agency consultation promising levels of police performance, with surveys of public opinion to judge the quality of service, dedicated officers to carry out social tasks and an emphasis on informing the public through the conventional and social media (O'Connor, 2005).

Sixth, the major terrorist assaults of 9/11 in the US and of July 2005 in the UK (see Chapter Four), as well as attacks elsewhere, largely against American and Israeli targets but also against foreigners at popular tourist spots in several countries, brought counter-terrorism to the forefront of criminal justice. The US, the UK and their allies saw this as a global effort – the 'global war on terror' – which has powerfully influenced criminal justice systems in a range of countries. This has been linked to an increasing focus on transnational organised crime, which is viewed as a substantial threat, while the boundary between transnational organised crime and terrorism is not easy to determine and can shift over time. This has influenced criminal justice in a significant number of ways. There has been emergency legislation creating new agencies alongside the necessity to work increasingly in transnational networks (Bowling and Sheptycki, 2012). This may involve officers working abroad with several nationalities or having a lead position in a multinational agency, such as Europol, or a peace-keeping force in a post-conflict situation requiring an understanding of cross-cultural management (Browaeys and Price, 2008; Bayley and Perito, 2010). The most disturbing issue arising from these complex developments is the possible growth of a 'security state' that threatens civil liberties and human rights (Bowling and Ross, 2006; Edwards, 2014).

Seventh, to a certain extent the emphasis on counter-terrorism has accelerated the push towards national initiatives and new units, which reinforces the tendency to centralisation. In the US, there was the creation of the behemoth of Homeland Security, and in the UK there was the Serious Organised Crime Agency (SOCA) which has been subsumed within the National Crime Agency (NCA). The remit of the latter, together with the new Border Agency, extends to the whole of the UK. Running through these initiatives are links between the intelligence services, the military and the police, with a blurring of boundaries and closer ties to government direction, with SOCA initially being led by a former official from the intelligence services (Hoogenboom, 2010). As with SOCA, the new NCA stands outside the regular police system; its officials are not police officers but can take on the office of 'constable' (see Chapter Two) to exercise the powers of that office when needed, and it reports to the Home Secretary. Such hybrid institutions containing personnel of different 'blood groups' from several agencies require considerable investment in processes to ensure a coordinated and productive functioning. And, again, this creation of a powerful force under direct political control awakens fears of sliding into a security state.

Eighth, ICT (information and communication technology) has greatly changed the techniques and resources of policing and the skills necessary for the new tasks. Computer-aided dispatch; technical apparatus in vehicles; advances in forensics at scenes of crime and with investigations; and the use of computer, mobile phone and internet data in the pursuit of crime have all combined to refashion policing substantially (Ericson and Haggerty, 1997; Manning, 2008). There has also been the outsourcing of certain areas of expertise with a high ICT component, such as forensic accountancy in the face of corporate financial crime and tracing the financial connections and assets of transnational organised crime. This requires internal expertise for the interface with the domestic and foreign accountancy firms, which relates to the next point in that increasingly such positions have been taken by civilians with specific qualifications and skills.

Ninth, there has been a major shift in the composition of the workforce. In the past, in the UK, for example, police forces had few civilians in service and virtually everything – catering, training, personnel management and public relations activities – was carried out by police personnel. With advances in technology and the need for expertise, allied to the pressure to economise and to enhance flexibility, an increasing number of civilians has been employed (Ericson and Haggerty, 1997). This has started to change the ethos of the institution, which some view as a 'straight-white-male-dominated, macho organization' (Paddick, 2008, p vii). An increasing number of women became civilian employees, which, along with the expansion in female police officer numbers, is changing the image of policing as an almost exclusively male occupation. In 2014, for instance, an average of 30% of Dutch police officers were women.[11] Civilians have not only brought diversity in terms of gender – including gay men and women – but also regarding ethnicity, religion, attire and political persuasion, which, in turn, has had an influence on the uniformly male culture of policing. In the UK, civilians were, and are, employed under different regulations from those for sworn officers who do not have a trade union with the right to strike. The important implication of this is that police leaders have to take into account that they are managing a diverse workforce under separate regulations and with potentially varying types of commitment to the ethos of policing.

Tenth, and finally, there has been the escalating impact of the media since the 1990s. The speed of response and resources of the media – internationally, nationally and locally – have rapidly increased, while coverage of police and crime issues has moved to the front page news or to lead items on television (Reiner, 2007). Of particular significance has been the rise and impact of the social media and social networks. This pervasive and intrusive scrutiny and coverage has become of fundamental importance for police organisations and for police leaders in particular.

There are diverse implications arising from the multiple macro developments touched on here, along with organisational issues related to effectiveness and cohesion in these newly structured systems with their ambitious aims and enhanced powers (Reiner, 2010). The measures arising from these combined developments doubtless seem justified to the policy and law makers but, given the unanticipated consequences of any system change, can be viewed as potentially threatening to the essential notion of policing in the two societies under consideration. Indeed, there is a sense that these system changes are being conducted with a number of key issues unresolved. The speed, complexity, ambiguity and neglect of the long-term consequences of such developments in diverse societies foster an uncomfortable sense that policing is developing in ways that profoundly alter our conceptual map of what 'policing' essentially means (Shearing, 2007). These developments have, in turn, significant implications for the 'profession' of policing in terms of control over itself as an institution, over the content and style of its knowledge base and skills, over quality in the delivery of services and over its relationship with the public.

Inhibitions to change

Worryingly, the change process may not be quite as coherent and controlled as it is meant to appear (Watson, 1994). This is not surprising, as typically plans for system change and accompanying organisational development programmes are by their nature overly optimistic and often fail (Kotter, 2012). That makes it necessary to bear in mind the realities of organisational life in general, and of the police organisation in particular, which might temper, divert or even undermine the reform process (Bayley, 2006b). For instance, a number of sources in the US, including Manning (2003, 2010) and Skogan (2008), are especially sombre, and maintain that the reform movement of recent decades has largely failed. Walker (2005, pp vii and 17) remains 'deeply skeptical about the possibilities of lasting change' and further states that 'the history of police reform is filled with stories of highly publicized changes that promised much but evaporated over the long run with minimal impact'. Indeed, he refers to cynics who feel that 'the American police are incapable of reforming themselves' and that 'the police subculture is resistant to all efforts to achieve accountability'. This is particularly relevant given the crisis of trust in US policing, with its issues of discrimination and undue violence, which has arisen yet again in 2014. This holds even more so for policing systems in fragile states with an espoused reform agenda but that are seemingly incapable of implementing the necessary changes despite at times substantial injections of funds and plane loads of imported expertise (Hinton and Newburn, 2009).

One element of resistance to reform is precisely that it is from abroad and is viewed as incompatible with local circumstances and mores. Hornberger (2007), for example, writes of the difficulties of transplanting a human rights perspective, with experts coming in droves from advanced democracies to reform post-apartheid South African policing. This rejection can also apply domestically, with a 'not invented here' disdain in one force for innovations emanating from another force. It is not uncommon for the leading force in a country to be taken as a negative reference point precisely because of its dominance, despite the value of what it has to offer; equally, the lead force may be reluctant to adopt anything developed successfully elsewhere. Another limiting factor is reform fatigue, as officers with long service laconically lament that they have been through several change cycles with the same old concepts being enthusiastically rebranded by those lacking an institutional memory or suffering from selective amnesia. A decade back in the UK, notions of community-oriented policing (COP) and problem-oriented policing (POP) were being resuscitated and the good old British 'Bobby' was, once more, being 'reinvented' (Savage, 2007b). And a Dutch officer of long service who was asked to speak about the 'reorganisation' relating to the new National Police asked 'which reorganisation?'. For some 40 years, he had known nothing else but reorganisation (Bangma, 2014).

Furthermore, Boin and colleagues (2003, p 144) conclude that 'one of the most important and most uniform findings of half a century of political science research is that even implementing the most simple aims always turns out differently than anticipated'. They illustrate this with a range of studies where promising and ambitious change projects, including some relating to crime control, met with disappointing and even meagre results. The Appendix to this volume presents two case studies to illustrate this. In one study of a large metropolis, Fitzgerald and colleagues (2002) conveyed the concerns of Londoners and police officers about the delivery of services by the Metropolitan Police following two decades of reform. Organisational size and complexity along with overly centralised direction – making the Met a 'bureaucratic nightmare' (Paddick, 2008, p 242) – was undermining the quality of local policing provision (O'Connor, 2005). And at the micro level, Herbert (2006) illustrated the dilemmas of operationalising community policing (COP) in three areas of Seattle at a time when COP was viewed as the panacea for all the ills of US policing (Skogan, 2008). Although the focus in this book is primarily on the UK and the Netherlands, it draws on this case study from the US as community policing was strongly promoted by massive federal funding through COPS (the Office of Community Oriented Policing Services within the Department of Justice) and with a veritable COP industry of academics, advisors and practitioners. Yet the case illustrates that even in the relatively benign environment of Seattle, community policing encountered persistent resistance within the police organisation and difficulties with implementing it in practice.

This is not to dampen the enthusiasm for change but to draw on the body of knowledge about change in order to prepare senior officers for managing and dealing with it and particularly its unanticipated consequences. Crucially, changes in structure and resources can be imposed by decree, while this is fundamentally not the case with changes in culture and behaviour. And changes in structure and resources might have very real consequences that touch on the essence of policing, and these might very well contradict espoused professional goals. For example, in the Netherlands the reorganisation relating to the formation of the National Police was presented as leading to economies with, in the early phase, no enforced redundancies – and the police unions still remain powerful – but the restructuring and budget restrictions will doubtless have a more significant impact on the development of the police organisation and its future than indicated in the proposals (van Dijk and Hoogewoning, 2014a). This reorganisation is the most significant one in the recent history of the Dutch policing system. The espoused aim is a 'leaner' and more effective, efficient and 'professional' police service. There can then be little doubt that the pressure on all ranks to achieve this aim will increase. Yet in many respects the demands on senior staff are likely to be particularly weighty in the coming period of complex institutional change, with new challenges and pressing demands on those leading it. At the same time, the leadership of the senior officers can potentially be very important in shaping the future of the police organisation and role. And it is on the senior officers that this work will focus, with the understanding that leadership applies in different ways to different people throughout the organisation given the complex nature of the policing enterprise. The next section will set the stage for the discussion on police leadership in Chapter Five by defining some basic premises.

Leadership in policing

The two short overviews for the Netherlands and the UK presented so far in this chapter make one ponder on exactly what sort of leadership there should be in relation to system changes. It is alas the case that leadership is a notoriously vague subject, if not a semantic sponge, leading to different meanings for different people in different contexts. While taking this into consideration, the authors view 'leadership' pragmatically by drawing on what police have to do and what competences are needed, given the unique nature of the police organisation and the range of challenges it faces operationally and institutionally. In generic terms, leadership typically refers in contemporary society to those in senior roles in organisations who are in charge of institutional change and development, endeavour to achieve results through directing personnel, and have to cope with the demands and restraints of specific environments. Of course, it is much more complex than that, but of the essence is that while there are some universal elements to leadership in organisations there is also a broad sweep of organisational types requiring a diversity of leadership approaches tailored to the specific nature of each type and varying context in which it functions. The meaning of leadership will have varying connotations in a multinational oil firm, university, non-governmental organisation (NGO), retail chain, low cost airline, charity, political party, aircraft carrier, orchestra, government ministry, industrial laboratory, professional sport club, agricultural enterprise, monastery or innovative ICT firm. And there will even be variety within those categories, along with differences in national and local cultures and in differing operating environments. Some humanitarian NGOs, for example, engage in massive logistical operations within vulnerable states where there are conflict-ridden, high-risk environments; yet they do so partly with young professionals who often do not fit a conventional leadership profile and have not enjoyed the leadership training associated with the military or with major corporations. Then some contemporary 'virtual' enterprises claim to have no leaders, hierarchy, headquarters, fixed salaries or hours of work, and no delineated assignments. This may seem to usher in the 'end of leadership' (Kellerman, 2012), but that would doubtless not apply to those in charge of a global merchant bank, the US Navy Seals or Human Rights Watch.

But equally it would not apply to police facing rival fans from two countries who have clashed before a crunch football game, have started fighting each other, have turned on the police and have begun to run amok through the city centre on a busy shopping day. Neither would it apply in the case of a special unit within the force being exposed for falsifying statements and using intimidation to gain convictions, leading to an external inquiry, criminal charges against officers, civil claims for unlawful arrest, the quashing of numerous convictions, legal action by sacked officers for unfair dismissal and a media campaign demanding that heads should role at the top of the organisation. This is reinforced by the perspective adopted here, which, having taken the wider leadership material into account, focuses on the unique and highly specific nature of policing, and on the exceptional demands on leadership within policing. In brief, the police organisation is a public agency with vital functions in a democracy under the rule of law. It has a (near) monopoly of violence; is a major processor of people and cases for the criminal justice system; is called on to aid people in need; and deals with disasters and emergencies. Policing covers in fact an almost 'mindboggling' assortment of functions, according to Bittner (1970), with activities ranging from dealing with dog poo to disasters and from 'parking tickets to class repression' (Marenin, 1982). This makes policing an irreducibly complex business with multiple functions that are defined by law, regulations and custom, that are implemented with diverse publics, that attract constant scrutiny and that – crucially – require the routine giving of accounts in a number of arenas, including the courts, government, oversight agencies and media, as well as to a bevy of stakeholders.

The sensitive nature of many of the issues to be dealt with implies that the nature of leadership within the policing enterprise has an intrinsic 'moral' or values component. It also requires proven competency in dealing with a cluster of routine affairs but especially in managing the institutional shift to emergency response. For the police organisation is a 'front-line' institution with a measure of autonomy and discretion for the lower ranks that has to shift to a more central organisational mode for major pre-planned or sudden emergency operations. Indeed, leadership is not confined to the senior ranks but is to be found, and is required given that 'front-line' nature of the organisation, at all levels (Vinzant and Crothers, 1998). This makes the police organisation very different from the typical business organisation, most other public service organisations and not-for-profit organisations; and it requires different leadership values and skills from all those other institutions. There are, for instance, three essential roles and sets of functions that are required at the senior officer level in running a police organisation:

- *institutional leadership*: here the police leader role is a figurehead, a carrier of the institution's philosophy and the face and voice of the organisation at key moments;
- *concern leadership*: this 'CEO'-style role carries mainly managerial responsibility for setting goals, performance targets, budgets, acquisitions, infrastructure, personnel and diversity;
- *incident leadership*: this role relates to all operations and key emergency situations with the need to be able to respond to, and take the lead in, major incidents and large-scale operations, including big events and investigations.

These are functional areas – and not three types of leader – while it is assumed that there is the capacity and expertise to carry them out effectively in the division of labour within the leadership team. In implementation there is probably an advantage in having a diversity of backgrounds and skills, with multi-tasking within the team to ensure that there is combined strength in all areas. The three roles take on a special flavour within the policing context. It could be maintained that the first two are more 'generic', whereas the third one is specific and essential to executive policing, and that all in the senior team should be capable of carrying it out or have sufficient experience to support those in that role. Furthermore, the following basic elements need to be taken into consideration in the wider organisational context. To begin with, as opposed to many other organisations, there are formal leadership and supervisory roles throughout the organisation at the force, unit and team levels. Much routine policing is conducted in small teams within devolved units under low-level, supervisory leadership. Leading teams – at all levels of the organisation including the top – forms a key function and a crucial skill. Next, in emergency incident and pre-planned event mode, the organisation shifts to central direction, requiring many people to change roles and to function under the diverse levels of non-routine incident leadership.

The implication is that there is a complex matrix of formal managerial and operational roles and functions. In pre-planned operations, the formal leadership roles are obviously defined in advance. In unfolding incidents, however, the dynamic is of lower-level personnel arriving on the scene first and taking on the primary operational response role, while the higher-level operational leaders are mobilised where appropriate. It may even be the case that a single officer on routine duties is confronted with a serious incident – say a major road accident or a train crash – and has to take on the leadership role temporarily until reinforcements arrive. The first responder has an informal 'holding' leadership role until this responsibility has been taken over, at which point he or she becomes an active 'follower' to a superior officer within the higher operational chain (Chaleff, 2003). In that sense, *every* officer may have to take on unexpectedly an informal incident leadership role, and may be required to do so when not on duty. And even those with primarily a 'managerial' leadership role may have to take on incident leadership roles under certain circumstances. This is of significance for institutional leaders in the force senior management team who, alongside 'taking charge and directing' the organisation at the strategic level, all remain potentially leaders of major incidents. In essence, 'emergency response' and 'major incident deployment' in the widest sense is a crucial and core area. The organisation has, then, to be suffused with awareness of the dynamic of both the organisational shift required and the predicament of lower-level personnel taking operational roles and needing support. Everyone without exception has to have a close understanding and affinity with the dilemmas associated with operational policing, from patrolling, investigations, traffic, community liaison, specialist units (say firearms, counter-terrorism or scene of crime) to major incident management. A fundamental implication, moreover, is that while each officer remains individually accountable for his or her actions, there is also institutional accountability, with possible corporate liability, which should be delivered by those who have taken institutional responsibility for policy and practice as leading officers and those who have taken senior operational responsibility.

Those in a nutshell are the premises developed during this explorative research and that will inform the rest of this work. 'Leadership' is seen pragmatically as what is needed given the nature of the police organisation and the challenges it faces operationally and institutionally. There is, then, a need for officers who are competent, confident, tried and tested, and whose leadership is rooted in the values of an accountable public service within a democracy.

Matters of concern

Permeating this work, with the major restructuring effort of the new Dutch National Police in the background, is the insistent realisation that in many Western societies police systems are facing multiple and demanding challenges that may have serious consequences for those societies. For the socio-political environment in which police function is becoming increasingly unstable and unpredictable. Police systems face fundamental structural change, with some facing stiff austerity measures and downsizing. There is, moreover, a sense in the literature that the devastating terrorist attacks in the US (2001) and UK (2005) have skewed policing and the wider criminal justice system towards a dominant security agenda based largely on counter-terrorism. And with increasing globalisation, there is a near comparable focus on transnational organised crime (Allum and Gilmour, 2012). The concern, then, is that the obsession with the external global threat from terrorism leads domestically to a massive investment in new measures and institutions that have considerable consequences for civil liberties. Yet these seem hardly justified by the actual level of threat and by the small number of suspects located in the home country (Brodeur, 2010). There has emerged, furthermore, a degree of institutional fragmentation in the US and the UK, with new national agencies with enhanced powers and involving increased transnational cooperation raising issues about accountability (Hoogenboom, 2010). In this process, nation states are even held to be 'losing the monopoly over policing' (Bayley and Nixon, 2010). Given the sensitivity of these largely concealed areas in new and older agencies to 'mission creep' (informally or illicitly expanding the legal mandate) and abuse of power, which arise constantly within security and intelligence services, there is concern about inroads into privacy, dubious if not illegal methods in countering terrorism and unregulated contacts between police and other agencies across national boundaries (Priest and Arkin, 2012; Edwards, 2014). This poses urgent questions about human rights, governance and accountability. This of particular concern in the UK, given that a number of politicians and segments of the media are waging a campaign that is critical if not hostile to human rights. Prime Minister Cameron even talked in 2014 of repealing the Human Rights Act, and others have proposed withdrawal from the European Convention (*Telegraph*, 1 October 2014). There is, then, a great deal going on in the turbulent environment of policing and within policing in both societies under consideration. In policing in England and Wales, for instance, the Chief Inspector of Constabulary writes in his annual report that policing has been damaged – 'but certainly not broken' – by scandals and affairs, and states that loss of trust is corrosive of the British policing model and clearly needs to be restored (Winsor Report, 2014).

Given the pressing concern of many about the direction policing is taking, it is, then, both essential – and a professional obligation – to examine the lessons from research through the lens of 'what matters?'. Without that critical and persistent exercise, it is nigh on futile to discuss and determine what police leadership should entail. For in this perilous time of significant system change – with doubtless fresh hazards ahead – it is vital to engage with the fundamental issues relating to justice, equity, diversity, privacy, use of force, abuse of power, discrimination, rights, accountability and paradigms in policing. And allied to those are the equally fundamental questions of how independent the police service should be; how independent the police chief should be; how independent the individual police officer should be; and to whom they should be accountable. Encapsulated in these issues – in the Netherlands, the UK and elsewhere – is the pivotal factor as to what sort of policing is appropriate for citizens in a democracy in an advanced society. And within that crucial public service agency, what sort of leadership is appropriate? Furthermore, if trust is the overriding concern, how does leadership gain, and retain, trust – and restore it if it has been damaged or lost?

The approach taken in this book is based on the conviction that we cannot fruitfully ponder on police leadership without considering the future of policing in the light of the accumulated body of knowledge on policing. In ruminating on this, one has to remain aware that politics determines policy and that policy decisions are often driven by ideology, partisan and personal interest, opinion polls, scandals and even the day's headline. Nevertheless, the police institution is so fundamentally important to democratic society and the well-being of its citizens that it is essential to take into account the lessons from over half a century of academic research – from Bittner (1967) to Brodeur (2010), from Skolnick (1966) to Shearing (2007) and from Reiss (1971) to Reiner (2010). While these lessons are open to interpretation and debate, they convey clear and valuable indicators that cannot just be ignored. That accumulated material can usefully be trawled to satisfy the growing demand from policymakers and practitioners for 'what works?'. This can undoubtedly be a valuable exercise provided it is not accompanied by a simplistic, unreflective, reductionist 'one size fits all' approach. This only encourages lazy thinking and copy-cat policies whereby people overlook the insistent but apparently inconvenient messages from the wider evidence. The authors argue, in contrast, that the exercise needs to be accompanied by critical scrutiny and serious reflection, driven not only by 'best practice' but also by 'best thinking', as illustrated by the innovative approaches of Cartwright and Shearing (2012) in *Where's the chicken?*.

With a strong sense of urgency, then, the following chapters will touch on a range of material regarding policing, paradigms, accountability, reform and the future of policing (compare Boin et al, 2003; Newburn, 2003, 2005; Vlek et al, 2004; Savage, 2007a; Maguire et al, 2012). Chapter Two examines a subject of key importance in assessing the significance of change in contemporary policing – namely the conceptual nature of the two dominant 'paradigms' of policing – and how 'paradigm lost' and 'paradigm shift' have occurred in the two countries focused on throughout. Chapter Three deals with the nature of policing and endeavours to summarise the key findings from research. To discuss realistically police leadership, one has to appreciate the nature and culture of police work and the police organisation; the challenges that policing faces in its institutional and operational functioning; and how, within a complex, shifting and at times perilous environment, police leaders have to juggle constantly to cope with the sometimes wrenching dilemmas and resilient issues that confront them. Chapter Four examines the vital area of commanding operations. This will serve as an essential backcloth for the detailed focus on the central topic of leadership and leadership education in Chapter Five. The authors propose, in the concluding Chapter Six, a comprehensive paradigm and sum up their views and proposals as a tentative answer to a fundamental underlying question.

Finally, in the light of the daunting situation sketched, and of the acute dilemmas and pressures facing police systems and their leaders, this crucial question has to be, what matters in policing?

Notes

[1] Others use the term policing for all those activities and agencies – including private police and security, regulatory institutions and the intelligence services – engaged in diverse ways with law enforcement, maintaining order, surveillance and so on (Wood and Shearing, 2007; Reiner, 2010).

[2] The New Zealand government and police engaged in an extensive review with expert seminars, surveys of the public and of police officers and visits to forces abroad: *Policing directions in New Zealand for the 21st century* was prepared for the government and police by the Police Act Review Team in 2007. In Canada, there was the *Economics of Policing: National Policing Research Symposium* at Vancouver in March 2014 to debate a policy proposal for change, and in the US there was the *New Perspectives in Policing:*

Harvard Executive Session on Policing and Public Safety, with Harvard University, Kennedy School of Government and the National Institute of Justice, in 2010.

[3] Instead of the classical approach in terms of most different or most similar, see Anckar (2008).

[4] The *Rijkspolitie* developed central investigatory units, was responsible for diverse resources (boats, equipment, later helicopters) for patrolling the motorways, and also delivered some local policing. It was not a single 'national' force like the new National Police (from 2013) but was a centrally led agency next to the city forces (*gemeentepolitie*).

[5] The *Marechaussee* is a *gendarmerie* and a separate policing formation within the military that performs tasks within the military at home and abroad and has become responsible for border control, security at airfields, royal and diplomatic protection and protecting money transports for the Dutch Central Bank. Its members receive a military and a police training. It has in the past conducted general policing duties in certain areas and can be called on by the public police in time of need. It answers primarily to the Ministry of Defence, but also to the Ministries of Justice and the Interior, depending on the specific function its units are performing.

[6] *Wetsvoorstel nationale politie* (Ministry of Security and Justice, 2011): this is the proposal to Parliament for a change in the law to create a new national police force. In effect, the NP is legally a completely new organisation, replacing the former one on 1 January 2013.

[7] The 'Troubles' refer to the conflict (1968–98) between British security forces – police, army and intelligence agencies – and the Irish Republican Army (IRA; mainly the 'Provisional' IRA), which launched a campaign of violence aimed at the reunification of Ireland and the removal of the British administration from Northern Ireland (Punch, 2012).

[8] Formally the *Stephen Lawrence Independent Review*. Stephen Lawrence was a black youth who was the victim of an unprovoked attack in London in 1993 by a gang of white racists. The ineffectiveness of the police response brought intense media attention and a commission of inquiry that referred to 'institutional racism' in the Met (Macpherson, 1999). The repercussions of the murder continue to reverberate some 20 years on, with Stephen's parents playing a prominent role in keeping his case and the issue of racism in policing in the public arena. There have also been allegations of police corruption undermining the investigation.

[9] 'Anon' is a serving officer who wrote a paper for a UK degree programme. It conveys wide disillusionment about changes to pay, pensions and cuts to the police service.

Some recruits who joined with eagerness and motivation are now, it claims, thoroughly discouraged and demotivated and are leaving the service prematurely.

[10] For Northern Ireland, Scotland, the Metropolitan Police, City of London Police and for the other forces in England and Wales.

[11] In the Netherlands during the 1990s there was increasing criticism of the closed, masculine nature of the police organisation in relation to gender and diversity. Police chiefs were almost exclusively WASP – 'White Anglo-Saxon Protestant' – males who were formed by a career confined solely to policing. There was growing dissatisfaction about the inability of the system to develop and promote women, and those with a minority ethnic background, to the higher ranks. This led to several women being recruited through lateral entry to senior positions of whom a few became chiefs in the regional system. In 2015 at the time of writing, of the 16 most senior officers, four are female.

TWO

Police systems, perspectives and contested paradigms

There is a range of policing systems in various societies and it is useful to clarify briefly what formed them, what they look like and how they differ (Mawby, 1999). For there is a tendency, which many follow, to ignore history and to generalise sweepingly about policing. The systems do have universal elements that cross cultures, but we should remain conscious of the dissimilarities and bear in mind system and cultural differences. Police research has been conducted predominately in the English-speaking world and often to the neglect of material in other languages which could provide access to a rich variety of systems (Hoogenboom and Punch, 2012). Brodeur (2010), for example, was a French Canadian whose work fruitfully draws on sources in French, both historical and modern, which he employs to chart the differences between the two dominant 'French-Continental' and 'Anglo-Saxon' criminal justice systems. Students of policing can be much aided by his insightful work. Also it remains the case that, despite change, police systems often continue to display genetic features reflecting their society's history and culture. Therefore, this chapter takes a closer at different police systems and deals with the important distinction made by Brodeur (1983, 2010) between what he calls 'low' and 'high' policing and his insights on 'militarised' policing. The chapter then examines the concept of policing paradigms as well as paradigm change in the UK and the Netherlands.

Police systems

It is possible to discern five main types of police systems or policing styles in existence since the start of 'modern' policing some two centuries ago. First, the French – or 'Continental' – model can be traced to the 17th century. In France, high-level magistrates working on behalf of the absolute monarch were tasked with a broad form of 'government' in regulating matters to protect the monarchy and ensure order in the cities where there was a continual threat of disturbances. The term 'police' was not then used and the broad concept of government was not at all like the modern notion of police; rather, it was an all-encompassing mandate utilising in practice a combination of central surveillance by spies and informers and of urban order maintenance by military-style units (Brodeur, 2010). There later evolved in France a system of local and national policing agencies falling under diverse ministries and with a national, centrally led *gendarmerie* for maintaining state control that was formally part of the military. From early on in revolutionary and post-revolutionary France, the focus remained on bolstering central government and later presidential control, by maintaining public order along with an emphasis on the covert surveillance of perceived threats from political opponents and from 'subversive' groups within the population. This model survived after Napoleon's defeat within the countries emerging from French occupation, particularly in Spain, Italy, Belgium and the Netherlands. Such systems still tend today to be strongly geared to serving the state through several agencies, central and local control of public policing through dual civil–judicial authority and a narrow focus on public order and crime control. Those 17th-century origins when power was concentrated 'in the hands of a police magistrate begat an administrative culture of top-down centralized authority characterized by rigidity, which has lasted until this day in France' (Brodeur, 2010, p 51).

Second, there is the Anglo-Saxon model, which is held to date from the founding of the Metropolitan Police in London in 1829 when an unarmed civilian police was created, with this model, subject to local variations, spreading to the forces formed outside of London (Critchley, 1978). This has strongly influenced the common-law, 'Commonwealth' countries (especially Canada, Australia and New Zealand) as well as the US and has, in recent decades in its modern form, had an impact on other countries including the Netherlands. We look at this model in more detail later in this chapter. Third are the colonial policing models, which are typically a military variant of police in the home country. The Royal Irish Constabulary (RIC), for example, was an armed force with its roots in the Peace Preservation Force created in 1814 in Ireland, hence predating the Metropolitan Police in London, and formally founded in 1836 (Conway, 2014). Much British colonial policing in Asia, Africa, the Middle East and parts of North America and the Caribbean was subsequently based on this RIC model. This was true of the Royal Canadian Mounted Police (RCMP), which, like the other forces in the British Empire, sent its senior officers to Dublin for training and also recruited officers from the RIC. Colonial policing was clearly a central control apparatus over indigenous peoples reflecting features of militarised policing in a number of countries, including Germany, France, Portugal, Italy and Spain, but the agencies could also perform diverse civil functions. There was traditionally no question of 'consent' from indigenous populations and at times there was severe repression and even 'excesses' (Newsinger, 2006). Fourth, there have been highly repressive police systems serving authoritarian, dictatorial states. These include systems in Spain (under Franco), Portugal (under Salazar), Greece (under the military junta) and Germany (under Hitler), as well as in the countries occupied by Nazi Germany in WWII and the Eastern European societies occupied by the Soviet Union after 1945. The latter were forced into Soviet satellite status where policing was geared to protecting the state from subversives. Police powers were effectively unlimited and accountability non-existent, as with the Stasi in Eastern Germany and its ubiquitous apparatus of covert surveillance. Appelbaum (2012) gives a chilling overview of repressive policing in Eastern Europe under post-war Soviet influence and control. In Africa, South America and Asia there are, and have been, strongly repressive police systems that at times have supported dictatorial regimes and fought 'dirty' wars against left-wing, radical movements; and in South Africa, units within the police system have been employed to suppress brutally domestic opposition to the white-dominated apartheid regime but also to fight in counter-insurgency campaigns outside of the country (Ellis, 1988; Marks, 2005).

Fifth, and finally, one can speak of a transitional model in those societies that have experienced regime change following armed conflict and/or political developments and have had to alter their genetic features, structure and culture. This happened following Irish independence in 1921 when the Irish Free State distanced itself from Britain, abandoned the RIC model and formed the *Garda Síochána* (Guardians of the Peace). This unarmed national police force was viewed as one of the central cultural pillars in establishing the new Irish state (McGarry, 2007; Conway, 2014). Then WWII was crucial in the foundation of a decentralised policing model in West Germany after 1945 for clear historical reasons. Policing had to recover from the appalling years of Nazi tyranny based on pervasive state control, and restructure itself in a democratic society suffused with a profound fear of undue central power. Having gone through that transition, the system went through another massive change when West and East Germany were united and two dramatically different police systems were merged to conform to West Germany's decentralised *Länder* model within a democratic state under the rule of law. The demise of the Soviet Union also strongly influenced policing in the former Soviet Bloc countries following their independence from 1990 onwards. Like those countries emerging from armed conflict and receiving support from Western countries, these systems ostensibly adopted a model of democratic, accountable policing with respect for human rights on the lines of the consent model (Bayley, 2006a). This was greatly stimulated by encouragement and finance from the US, EU, Council of Europe and private foundations. But systems do not change their spots that easily, and, for some, the transition has proved, or is proving, a long and demanding process. In South Africa, for instance, the police had, as mentioned, been a vicious element in enforcing the apartheid laws and also in pursuing and eliminating activists of the African National Congress. This legacy has continued to bedevil the efforts to establish a new force under a democratic government. As Steinberg (2008, p 22) stated, '13 years after the inauguration of democracy, South Africa's general population has yet to give its consent to being policed'.

Brodeur: low and high policing, militarised policing

Alongside this typology of police systems, there is an important conceptual distinction made by Brodeur (1983, 2010) between 'low' and 'high' policing. It will be evident that the prime focus throughout this book is on 'low' policing and that this will inform the material on organisation, culture, deviance, operational challenges and leadership. Brodeur's terminology will also be adopted when speaking of police agencies carrying features of the military with regard to structure, culture, ranks, training, uniform, tasks and ethos. Nearly all policing systems have drawn on the military to a degree, but some more than others. Brodeur refers to those agencies with a strong affinity with the military as 'militarised' police.

Low policing

Low policing is primarily the routine, everyday, authorised work of public police (including patrol, investigations, public order, traffic and emergency response), which is largely visible through uniformed personnel in public places and largely legal in implementation while being ostensibly subject to public accountability. Importantly, the vast majority of police research has been conducted on low policing and within that mainly on uniformed police work. This means that substantial areas of low policing still remain to be researched. The main focus in this work is on low policing so that the sections on 'paradigms' later in this chapter should be viewed as applying predominantly to low policing.

High policing

High policing draws on the concept of *haute police*, which in 17th-century France was for the preservation of the regime, and in modern societies refers to police activity to protect national security. For obvious reasons related to secrecy and confidentiality, high policing is under-researched but comes under occasional scrutiny through special commissions, journalism and whistleblowing. Although considered fairly rudimentary and in need of revision by most commentators, the strength and utility of the high–low distinction when first published in 1983 was to draw attention to the neglect of 'high' policing among most of Brodeur's colleagues in the US and the UK. In the predominantly Anglo-American body of knowledge available at the time, the central state was – with a few exceptions and then mostly in the radical 1970s – rarely mentioned, despite the fact that in many societies policing was subject to direct state control. Typically, this high policing is found within the intelligence agencies of the 'security community', but not exclusively. In the UK, for example, public police forces have a 'Special Branch' for investigating political crimes and crimes against the state that has ties to MI5, formally the 'security service' for internal intelligence activities (Allason, 1983; Porter, 1987). And in Dutch policing there was in every public force a Political Intelligence Department (*Politieke Inlichtingendienst* or PID). Intelligence Departments operated from 1993/94 at the regional level and since 2013 have been integrated within the National Police while retaining some regional functions within the 10 new 'units'. Like its British Special Branch counterpart, the Intelligence Department has strong links to the Dutch General Intelligence and Security Service (*Algemene Inlichtingen- en Veiligheidsdienst*, or AIVD).

The key point that Brodeur makes about the two types is that high-policing agencies tend to slide into, or almost routinely adopt, illicit means, and that this is partly related to the opportunities afforded by the ambivalent or vague phrasing of legislation and/or passing of special legislation, and partly to political encouragement and judicial approval of such means, particularly in periods defined as a national emergency. This means that they frequently evade the accountability imposed on low policing. Such agencies, moreover, employ the devious arts of infiltration, active informants, covert surveillance, disinformation, 'black propaganda', entrapment, intimidation, violence and blackmail, and can do so largely under a cloak of secrecy and with an absence of accountability (Marx, 1988). Brodeur argues that the state often condones the tendency in such agencies to go outside the law, either because it is viewed as necessary to protect the interests of the state or is in the interests of leading members of the state. This was the case in the US where the FBI, in the absence of an internal security service, was used for decades not only to investigate any group considered 'subversive' – and the net was thrown pathologically wide – but also as a kind of 'private political police' for presidents (Summers, 2011, p 409). This granted near absolute power to Edgar Hoover, who headed the FBI for 48 years and who systematically used widespread surveillance and blackmail against those considered opponents of the state and anyone he considered a personal opponent. The dubious licence granted to him to bend and break the law by a succession of presidents meant he can be considered to have 'subverted the democratic system as ruthlessly as any secret chief police in a totalitarian state' (Summers, 2011, p 323). This may be an extreme case, but it graphically illustrates that high policing carries the danger – even in an established democracy with ostensible checks and balances – of certain agencies being given the freedom to employ illicit means that undermine the rule of law and the democratic process (Ermann and Lundman, 1996). The agencies effectively act as covert judges and juries and, at times, executioners; this can apply to the formal state security agents, and especially to the aggressive para-military units that combat those classified as enemies of the state and engage in ruthless counter-insurgency campaigns.

The importance of Brodeur's distinction between high and low policing is threefold. First, it draws attention to an area of law enforcement and 'policing' in the wider sense that has a tendency to use illicit means in the interests of the state while evading the public accountability essential to the oversight of government agencies in a democracy. Second, that tendency applies not only to the security agencies but also to public policing. As mentioned, both countries under consideration in this book have 'political intelligence' units within regular police forces. In Northern Ireland, for instance, the Special Branch of the RUC played a key and highly controversial role in the counter-insurgency campaign against the Irish Republican Army (IRA) (Geraghty, 2000). Furthermore, in Canada during a state of emergency in the 1970s, when Quebec was threatening secession from the federal structure and a terrorist group – the Quebec Liberation Front – was committing acts of violence in the name of independence for Quebec, it was special units of the RCMP, Provincial Police and Montreal Municipal Police that engaged in devious practices during covert campaigns of infiltration and destabilisation. Brodeur (1981) conveys that the unlawful police activity that then came to light was effectively condoned by higher authorities and the judiciary under the blanket concept of 'national security'; this extracts malice from the intent in the criminal act (say in a burglary to attain evidence) and makes it legally justifiable. Third, and crucially, it is a matter of acute concern in contemporary society that there is both mounting evidence of major and structural abuses within the security services of Western countries and also among certain private security companies, along with the blurring of boundaries between public policing and security policing. For instance, some argue that there is a growing measure of interaction and of cross-boundary cooperation between low policing and high policing regarding responsibilities and accountability. Yet this is rarely explored and only addressed by a few academics (Marx, 1988; Hoogenboom, 2010).

'Militarised' policing

'Militarised' policing refers in Brodeur's work to policing shaped by the military ethos and style. For instance, some police systems have a separate agency for public order and special duties such as Special Weapons and Tactics squads in the US. The extent to which the US police have increasingly taken on a militarised style with training, tactics, equipment and weaponry – with automatic weapons normally meant for the battlefield and sophisticated armoured vehicles being almost gifted to them by the Army and government, especially since 9/11 – has been a source of critical comment and growing concern (Kraska, 2001, 2007). In France, there is the *Compagnies républicaines de sécurité* (CRS), which is part of the public police but distinguishes itself from it by looking and acting in a military fashion while only performing a limited range of tasks focused around large-scale operational deployment. Such units often have a reputation for tough enforcement as with the riots in the suburbs (*banlieues*) of Paris and other cities in recent years and largely involving youths of North African background protesting about high unemployment and police discrimination.

The Netherlands may seem relatively pacific, but has had in the past to deal with periodic large-scale popular or industrial unrest. To respond to such incidents, Dutch policing developed military-style units at the central and force levels. These operated from the 1920s onwards, with steel-helmeted squads riding in tenders and equipped with rifles, submachine guns and machine guns; they were almost indistinguishable from soldiers. Indeed, there was for a time a policing unit for public order within the Army, the Police Troops Force (*Korps Politietroepen*), which was under the direction of the Minister of Justice.

This Force (1919–40) was set up at a time of post-war concern about possible revolution and industrial unrest in the wake of the 1917 Russian Revolution. The *Marechaussee* was also part of the Army and had a public order capacity. Both were notoriously heavy handed and on occasion large-scale unrest was dealt with harshly, leading to deaths and injuries from firearms and other weapons. During the riots in the *Jordaan* district of Amsterdam in 1934, for instance, there were five fatalities and 47 people were seriously injured (Fijnaut, 2007). At a time of high unemployment, the benefits for the unemployed were cut, leading to protests with people breaking up streets in Amsterdam and throwing up barricades; the police, military with armoured cars and the *Marechaussee* replied with live ammunition to quell the disturbances, which lasted a week. It is clear that this hard enforcement in the face of mass violent unrest that the local police could not contain, was strongly encouraged by the authorities.

It was only from the mid-1930s onwards, in the wake of the *Jordaan* disturbances, that Amsterdam and other city forces wanted to cope with public order without calling for assistance from external units. Militarised squads were set up from the mid-1930s and became known as Carbine Brigades (*Karabijnbrigades*), equipped with carbines but also submachine guns rather like the Police Troops Force. These were the forerunners of the later riot squads that developed in the 1960s; in Dutch, these are known as the Mobile Unit (*mobiele eenheid*), referred to as the ME. These were meant to be for more general public order situations while *all* officers went through Mobile Unit training and could be mobilised at any time. They had to drop their regular duties, change uniforms, take a shield and long baton and instantaneously slot into a squad with a near military-style functioning. But those early ME units remained rather crude and blunt instruments that failed dramatically in the mid-1960s and that failure in public order ushered in significant change.[1] The early Mobile Units had mounted officers and water cannons and could employ tear gas, with some squads using motorbikes with side cars or light jeeps to pursue rioters. One can clearly see the French-Continental model at work here. This exemplifies almost a distrust in the regular, local police when dealing with major disturbances; a predilection for central surplus capacity that can be rapidly mobilised; several units under diverse ministries – with at one stage even two militarised 'police' units within the Army; and harsh methods including the use of firearms when suppressing riots. And those methods were long condoned by the local and national authorities (de Rooy, 2011).

That operational style – and especially the military imagery and equipment – would not have been seen as appropriate in post-WWII mainland Britain. The failure of the military in the realm of public order had been one of the reasons for opting for the New Police in the 1820s, and Peel as Home Secretary made it clear that the Army in public order situations was always subordinate to civil control through the magistrates (Hurd, 2007). This deep-rooted apprehension about military intervention in British society was clear in the 1970s, when regular army units with armoured vehicles were occasionally employed to protect public facilities in an emergency. Indeed, the reluctance to establish military-style squads with special training and gear is plainly evident in the TV footage of the 1981 Brixton riots, showing officers with no protective equipment having to use dustbin lids as shields. It was largely as a result of that experience that protective gear and equipment was introduced. Yet there remains a deep institutional reluctance to use baton rounds ('rubber-bullets'), CS gas and water cannons in mainland policing. These have been employed in Northern Ireland; indeed, at one stage in the Troubles, the RUC employed armoured vehicles equipped with machine guns to fire indiscriminately at buildings in Belfast (Punch, 2012, p 71). This would have been unthinkable in other parts of the UK. The RUC always had, for historical reasons, a large public order capability, as does the PSNI. There is and has not been a standing equivalent of the French CRS on the British mainland, so individual forces have developed specific units for public order and special duties. These units started on the mainland with the Special Patrol Group in the Met in the late 1960s, which was sometimes armed, and similar units in other forces. Since then, the police have developed the capacity for large-scale public order operations, as was evident in deployment and equipment during the extensive 2011 riots in London and other cities, which were unanticipated and stretched the police response considerably (LSE, 2011). Such semi-military formations and their tactics often attract adverse comment, as in recent years for 'kettling', which involves penning in groups of people to control their movement.

Brodeur reserves the term 'para-military' for those special units within state policing set up specifically to tackle organised, armed, anti-government groups with a radical political agenda aimed at regime change and out-groups perceived as disruptive and dangerous. He argues that typically they adopt extra-legal measures that are tolerated or even encouraged by the state. This type of state-driven, systemic illegality has been a frequent occurrence in South America under military regimes in which such units conducted a reign of terror with abductions, torture, rape and murder. But this also happened in South Africa during the counter-insurgency campaigns of the South African Police in the apartheid era (Ellis, 1988). Such campaigns were instigated by the state and the systematic 'excesses' committed were condoned by the state. And at times such units have been equipped and trained, formally or illicitly, by the US (Huggins, 1991).

Policing paradigms

Both the typology of police systems and Brodeur's distinction between high and low policing are conceptual lenses through which we can look at policing and police systems. To gain further insights and to provide an alternative lens, this chapter will now attend to the concept of policing paradigms. 'Paradigms' of policing at the system level reflect deep-rooted, societal worldviews on the conservative-liberal socio-political spectrum. Excluding as extreme those repressive systems under dictatorships, or the highly undemocratic government found in Russia and elsewhere (Rawlinson, 2010), the focus here is on the two main paradigms of 'control' and 'consent' at the police institutional level in Western democracies. The control paradigm is geared to a narrow mandate focused primarily on crime control and maintaining public order through reactive policing where there is distance from the public and a disassociation from problem solving and 'peace keeping'. The consent paradigm is based on a broader mandate that seeks the consent of the public for legitimacy and is more oriented to service to the community and a wider stance of societal engagement, including prevention of crime alongside crime control and public order. Plainly, there is a relation here to the nature of the political system, and the control paradigm probably was, and is, prevalent in many societies and policing systems with high central control and with a political fixation on crime and order issues. The consent paradigm, in contrast, is most likely to be found in liberal, democratic societies or cities. Thus, these two paradigms are reflected in ideological approaches to governance, justice, crime, deviance, sanctions and control measures and the role of policing in society. The choices made on the basis of a paradigm are then transmitted in the mandate of a police system through legislation, policies of governments and ministerial guidelines. They are often explicit in government documents, can be discerned from statements of common purpose by police systems or are conveyed in the mission statements of individual forces. In those societies that are highly decentralised, as in the US, or allow a measure of autonomy to forces as in the British policing model (O'Connor, 2003, 2005; HMIC, 2009), there may also be variety in the institutionally dominant paradigm at the individual force level. There may well be a discrepancy between the 'espoused' paradigm and the actual paradigm 'in use', and perhaps also a measure of conflict or competition between 'paradigms in use' in diverse segments of the system or between and within forces.

Control paradigm

In Continental Europe and elsewhere, most systems and forces were, and are, based on the control paradigm. For it is largely the case that in many societies the police organisation is viewed as primarily an agency of state, or local control, which is distant from the public and devoid of any notion of service. And in some countries the police are violent, untrustworthy, indolent, discriminatory and corrupt. There is a historical explanation for this predominance and resilience of the control paradigm. The influential French model was based on magistrates and the military with tight central control. With slow communications and long distances in the Empire, it was imperative for France, and later other states, to have federal forces dispersed in barracks, with *gendarmes* who were not from the region and who would act dispassionately. The French *gendarmerie* was part of the Army, was ready to subdue local dissent and could be relied on for its loyalty. Only in 2002 did it become accountable to the Ministry of the Interior for domestic duties while remaining part of the Army under the Ministry of Defence. There also emerged a policy of 'divide and rule' in France as municipal and national police along with the *gendarmerie* fell under diverse ministries; hence no single ministry could control the police.

Importantly, that structure was adopted in the countries France had occupied. Its emphasis on central control and public order was useful for the state as there was fear of the mob and of revolution throughout the 19th century, with the 1848 revolts, 1871 Paris Commune and the threat from socialist and communist movements culminating in the Russian Revolution of 1917. Furthermore, before the French Revolution, most law was local with a jumble of near autonomous jurisdictions. The French model of a codified law and highly structured agencies for policing and justice was retained elsewhere because it brought central organisation and clarity to disorganised systems and to non-codified and disparate laws. In the Netherlands, there was also a structure to ensure that a local police force did not become too independent as the mayor held the formal authority over the police for matters of public order and the public prosecutor for criminal investigations. The former was linked to the Ministry of the Interior and the latter to the Ministry of Justice. In effect, the Dutch police chief had a civil and judicial boss at the local level and also at the central level, and ultimately the state controlled the police system.

This helps to explain the dominance of the control paradigm in much of Europe up to modern times. This paradigm, with its focus on central control, maintaining order and forcefully tackling crime, has continued to prove highly attractive to many governments, politicians, city mayors and police chiefs. It particularly suits those with a conservative worldview and mindset – in politics, the media and among the public – but can also be advocated for various reasons by those of a more liberal persuasion to gain electoral advantage.

Consent paradigm

The Anglo-Saxon model has become associated with consent and can be traced to the 'New Police' in London in 1829, although forces were founded earlier in Ireland and Scotland (Ascoli, 1979). In the UK, this has become known as the British policing model, although as emphasised earlier there were three separate systems. A great deal of mythology surrounds the shaping of the Metropolitan Police in the 1820s, which is at times presented as if there was some grand, intrinsically liberal and typically 'English' strategy defining its innovative contours. The reality is more prosaic, in that it was the result of a pragmatic compromise on the part of Sir Robert Peel (Home Secretary) to get his Bill through a sceptical Parliament after several efforts in previous decades to establish a police force by statute had failed. For political reasons, Peel exempted the City of London from his proposals and there is still a small, separate force for what is now the financial heart of the capital. Crucially, there was in that period in British society a widespread aversion to the notion of 'police', which was seen as intrinsically French and as intrusive to personal liberty. At the same time, there was an increasing demand for policing in terms of safety of property and personal security (Emsley, 1996, 2009). There was growing concern about the rising economic and social costs of crime in a society going through a rapid process of industrialisation and urbanisation, and an awareness that at times of moral panic, say related to a brutal serial murderer, there was no effective policing to deal with the case. There was, too, an awareness of the crudeness of the military in public order situations in a period when large-scale disorder was a constant threat and when cities were still relatively small, allowing the unruly 'mob' to take over cities or parts of cities for days and attack public buildings and the houses of the wealthy (Hurd, 2007).

The French-Continental model was deeply contaminated as France had been the enemy in the protracted Revolutionary and Napoleonic Wars (in the period 1792–1815). Peel had, therefore, to disassociate his plans from anything that reeked of France and of potential state repression if he was to succeed where others had failed.

What emerged – with considerable help from the first Commissioners, Rowan and Mayne – was something quite unlike policing in Continental Europe. Rowan was a soldier and Mayne a lawyer and they served long in office – Rowan 21 years and Mayne a staggering 39 years – so they were highly influential in shaping the disciplined and legalistic ethos of the force. Peel himself was not averse to that more traditional model because previously, as Secretary of State for Ireland, he had set up an armed, militarised force that later became the Royal Irish Constabulary (Conway, 2014). In his delicate juggling with Parliament, Peel had to persuade the members that his version of policing for the capital would be benign, accountable and not a threat to personal liberty or indeed to the state itself through a coup. In a nutshell, the compromise model he proposed for the Metropolitan Police, and which was later adopted elsewhere in Britain and abroad, was based on the following.

The primary focus was on the prevention of crime and preservation of order by a constant, visible police presence on the streets by patrolling uniformed officers. Officers were not routinely armed (although some occasionally were); even the wooden truncheon was later kept in a special pocket in the uniform trousers. They were not militarily trained and their uniform was deliberately designed not to be like that of the military. They were not led by 'gentlemen', meaning those who could claim their positions in public life on grounds of class and wealth; long before the setting of standards in recruitment for public office, here was 'the authentic voice of the Victorian reformer proclaiming the supremacy of merit in the public service' (Hurd, 2007, p 104). There was an emphasis on discipline and standards of conduct. Almost everyone started as constable and had to work their way up the hierarchy.[2] 'Constable' was not just a rank but also an office with a long history in the English legal system, whereby the holder was an independent legal official who could mount his own investigation and prosecution.[3] All police officers were in that second sense 'constables'. Officers owed allegiance to the Crown and were accountable to the courts rather than directly to politicians. The legalism was designed to convey impartiality which was reinforced by police not being allowed to vote in elections or belong to a trade union. Constables were identifiable by a number on their collar with a letter for the division they served in.

Importantly, the tradition developed in a number of common-law countries with police chiefs enjoying operational autonomy and a measure of freedom from direct political interference. In the early 1960s the 'tripartite' system that had developed in England and Wales was formalised with policing in local administrative areas being the responsibility of the local police authority, the Chief Constable and the Home Office. The Met Commissioner was exceptional in not being accountable to a police authority, but to the Home Secretary. However, the principle of constabulary independence was held to apply to all forces, and this principle was most explicitly expressed in 1968 by Lord Denning in a case referring to the Commissioner of the Metropolitan Police but extending to all chief constables:

> No Minister of the Crown can tell him that he must, or must not, keep observation on this place or that; or that he must, or must not, prosecute this man or that one. Nor can any police authority tell him so. The responsibility for law enforcement lies on him. *He is answerable to the law and to the law alone.* (Lustgarten, 1986, p 64; emphasis added)

In English common law, this set a precedent in jurisprudence, although its legal validity has been disputed (Lustgarten, 1986). From this tradition, British police chiefs saw themselves as having a high measure of operational autonomy, with a primary accountability to the law and the courts, while remaining institutionally accountable to the local police authority or, in the case of the Metropolitan Police, to the Home Secretary. It is debatable as to how far that autonomy went; one can imagine that traditionally there were polite requests rather than specific instructions that, in the British way, were implemented as a 'gentleman's [sic] agreement' whereby no-one felt that a direct order had been given. In the early decades after 1829, moreover, it was not unusual for a retired military officer to be appointed as chief constable in the county forces and some held office for 15 or more years; they may well have been fairly compliant with 'requests' from the central authorities.

Crucially, 'Peel's Principles' – which may have not been his and may have been penned long after 1829 – were geared to reassurance. The police officer was to be seen merely as a citizen in uniform – 'the police were the public and the public were the police' – and he would conduct himself with restraint. Those oft-cited principles attributed to Peel have longevity, being adopted in New Zealand as central to the new Police Act 2008, and lauded once more by Bill Bratton, who was Commissioner of Police in New York in the early 1990s and who, in 2014, after periods as a consultant and as Chief of the Los Angeles Police Department, returned to the New York City Police Department (NYPD). Peel and his associates were endeavouring to convey to the public that the police were a trustworthy rather than an alien force, and that the policing system was essentially benign, *as indeed was the state it represented*. In a period when undue state interference was associated with the despised French Revolution, this was a very important message.

It took a while for the New Police to become accepted (Bailey, 1981), but in time the 'bobby' (derived from Peel's given name, 'Robert') became an icon of restraint, approachability and helpfulness. This was not an effortless process, and it took time to establish disciplined forces. Some critics viewed with suspicion the collective deployment of police in public order situations as too 'militaristic', and were dismayed when the first case of undercover policing was exposed. In contrast, others within the establishment from a military background proposed arming the police and forming special units modelled on light infantry with artillery to deal with public order (Emsley, 2009, p 88). Fortunately, the Peelian model survived these disputes and proposals. It is best expressed in 'Peel's Principles', which reflect the working values that Peel, Rowan and Mayne propagated in the early years of the Metropolitan Police (Reith, 1956, p 140)

- The basic mission for which the police exist is to prevent crime and disorder.
- The ability of the police to perform their duties is dependent upon the public approval of police actions.
- Police must secure the willing co-operation of the public in voluntary observation of the law to be able to secure and maintain the respect of the public.
- The degree of co-operation of the public that can be secured diminishes proportionately to the necessity of the use of physical force.
- Police seek and preserve public favour not by catering to public opinion, but by constantly demonstrating absolute impartial service to the law.
- Police use physical force to the extent necessary to secure observance of the law or to restore order only when the

exercise of persuasion, advice, and warning is found to be insufficient.

- Police, at all times, should maintain a relationship with the public that gives reality to the historic tradition that the police are the public and the public are the police; the police being only members of the public who are paid to give full-time attention to duties which are incumbent upon every citizen in the interests of community welfare and existence.
- Police should always direct their action strictly towards their functions, and never appear to usurp the powers of the judiciary.
- The test of police efficiency is the absence of crime and disorder, not the visible evidence of police action in dealing with it.

It is not often that police become a positive symbol, but that happened with 'the great British bobby' (Emsley, 2009). More by accident than design, Peel and his associates had shaped a viable – and exportable – alternative to the then dominant French-Continental model.

In short, in the Metropolitan Police and the forces that soon followed, the system was based on one form of policing that had primacy over the use of force (including by the military); ostensible independence from direct government control; operational autonomy for the chief; a degree of legal autonomy for all ranks through the office of 'constable'; accountability to the courts and not directly to Parliament; no military training and no routine arming of officers; and no dual entry system with an officer caste, but rather a system whereby everyone had to start in uniform out on the streets. Brodeur (2010) emphasises that this was a veritable sea-change in the concept of policing. For really the first time there was a professional body of police officers, performing under statute a set of tasks for the criminal justice system. For quite some time, these tasks included the preparation of prosecutions, an anomaly given that elsewhere this was normally the preserve of other agencies, with investigations being led by magistrates.[4] And the Bobbies were subject to a degree, however rudimentary, of oversight and public accountability. Above all, the system exemplified that the legitimacy of the police depended on the consent of the public, and that without that consent the police could not function effectively.

However, that consent was further related to the willingness of the public to comply with regulation by the police. In many European societies, cities could be rowdy and disorderly, there was long a threat of political unrest and some societies remained politically unstable throughout the 19th century. Police could not always rely on compliance and were kept largely locked in control mode with an emphasis on maintaining order. Britain, in contrast, became increasingly prosperous, had an established parliamentary democracy and by mid-century was relatively stable politically and socially. In a way it could 'afford' to work according to the notion of consent, primarily because it had, after a difficult few decades, managed to negotiate with the public over their willingness to be policed, and gain their compliance. While that British consent paradigm emerged from the necessity to make opportunistic choices to charter the New Police legislation through Parliament in the late 1820s, it has become central in Britain to an almost mythical police identity that is subject to periodic reconfirmation in time of need. It found its icon in *Dixon of Dock Green*, a highly popular character in a film and a long-running TV police series that began in the late 1950s. Dixon came to represent both a golden age in policing as well as the unflappable, restrained, avuncular 'bobby', who was a peace keeper and problem solver of the finest sort (McLaughlin, 2005). Hence when the consent paradigm is under threat, the British constable re-emerges as a kind of Dixon incarnate who is 'approachable, impartial and accountable' and who with minimum force wins 'public support through tolerance and patience' (HMIC, 2009). Not only has that image altered – the bobby is likely now to be wearing a stab-vest and carrying an extendable baton, CS spray, speed-cuffs and a Taser – but also the mode of policing may be geared primarily towards sanctioning people and discouraging the exercise of discretion in order to meet targets linked to performance indicators.

British policing: paradigm shift

That traditional consent paradigm associated with the British policing model can be viewed as an 'ideal type' that may not fully correspond with the reality of practice at all times and in all places; indeed, it may even have a near mythical and unquestioned status. In its statement of intent, for instance, the newly formed College of Policing lauded the consent paradigm but there is no discussion about what it means, about alternative or competing paradigms, or about paradigm shift (College of Policing, 2013). In all organisations, moreover, there is always a discrepancy between the 'myth system', or ideal presentation, and the 'operational code', or how things 'really get done' (Reisman, 1979). Drawing on this distinction, there can be a considerable gap between the 'espoused paradigm' and 'the paradigm in use'. Indeed, the 'paradigm in use' is not necessarily a fixed element, but rather is subject to dispute, oscillation and differential adoption. This has certainly been the case in British policing, where there have been in recent decades cycles of assertive policing and/or loss of confidence in the police followed by a reassertion of the consent paradigm (O'Connor, 2003, 2005; Savage, 2007a; Flanagan, 2008). For example, there have been periodic 'crack-downs' on suspects of street crime in certain areas in times of moral panic often leading to inflammatory situations, especially in areas of ethnic tension. For example, in Brixton, London, in 1981, there was serious rioting by predominantly black youths as a protest against aggressive police behaviour (Bowling and Phillips, 2003). Some 300 officers were injured and about 60 police vehicles were destroyed. The influential Scarman Report (1981) on the disturbances argued that the police had become divorced from the community and had to return to the traditional 'consent' paradigm. This coincided with a rapid expansion of people with university degrees entering the service or gaining degrees while working in the police (Lee and Punch, 2006). Particularly at the top of the organisation, this and other developments led to more liberal views about policing – with top officers becoming 'Scarmanised' – implying a return to the consent paradigm. This was not to say that crime control was not important, but rather that chiefs started to see policing as having a broader mandate. However, many politicians and members of the public, fed by the populist media, tended to see this as too liberal and 'soft', favouring instead a 'tough on crime' approach. The tabloid newspapers are particularly influential in shaping opinion in the UK: they demonise in their eyes 'deviant' out-groups and individuals and have remorselessly pursued police chiefs, including in their private lives, who are held to be too progressive or unconventional (Paddick, 2008).

The public and political debate around criminal justice, moreover, had become something of an escalating competition between the two major parties. When the Labour Party under Tony Blair entered government in 1997, it energetically competed with the Conservatives on this issue by unleashing a campaign of intense pressure on the police to reduce crime and to perform to a set of centrally defined standards. This can also be seen as substantially reducing the operational autonomy of police chiefs by tying financing to results. To a large extent, the contours of a strong crime-control paradigm have been present for some time and this has been linked to more direct civilian control over the police since the Conservative–Liberal Democrat coalition took office in 2010. In commenting on the resort since then to a deterrent, reactive, crime-fighting model, Loader (2014, p 43) states, 'the government sees itself as releasing the police's inner crime-fighter. Inside every police force, it reasons, there is a lean, mean crime-fighting machine struggling to get out.' An issue of concern, moreover, is to what extent operational autonomy has become corroded and what the implications for governance and accountability are. The uniqueness of the notion of 'constabulary independence' based on the operational autonomy of the chief constable can be compared with the system in the Netherlands, where – and this would be true for most policing models – the police chief has never formally been granted such autonomy. And in the US, the police chief has typically had low autonomy because he or she is caught between powerful and intransigent unions and politically motivated, media-obsessed, vacillating mayors who may change a policy direction without warning, demand obeisance or fire chiefs at will.

This happened when the Mayor of New York, Rudy Giuliani, removed Bill Bratton in 1996 – only two years after he had recruited him as Commissioner of the NYPD – for being too prominently successful. Bratton had hogged the publicity around the so-called New York 'miracle' in reducing crime (Silverman, 1999). This led to his picture on the cover of *Time* magazine, much to the aggravation of Giuliani. Giuliani also later crudely sacked another NYPD Commissioner, Ray Kelly, for underperforming on crime control (Levitt, 2009, p 42):

> When Giuliani asked how he would reduce street crime, Kelly began discussing community policing. Hearing those two words, Giuliani looked up at the ceiling, then turned towards an aide, and in mid-sentence cut Kelly off. He rose, shook Kelly's hand, thanked him, and walked out of the door. The meeting was over. Kelly's thirty-one-year career with the NYPD, including his praiseworthy fifteen months as police commissioner, had ended in fifteen minutes.

But that brutal style of Giuliani reflects how the police organisation in certain American cities was, and is, a vehicle for the mayor's political ambitions. He or she may be facing re-election or may be aiming to become the state governor, a senator, or even, as in Giuliani's case, the president. The serious distortions that this unbridled egoism can bring to a police organisation are graphically portrayed for the NYPD during Giuliani's reign by Levitt (2009). Such almost unchecked political control over the police can lead to an abrupt *volte face* in reaction to moral panic sparked by specific violent crimes or perceived crime rises fed by the populist media. Skogan (2008, p 31), who has long been associated with implementing community policing in Chicago and witnessed just such an abrupt turnaround in Chicago, relates another instant change of policy, and of commissioner, in Baltimore:

> Baltimore elected a new republican mayor in 1999, one who ran on a tough 'law and order' platform. His predecessor had committed the city to community policing, and had selected a new police chief from Los Angeles to implement the program. The new mayor fired the chief at their first meeting. The deputy chief, who was present at the meeting, stood up and promised to push a 'zero tolerance' strategy that the mayor found more appealing. The mayor promoted him to chief of police on the spot.

To a degree, this external dominance and interference would seem to be the case in London where the Mayor since 2008 – Boris Johnson – is highly popular in Conservative circles and is viewed as a future Prime Minister. Although the Home Secretary had always appointed the Met Commissioner, changes in the local authority structure for London in 2000 gave more power to the Mayor as head of the new Metropolitan Police Authority. This was not an issue until the Conservative Johnson was elected. He seized on this opportunity and surprised many, including the Home Secretary, by asserting the Mayor's right to make the appointment. Then he clearly saw the sitting Commissioner, Ian Blair, as being too oriented to the Labour government and pushed him to resign by withdrawing confidence in him; mayoral staff later spoke of Blair being 'sacked' (Blair, 2009). Squeezing out a British police chief in this blunt way was alarming to some and seemed to ape the power of American mayors to hire and fire their police chief at will for political and personal gain. Mayor Johnson also boldly spells out ambitious goals for the police to reach: and with the Police and Crime Commissioner for the Met on his staff and located within the Mayor's Office for Police and Crime (MOPAC), he can also put pressure on the Commissioner. Plans for policing the capital draw on martial imagery – of all-out efforts, echoing the language used about mass bombing raids on Germany in WWII – and sport, in order to widen their appeal (Steve Savage, personal communication). For instance, the inclusion in the plans for a '20, 20, 20' mayoral campaign, intended to cut crime, cut costs and improve public confidence by 20% respectively, is a nod to the introduction of 'Twenty20 cricket', designed to appeal to a wider audience.[5] Enforcement appears to be based on large-scale deployment in selected areas, focusing on a specific offence with no leeway for exercising discretion. Even more grating is that the Commissioner has adopted the term 'total' policing for the Metropolitan Police approach: if this is viewed as a 'total war on crime', it is a war that – predictably – cannot be won.[6]

Typically, questions as to whether or not these mayoral goals are competing or conflicting, or whether the means adopted will alienate the public whose confidence is being sought, are not raised. In adopting this approach the Mayor of London, and consequently the Metropolitan Police, are conveying the impression that police efforts are akin to a battle or a sporting match, where one side has to 'win' in a competitive contest, where only the results count and where the victorious commander or captain is feted as heroic. But rather like the immodest and almost biblical subtitle of Bratton's book on his successful police career – *How America's top cop reversed the crime epidemic* – it is obvious that it is all about success on just one dominant indicator, cutting crime (Bratton and Knobler, 1998). In this scenario, the police chief is reduced to the role of football manager who is disposable if the club owner is dissatisfied with a team that is not scoring enough goals to bring in glittering prizes. It is highly debatable whether this is the sort of gung-ho, uncompromising message that is appropriate to policing a large, multicultural metropolis or indeed, any other environment, as it threatens to put the public in the role of 'the other side' or even 'the enemy'. Even when this type of approach is adopted in the name of the public, we know from previous campaigns that swamping, non-discretionary enforcement techniques tend to alienate those law-abiding members caught up in them, particularly if there is a sense of systemic discrimination, which there nearly always is (Bowling and Phillips, 2002). The lesson of Brixton seems to have been forgotten.

The common element in the trend for quantifiable policing goals in the US and UK is cutting crime, because this is what resonates with the public – which stubbornly refuses to accept that crime is falling – and takes prominence in political debate and media coverage. And increasingly in the UK it signifies a measure of redefinition in the traditional 'Peelian' model with regard to home-grown leaders rising from the ranks and to operational autonomy in three ways. First, the 'artisan' institution envisaged by Peel required a long period of practical experience starting at the bottom of the ladder before being promoted, and this was not likely to attract too many well-educated recruits. Indeed, there developed a strong, anti-elitist culture opposing any form of lateral entry and for a long time it was rare for a university graduate to join the police. By the 1960s, this was perceived as a problem and the service has endeavoured to recruit, and to accelerate promotion, for well-qualified candidates and for those with potential. Second, the relative freedom granted to chiefs led at one stage in the 1950s to a degree of venality and cronyism (leading to the last Royal Commission on policing in 1962) and later to the appointment of some rather 'strong' if not somewhat eccentric personalities. Reiner (1991) typified the generation he interviewed in the 1980s as 'barons, bobbies and bosses' but argued that they were already becoming 'bureaucrats', and later he saw them as more like businessmen (Reiner, 2007). Third, there was the issue of governance. That traditional autonomy of the chief frequently meant that the local police authority had little power or inclination to control or intervene in decision making and if it did, the chief could usually rely on support from the Home Secretary (Reiner, 2013, p 169). Some chiefs were clearly not too enthusiastic about accountability and transparency. The tripartite arrangement (police chief, local authority, Home Office) forged in the 1960s functioned well for some time, but did not really alter the chief's claim to autonomy.

Both the tripartite arrangement and chief's autonomy became bones of contention, with increasing central pressure on chiefs starting under New Labour in 1997. Since then, they have been pursued by relentless performance regimes, and have had Home Secretaries and their officials trying to bully and intimidate them. Indeed, when two police chiefs refused to accede to the government 'requests' in relation to breaking the petrol drivers' strike of 2000, the government brought in legislation enabling it to remove police chiefs. And as one chief put it (to one of the authors), 'at least Jack Straw [Labour Home Secretary] treated us like adults', intimating that others talked down to them. It seems the Conservatives view the police as 'the last great unreformed public service', according to David Cameron (*Telegraph*, 5 January 2006) and are impatiently badgering them to get a move on. For some time, the government imagery in Whitehall has been 'we steer and you row', which conveys a subordinate if not servile role. It could be concluded, then, that the notion of autonomy dating back for some time and made explicit by Lord Denning has been under continual erosion.[7] That process has culminated in a new system whereby an elected civilian Police and Crime Commissioner (PCC) can curtail that autonomy in certain areas and also hire, and perhaps even fire, a chief.[8] The very title suggests that the PCC's task is to keep the chief and the force focused specifically on crime control. There can be no better illustration of this shift than the narrowing of focus and hectoring style in the speech of Home Secretary May (quoted at the beginning of Chapter One). This was at the Conservative Party conference in 2011 where one might expect expansive statements, but it did convey a degree of hostility between her and the police, some of whom had behaved boorishly to her at a meeting. As a consequence, the Home Secretary responded fairly assertively. However, in reducing matters to one overriding goal, Home Secretary May overlooks the substantial body of academic knowledge about policing and crime control (Bayley, 1994; Manning, 1997; Tonry, 2004).

Indeed, at a time when influential figures in policing, academia and government are pushing strongly for 'evidence-based' policing (Neyroud Report, 2011; Sherman, 2013), she sidesteps that evidence that does not suit her and her government's ideological convictions and political ambitions. That may not be especially new in politics, but coming at this particular moment it threatens to undermine much that is valuable in British policing, with potentially grave consequences for the relationship between the state and its citizens. This would seem to indicate the effective end of the consent paradigm and signifies a clear paradigm shift to 'control'.

The Netherlands: paradigm lost

The Dutch police system, as mentioned earlier, was based on a model inherited from the French Occupation and subsequent integration of the Netherlands within the French Empire during the period 1795-1813. That model was largely retained and given form when the Netherlands began to evolve into a parliamentary democracy with, as under the French, several police forces answering to diverse ministries and with a central, militarised *gendarmerie* – the *Marechaussee* (Fijnaut, 2007). The resilience of this structure was still plainly visible up to the early 1990s. Local governance was based on dual control, with the mayor holding responsibility for 'public order' and the public prosecutor responsible for criminal investigations. Together with the police chief, who was formally subordinate to both of them, they formed the policy and decision-making 'triangle'. This division of authority was geared to not having a 'too independent' police or one ministry dominating, so that central authority was also dual, resting under two ministries – Justice and the Interior. The city forces (*gemeentepolitie*) were the responsibility of the Ministry of the Interior and the National Police Force (*Rijkspolitie*) the responsibility of the Ministry of Justice; the *Marechaussee* came under the Ministry of Defence. This was long recognised as a fragmented, unwieldy and unsatisfactory arrangement but there was a lack of political will, given the powerful vested interests at the local level, to bring about system change. But besides structure, there is also culture, along with a 'paradigm' of policing, and in recent decades Dutch policing has developed a highly specific style.

In the late 1960s and early 1970s, Dutch policing was still somewhat old-fashioned institutionally, with a highly reactive style, little sense of direction and a bureaucratic leadership where promotion was based on seniority rather than merit (Zwart, 2004, Meershoek, 2011). Moreover, the post-war period was dominated by efforts to rebuild the country's infrastructure, and this, combined with low levels of crime and disorder, resulted in a reduction in police resources, which were at an all-time low in 1968 (personal communication: Guus Meershoek). The Amsterdam Police, for example, was down from around 3,000 to 2,000 officers: this played a role in its failure during the turbulent events of the 1960s just when more personnel were desperately needed. At this point many Dutch forces had the hallmarks of non-thinking, authoritarian institutions which in time of need fell back on stereotypical, unrefined and un-nuanced practices bereft of internal scrutiny. This rigid, traditional model came under attack in the 1960s for being unresponsive to societal change, authoritarian, unreflective and not particularly competent; moreover, leadership was palpably weak if not absent. This is not to say that there were no enlightened or forward-thinking chiefs in Dutch policing, but that their efforts were usually confined to their own forces, leaving the wider system mostly unresponsive to their ideas and innovations. The police organisation was primarily a legally oriented agency for the criminal justice system, with rigid operational structures for categorising and processing those within its remit solely as victims, witnesses or suspects. Even in the 1960s, it scarcely bothered itself with anything like 'policy' or with formulating its own aims (van der Vijver, 2009). When the wave of criticism hit policing from the mid-1960s onwards, it came not only from without but also, importantly, from within.

The background was that Dutch society had reacted to the turbulence of the late 1960s with a leap to the left; politicians and others had become progressive and many policies were lenient – notably on drugs, homosexuality, pornography and prostitution. The anti-authoritarian and anarchistic 'Provo' movement of the 1960s had continually provoked the police, with playful 'happenings' that elicited a heavy-handed response. A crucial turning-point was the serious rioting in Amsterdam in 1966, which revealed a crude and hopelessly inadequate police response and which led to the unprecedented departure of both the Mayor and Police Chief (Punch, 1979a). The police organisation and its senior officers were widely held to be hopelessly out of touch with developments in a society where a youthful, assertive, post-war generation was thirsting for change (Verbij, 2005). One response to this incapacity to deal with societal and institutional change was that a new generation of vocal police officers started to emerge, kicking against the old-style, bureaucratic system that was buckling in the face of rapid change. In particular, three mid-career and ambitious officers accepted an assignment from the Ministry of the Interior relating to a specific organisational matter. This Project Group on Organisational Structure grasped the opportunity to write a wider, critical report on policing in general with the title *A changing police (Politie in Verandering)* (POS, 1977; Nordholt and Straver, 1983; Hoogewoning 1993). In essence, they argued for a more internally democratic police and for a stronger external orientation to societal change. Contrary to the intention of the minister who had appointed it, the group was primarily concerned with the legitimacy of the police in a society that required a paradigm shift (van der Vijver, 2004). All three of the young officers – Nordholt, Wiarda and Straver – later became influential and prominent chiefs in Amsterdam, Utrecht and Haarlem respectively. These 1970s rebels became the new progressive establishment and spread the word of renewal through their own forces and by teaching to future senior officers at the NPA (former Netherlands Police Academy).

The report, and the triumvirate that produced it, are of central significance in several decades of Dutch policing. For the call for reform had come from professionals within the system; it was not driven by government demands, but by a powerful, internal demand for change from critical, young, middle-ranking officers aspiring to top positions. The report acted for many years as a leitmotiv for policing in the Netherlands and gave it a strong 'social' character – geared to societal change, internal democracy and the wishes of the public (Boin et al, 2003).

Although this report was essentially a reflection of particular 'progressive' changes in Dutch society, it drew importantly on organisational concepts from the US. In particular, the Dutch model saw an affinity with moves by American policing agencies towards community policing and problem-oriented policing (Goldstein, 1979). These imported models fostered a series of experiments that were stimulated by the Department of Research and Development at the Ministry of the Interior. The projects were oriented to both internal and external change in the police organisation; internal efforts were geared to better communication, less hierarchy, decentralisation and enhanced problem solving; external efforts were centred on improved relations with the public, a service-oriented mentality and a focus on societal problems. Hence the new-style policing and paradigm came to be encouraged from the political centre and a range of change projects were funded by central government. Furthermore, the Foundation for Police and Society (SMP) – rather like the Police Foundations in the UK and US – became an influential stimulator of change. The SMP (later SMVP) had been set up in 1986 and it pushed for an emphasis on community security and safety, on increasing the self-reliance of citizens, on bringing back visible control agents (in public transport, schools and on the streets) and on informing the public on safety and prevention. Through conferences, projects, research, publications and publicity, it strongly pushed two themes – the need to focus continually on the relationship between police and society, and the importance in communities of a proactive, 'integrated safety policy' with multiple agencies. And security ensuring safety of the public was a task to be shared with others and could not be the sole responsibility of the police; this was clearly a forerunner of 'community safety' and 'plural policing' elsewhere (Crawford and Lister, 2005).

In short, there has been continuous innovation since the early 1980s, with a substantial investment in socially conscious, locally oriented policing with an external focus in the community. Much of the conceptual content of the change came from the US, and to a lesser extent the UK, but became mixed with a strong 'Dutch flavour'. For Dutch society was quite unlike American and British society. It was at that time stable and affluent, had low levels of violent crime, had an advanced welfare state, stimulated a range of community development projects with a high level of consultation, granted security of employment to many and benefited from low levels of racial tension. Furthermore, governments and leading public officials in ministries and cities had – in response to societal developments – largely shifted to progressive, 'tolerant' views and supported enlightened policies. In particular, criminal justice in the Netherlands came to be viewed as an alternative paradigmatic model to that in the US, and to a lesser extent in the UK. In his analysis of Dutch penal policy, for example, Downes (1988) showed that the judiciary had taken professional views on rehabilitation on board: few people were imprisoned compared with the US and the UK, even though crime was rising, and most prisons had liberal regimes. On the streets, beat officers were generally prepared to overlook the minor infringements that might attract swift police attention and sanctions elsewhere.

This alternative paradigm in criminal justice – the 'least inhumane in Europe' (Bianchi, 1975, p 1) – reflected the values of a liberal democracy at its progressive high point. Rather like Canada, New Zealand and the Scandinavian countries, the Netherlands followed relatively progressive and humane policies on social issues that fostered, as Downes (1988) shows, a genuinely enlightened position on crime and punishment shared by most police chiefs, prison governors and judges. In addition, the Dutch structurally turned a blind eye to certain illicit but generally accepted practices. This is referred to as *gedogen*, meaning a kind of conditional acceptance that can be seen as a pragmatic or even an opportunistic way of condoning matters. Brants (1999) speaks of 'regulated tolerance' on certain practices, such as prostitution and drug use, that was informally agreed by officials. Police chiefs, together with the mayor and public prosecutor in the local policy triangle, often tolerated practices that would have attracted harsh enforcement in other countries. But this *gedogen* happened without altering the law, which remained as a sanction in case of anyone abusing the agreement. There was a downside to this *gedogen* in that what appeared to be pragmatic liberalism could mask non-decision making and rationalising the postponement of tackling problems (Hoogenboom and Vlek, 2002; Pakes, 2004). This later became one of the criticisms of the criminal justice system.

In general, then, the espoused and working Dutch policing paradigm well into the 1990s was based on progressive values, the minimisation of violence, the avoidance of conflict by negotiation with groups, and close involvement in society to generate legitimacy and to increase the confidence of the public. The functioning orthodoxy was that virtually all basic policing was in decentralised, multi-tasked teams with a geographic base, with specialised community beat officers geared to problem solving ('area managers') and with deep engagement in multi-agency arrangements employing a high measure of discretion and 'social' skills (Punch et al, 2008). Dutch policing displayed a distinctly social face. This was one of the most serious attempts anywhere in the world to develop constructive ideas of community policing, problem-oriented policing and the consent paradigm (Punch et al, 2002, 2005). This approach had already begun to attract criticism in the mid-1990s, and that critical pressure increased. The leading chiefs had become public figures in the 1980s and early 1990s, with strongly expressed notions of reform, attracting considerable media coverage. They had helped to develop a paradigm favouring a value-driven culture, with decentralisation and an emphasis on external collaboration with multiple agencies. Their prominence in the media clearly displeased some in the establishment who wanted to put them firmly in their place; they had become 'too big for their boots' and had to get back in 'their kennel', as some critics put it (Punch, 2007). Indeed, there was increasing critical scrutiny of the criminal justice system fed by a number of failures, as if the years of *gedogen* had encouraged an influx of foreign criminals and fostered a rise in crime and feelings of insecurity. There were revelations that large amounts of drugs were passing through Schiphol Airport almost unhindered; that organised crime with foreign connections was flourishing, resulting in gang warfare and shoot-outs; that Amsterdam's red-light district, a major tourist attraction, was in fact mostly controlled by criminal gangs and that its sex workers were likely to be trafficked sex slaves (Weitzer, 2010, 2012; de Koning, 2012).

But, in particular, what became known as the 'IRT affair' proved crucial in the disenchantment with a liberal, and somewhat easy-going, justice system. The IRT was the Inter-Regional Crime Squad, which was a new proactive unit set up in 1989 involving several forces which aimed to use active informants to penetrate the hierarchy of internationally operating drug dealers. Amid disruptive inter-force rivalry and vitriolic squabbling among police chiefs regarding control of the unit, there emerged accusations of questionable police methods in arranging controlled deliveries of drugs with the aid of an active informant (Naeyé, 1995). Some shipments inadvertently ended up on the market, with the informant also dealing on his own, so that the Dutch government had, in effect, become a major importer of drugs. This met with disapproval from other EU member countries, particularly neighbouring France and Germany, where many of the drugs entering those countries came from the Netherlands. These revelations, alongside damaging leaks in the media, led to a high-profile, parliamentary commission of inquiry whose sessions were televised to an intrigued audience (van Traa Commission, 1996). The sittings exposed deep disputes over the IRT's methods, which seriously bent the law; persistent and often petty arguments about control of the squad; and systemic failures of control over events within the Public Prosecution Service and police force leaderships. The events of this period had a deep impact on the criminal justice system and on the influence and standing of police leaders (Punch, 2003). Part of the dissatisfaction that predated this affair was a series of incidents that established the failure of those within the system to cooperate. This was seen to have its roots in the strong element of localism in a structurally fragmented system.

The long-standing concern about fragmentation, linked with increasing dissatisfaction with police performance in certain matters and cases led in 1993/94 to the reorganisation of the police service into 25 regions and one central agency – by merging the then National Police with umpteen city police forces, and retaining the central body,

KLPD – with the promise of enhancing coordination, coherence and professionalism (Punch et al, 1998). For a short period in the mid-1990s, the Ministry of the Interior gained primacy over policing, hence seemingly ending the dual responsibility for institutional control with the Ministry of Justice. Furthermore, there was a discernible movement from the late 1990s onwards to more structured, assertive and proactive policing that drew from the trend set by zero tolerance policing in New York and elsewhere. This was reinforced by intelligence-led policing from the US and the UK and encouraged by the precepts and practices of New Public Management. Some of the enforcement methods developed in New York attracted Dutch attention, although the aggressive command style did not suit Dutch professional culture (Punch, 2007). Nevertheless, most forces implemented aspects of zero tolerance policing, which by then had become fairly universal – with more uniformed officers on patrol directed by up-to-date information – while the community renewal feature of 'Broken Windows' (Kelling and Coles, 1996) complemented what the Dutch had been doing for years.

In system terms, there were initially advantages to the regionalisation of the mid-1990s, but gradually most regions developed into what could be dubbed 'QAKs' – quasi-autonomous kingdoms (*koninkrijkjes*). There was also a gradual power shift in these new regions, with the 'force manager' – the mayor of the largest local authority who led the regional 'triangle' – starting to play a more prominent role in the triangle. This sometimes thrust the police chief back into a 'subordinate and obedient' role as opposed to the more collegial 'consultative and cooperative' role (Marshall, 1978) of previous decades. There was a clear tendency in a number of forces to put chiefs 'in their place', at times in a near belittling manner, and to enhance the public exposure of the mayor as force manager. This caused much dissatisfaction among chiefs and later made some of them favourable towards the idea of a National Police in which they would be less under the control of the local officials. Added to this, and of prime importance, was the rise of populist politicians after 2001, which signified, in a traditionally liberal society, a sharp shift to the right in politics, with increasing emphasis on crime, safety, security and immigration as major issues (Wansink, 2004).

The prevailing mood was reinforced by two murders that sent shock-waves through Dutch society. The first was that of Pim Fortuyn, who was murdered in 2002; this was the first political assassination in 300 years. Fortuyn's death at the hands of a Dutch environmental activist acting on his own was one of the most dramatic developments in Dutch politics in decades (Storm and Naastepad, 2003). Fortuyn's new, right-wing, populist party – the List Pim Fortuyn (LPF) – had come out of nowhere, and Fortuyn was even viewed as a serious candidate for Prime Minister. Indeed, despite Fortuyn's death just before a general election, the LPF became one the larger parties in Parliament and even entered into a short-lived coalition. Fortuyn had broken open the progressive consensus, stimulated a swing to conservatism and fuelled the growing polarisation between the main parties and a degree of anti-immigrant feeling among the electorate. The anti-immigration and anti-Muslim sentiment was fanned by the second and highly dramatic murder – of the controversial writer and film-maker Theo van Gogh, who was killed in Amsterdam in 2004. He had enflamed certain Muslims by a film, *Submission*, which aimed to expose the largely hidden issue of domestic violence against Muslim women, using texts from the Koran projected onto the bruised, naked body of a woman wearing a transparent veil. The film was conceived by Ayaan Hirsi Ali, an asylum seeker from Somalia brought up as a Muslim, who had made it into Parliament and had become highly critical of Muslim religion and culture. Both she and van Gogh had received death threats. Cycling to his office in Amsterdam in November 2004, which he did routinely despite warnings while he rejected protection, van Gogh was attacked by a young man in traditional Moroccan attire who shot him several times, calmly cut his throat with a large knife as if to decapitate him and then stabbed him in the chest with another knife which had a text attached to it (Buruma, 2006, pp 2-3). The assailant's real target had been Hirsi Ali but she had accepted constant protection. The callous, bestial manner of the slaying caused great public outrage. In both murder cases, the suspect was arrested, tried and convicted.

It is difficult to convey the massive impact these two crimes had on Dutch society and Dutch politics. The political system has long been based on proportional representation, with a range of parties typically forming a multi-party coalition, always implying a measure of policy compromise. This is quite different from electoral practice and the traditional two-party, adversarial systems of the UK and the US. In addition, the main parties in the Netherlands have long relied on fairly predictable voting patterns and an entrenched cadre of party leaders (Wansink, 2004). These established parties, which had become more progressive in varying degrees since the end of the 1960s had moved to the centre in the 1990s with two highly successful 'purple' coalitions (referring to the party colours), with an unusual combination of social democrats (Labour Party–PvdA), conservatives (People's Party for Freedom and Democracy–VVD) and progressive liberals

(Democrats 66). This new consensus 'polder' politics, implemented in two cabinets led by Prime Minister Wim Kok (1994–2002), reinforced the high degree of smugness and complacency found in Dutch political culture. Suddenly in the early 2000s the main established parties were confronted with right-leaning populist parties attracting votes that, through the proportional representation system, translated directly into seats in parliament. This voters' revolt against the main parties and their parliamentary elites not only shook up the vested political order considerably, but also caused politicians to take on board some of the populist rhetoric and proposals – for example, on immigration, integration of minorities and crime – in order to compete with the newcomers. As part of this societal-political shift to the right, the police were increasingly being pressured to tackle crime more forcefully, while at the same time coming under tough criticism for their part in a number of bungled investigations and miscarriages of justice (Pakes 2004). It was becoming increasingly clear that a range of factors were exposing the 'social' policing paradigm, and the police institution itself, as outdated and in need of reformulation.

In this context, a group was formed in December 2003 by the then Council of Chief Police Commissioners (CCPC) that, with aid from outside expertise, framed a new document called *Police in evolution* (CCPC, 2005). The project was chaired by Bernard Welten, who became Chief Commissioner of the Amsterdam Police one day before Theo van Gogh was killed on 2 November 2004. Welten typically represents the 'assertive yet thinking' strand in Dutch policing. It was the second time in the history of Dutch policing – following *A changing police* (POS, 1977) – that the profession came up with a strategic position. And again it was societal developments that 'forced' the police to redefine the profession (van Dijk and Hoogewoning, 2014b). It was a serious effort to produce a new, wide philosophy that tied the long-standing social paradigm to the starker realities of tackling new forms of crime and coping with a persistent public sense of insecurity. In a way, it was an attempt to construct a comprehensive paradigm, but, unfortunately, the political tide was turning against this approach, with the new-style, media-conscious populists painting a picture of the police as soft and overly politically correct (van Swaaningen, 2004). In their eyes, the police were there only to enforce the law fully and without discretion – meaning especially against the foreign-born, Muslim out-groups they demonised – which was a reversion to the rigid views of the 1960s. This broad move to the right was allied to a determination to get more effectiveness and efficiency from the police, along with proposals to reduce the number of forces (de Koning, 2012).

This contributed to the reorganisation of the regional forces into one force with one chief under one minister, but now (since 2010) under the renamed Ministry of Security and Justice. This Ministry is widely taken to be more legalistic and oriented to crime control than the Ministry of the Interior: and both the first Minister and the first Junior Minister (in office from 2010 to 2015) were renowned crime fighters. The former 25 regions have been recast into one national agency with a smaller cadre of top officers, larger units and a restructuring of governance.

This is the most drastic change in Dutch policing in over 150 years and it has potentially sounded the abandonment of the dominant 'social' paradigm of the past 30 years. This reflects how global economic change, migration, concern with external threats and a focus on crime and security have been changing the policy agenda for some time and how major political change fostered by the rise and strength of populist politics has led to major and rapid alterations in the political landscape in general and to views on policing, crime, security, justice and punishment in particular. But it could be argued that in practice most forces had been operating with an uneasy mix of paradigms for some years and that the arrival of the National Police has simply signified the awareness of 'paradigm lost' (Punch et al, 2005).

Contested paradigms and fuzzy rhetoric

In practice, policing comprises a wide range of activities associated with both the control and the consent paradigm. However, the paradigms refer to fundamentally different worldviews, and at the system level one tends to dominate the other. Broadly it can be posited that the control paradigm was long in the ascendancy in many forces outside of the UK but that the traditional consent paradigm attributed to the UK and the British policing model has resurfaced periodically in the past 40 years along with strategies associated with community policing, problem-oriented policing and neighbourhood policing (Tilley, 2003). A number of forces took this consent style on with enthusiasm or embraced it partially and only in certain segments of the organisation. But with the rise and popularity of the zero tolerance movement in the US and its transfer abroad from the late 1990s onwards, along with a political-economic shift to the right in many Western democracies, there has been a broad resurgence of the control paradigm (Hopkins-Burke, 2004; Newburn and Sparks, 2004; Jones and Newburn, 2007). In rhetoric for public consumption, police chiefs may try to propagate both, but it is plain that in most of the UK, and in the Netherlands and the Nordic countries, the political choice is now primarily geared towards control. Policing cannot, however, be reduced to one of the two paradigms and their related activities. The two are not necessarily incompatible and should ideally be complementary. However, systems and sub-systems tend to operate according to one dominant 'paradigm in use' even where the rhetoric of the 'espoused paradigm' maintains that both are equally valid.

For example, there is plainly a measure of ambivalence in the Netherlands, where the formal plans for the National Police seem to express a preference for the first paradigm alongside a reluctance to cast aside, at least out loud, the second. In the UK, in contrast, it is plain that the Conservative-Liberal Democrat government favours the first paradigm and effectively disparages the second. The assumption is that the control paradigm can stand on its own to the exclusion of the consent paradigm. Then again, the Stevens' Report clearly prefers the second without abandoning the first. But the authors of this book maintain that it is essential to be fully conscious of the significance of the actual model of policing to be adopted and the accompanying leadership style. This is important for communications with the public in conveying what they can expect from the police organisation and its officers. It is noticeable, moreover, that the two paradigms are highly diffuse and open to multiple interpretation. They are continually recycled with seeming amnesia about the past leading to periodic oscillation. The reality would seem to convey that the control model is the paradigm of choice, allowing people to slip back into the comfort zone of taken-for-granted and non-reflective practices, and that it is difficult permanently to convert police systems to the consent model. In Britain, for instance, John Alderson (1979) who was Chief Constable of Devon and Cornwall, attempted to champion a more liberal, community-oriented policing style in the 1970s and 1980s. But his ideas were ridiculed by hard-line chiefs who felt that what might be good for the rural counties might not be appropriate in the large, urban forces. It took two decades for neighbourhood policing, with a resurrection of some of his ideas, to become the new orthodoxy for local delivery, with the Home Office promising to fund it in every force. But that impulse has largely now been swamped by the blinkered and uncritical rush to re-embrace the control paradigm by the 2010 Conservative-Liberal Democrat coalition.

What one observes in practice is oscillation between paradigms over time, accompanied by ambiguity, mixed messages, hollow rhetoric and double speak. For example, when Kelling, who was associated with the introduction of zero tolerance policing in New York, calls the 'broken windows' element in it a 'new paradigm' of community policing when it was predominantly a crime control strategy, this amounts to obfuscation (Bowling, 1999; Karmen, 2001). Both Bratton and his adviser Kelling had soon abandoned the 'zero tolerance' term in favour of the more benign sounding 'broken windows' approach (Kelling and Coles, 1996). But the rhetoric of Bratton – even allowing for a commercial ghost-writer and grating mixed metaphors – sounds all but benign when referring to 'Operation Juggernaut', a campaign against drug dealers:

> Prior to Juggernaut, the city's war on drugs had been our *Vietnam*: we were fighting a *hit-and-run enemy* and had gone in and made a lot of contact when we could, but we couldn't hold the ground. We didn't have the tactics or the *will to win*. Juggernaut was *the Normandy invasion*. We were going to *overwhelm our opponents*, take the ground and never leave, and systematically take them out…. We would *systematically take out* the low-level street dealer, the mid-level operator, and the high-level kingpin. *We would attack them* consistently on all fronts at all times. If you were a drug dealer, you were a *marked man*. (Bratton and Knobler, 1998, p 275; emphasis added)

And Bratton's right-hand man in the NYPD, Jack Maple, boldly stated: 'We are doing something that to my knowledge has never been done before. We are fighting the war on crime as if it were really a war' (Punch, 2007, p 22). There is no doubting Bratton's achievements as a police leader[9] – but his agenda in New York was plainly dominated by crime control and order maintenance and this was achieved by aggressive methods internally and externally (Greenberg, 2014).

Community policing and problem-oriented policing may, then, be presented as seemingly benign approaches to solving community problems, but they may be compromised by internal ambiguity and conflict and may even be used by police organisations to promote a contradictory paradigm. For example, after 9/11 in the US (with cataclysmic suicide attacks on targets in New York and Washington DC with great loss of life), 7/7 in London (with horrendous suicide bombings on public transport with high casualties) and the murder of Theo van Gogh in Amsterdam, community policing and neighbourhood-oriented policing were seen as the front-line 'eyes and ears' of counter-terrorism in the UK and as essential to keeping an eye on matters in the Netherlands. At the time, leading officers stated that counter-terrorism began in the community and that community beat officers should be oriented to signs of radicalisation (Blair, 2009). Then in Amsterdam, following the murder of van Gogh, community beat officers were lectured by agents of the AIVD on how to recognise radicalisation in immigrant communities (Punch, 2007). Forces have, therefore, to be careful here about maintaining certain boundaries and be perfectly clear in their dealings with the public over such sensitive matters. Otherwise, this ambiguity and juggling of concepts may confuse the public and foster competition or conflict within the police organisation. There can also be differential adoption between various units, with, say, a hard-line leader in one segment insisting on the control paradigm with a colleague in another segment propagating the consent paradigm. Furthermore, to a degree, all policing is 'political' and police systems ultimately function in the interests of the state. Even ostensibly 'benign' policing labelled as 'consent' will contain the option of shifting to 'control' if the state so desires and the context is held to demand it. And the notion of autonomy for chiefs in those countries that espouse it will also be limited at times, as in national emergencies or in wartime. In the mid-1980s, for example, UK policing was experimenting with community policing but at the same time was being used in a near militarised style with aggressive deployment, and dubious restrictions on movement for citizens, to break the miners' strike in the interests of the Conservative government (Adeney and Lloyd, 1986).

Finally, we conclude that the two paradigms can best be viewed as an internally and externally contested matter, open to ambiguity and oscillating redefinition. They can be switched, discarded, misrepresented and recycled according to circumstances and government regimes. The community policing (COP), problem-oriented policing and neighbourhood-oriented policing concepts, for instance, carry the promise of caring, involved police officers who are deployed locally and are, in a way, 'on the side' of the public, available and approachable and geared to aiding with diverse 'problems'. They convey that there will be police who know the area and the inhabitants, and are known to the public. This is encapsulated in the concept of 'proximity policing' – a French term to avoid using the Anglo-Saxon COP concept – and 'reassurance policing' promoted by O'Connor (2003, 2005) as Chief Constable in Surrey, in collaboration with Fielding and Innes at Surrey University, and at the HMIC when O'Connor moved there. Manning (2010), however, strongly argues that these leading concepts are almost never fully internalised and are adopted primarily as tactical options with presentational value and leave the underlying control paradigm

– meaning police-driven, centralist, top-down, and oriented to crime fighting and order maintenance – intact. There are highly professional forces in the US, but the mainstream American policing that Manning portrays seems to be a recalcitrant repeat offender.

Centralisation and regression to the mean?

There is no necessary and uniform relation between up-scaling the police organisation and a shift towards the control paradigm, although both are strongly linked in recent reorganisations of forces (Fyfe et al, 2013). It is, thus, very interesting that there are five societies – Denmark, Norway, Sweden, Scotland and the Netherlands – that can be considered relatively, if not strongly, liberal but have reorganised through centralisation in the period 2010–14 (as have Finland and Austria). All had invested to varying degrees in forms of community policing with long-standing local administrative involvement. The three Scandinavian countries – Denmark, Norway and Sweden, which have national forces – also engaged in a centralisation process by increasing the size of policing regions to enhance coordination and effectiveness (Halstrom, 2013). This was generated (variously) by dissatisfaction with police performance but financial retrenching was not really a factor with policing in Norway and Denmark, which even received extra funding. Perceptions of changes in crime patterns, especially relating to organised crime, played a role, while in Norway there was understandably a critical debate on policing following the police response to the Oslo bombing and shootings on Utoya by Anders Breivik in 2011.

The Netherlands and Scotland, as mentioned earlier, have both formed national forces (both operational in 2013). It is noticeable, however, that the local dimension in policing – which is habitually a concern with centralisation – was left largely undefined in the Dutch reform proposals, even though it had long been central to Dutch policing, at least formally if increasingly less so in practice. Although the importance of the local dimension of policing is stressed, it is not translated into concrete proposals with the exception of the policy norm of one community policing officer per 5,000 citizens. This can be contrasted with Scotland, where there were explicit proposals for local policing embedded in the legislation. Combining eight Scottish regional forces into one central force had raised concerns about imposing one model, cutting back on policing rural areas and diminishing oversight (Cochrane, 2014). Economising was an important factor in enforcing change throughout the UK, but there was no groundswell of dissatisfaction with Scottish police performance; indeed, views on Scottish policing tended to be positive, drawing on the strong, but ultimately unsuccessful, movement for independence. There is now one chief constable, the Association of Chief Police Officers Scotland no longer exists, and an unelected Scottish Police Authority has replaced the local police boards (Terpstra and Fyfe, 2014). In Scotland the first Chief Constable clearly favours centralisation, uniformity and a more assertive policing style geared to enforcement, which conflicts somewhat with the promise of the legislation with its adherence to continued local engagement and diversity of approaches. There has been some concern that lean has amounted to mean: and with less oversight. For example, there have been raids on saunas in Edinburgh without local consultation although these houses of disrepute had long been tolerated; more officers have appeared in public displaying firearms; there are fears of a diminution in local policing in the large rural areas with their specific problems such as wildlife crime; and one style of policing – that of Strathclyde, the chief's previous force – seems to being imposed through what has been dubbed 'Strathclydification' (Terpstra and Fyfe, 2015).

The new arrangements are still in this fluid stage of implementation and in both Scotland and the Netherlands some local administrators are complaining of being deprived of information and consultation and of decision making being drawn to the centre. This is felt strongly in the Netherlands, where the mayors always had authority over the police and were kept fully informed; now they are suddenly deprived of information and kept out of certain decision-making processes. There is, however, a big difference between the small municipalities and the bigger cities and it is the latter that are complaining most. This is because in the former regional system, the mayors of the smaller municipalities, already had great difficulty in getting their interests on the regional agenda, and in that sense there was a so-called 'democratic gap' within the regional system. Informally, some speak of the 'Alkmaar norm', a city with approximately 95,000 inhabitants. If a municipality is smaller than Alkmaar it is likely to welcome the police centralisation; if larger, most mayors are unhappy with losing influence. And it does not help when the new policy is that half the police stations in the Netherlands will close in the coming years, something that is also likely in the four other societies.

Whatever the promises are in the diverse reform proposals, it does appear that centralisation in policing tends to foster uniformity – as if one size fits all – and also a tougher enforcement emphasis, even in these relatively liberal societies. Indeed, a central theme uniting these cases – the Netherlands, Scotland and Scandinavia – is the retreat from the concept of community policing and a reduction of local involvement, however much this is denied. Halstrom (2013, p 455) remarks of Scandinavia: 'Interestingly, in all three countries, the concept of community/proximity policing has been more or less abandoned in the wake of reform. The Norwegian reform proposals hardly mention proximity policing at all, and the Danish report focuses on local policing instead.' Terpstra and Fyfe (2015) – referring to Scotland and the Netherlands – conclude: 'The implementation of national police forces in both jurisdictions has thus resulted in a centralization of decision-making and more weight being attributed to national priorities which have significantly weakened the position of local authorities.' Importantly, instead of proximity, there is distance and the 'local' officer is increasingly far away. It seems that in these five societies that policing has changed direction on the highway without using indicators; the implicit contract with the public enshrined in the various forms of community or 'proximity' policing has been abandoned without consulting the public.

Conclusion

This chapter has dealt with the variety of police systems, the distinction between Brodeur's concepts of high and low policing and the nature of the two dominant policing paradigms – control and consent. A clear distinction is noticeable between the Anglo-Saxon model as exemplified in British policing – with one agency, primarily under local control and based largely on consent – and the French-Continental model adopted in the Netherlands. In the latter, there were historically several police organisations falling under different ministries with local control but central, ministerial direction; a militarised capacity for public order next to the regular forces; and, until comparatively recently, public police functioning within the control paradigm. In the light of rapid societal change, the Dutch police enthusiastically embraced consent and the accompanying structure and culture of community policing, as did some other forces in Europe, although to a lesser degree. It has been argued that there is often ambivalence and fluctuation in the adoption and operationalisation of the two paradigms, and, furthermore, that there has been a clear element of retreat from 'consent' within the last decade, both in the two main societies under consideration and also several other societies facing significant restructuring as in Scandinavia. Finally, the authors believe that a choice for either the control or the consent paradigm will not suffice, and that the described oscillation between the two – and the related ambiguity – is becoming less acceptable. In the final chapter, there will be a proposal for a comprehensive approach, after examining in the coming chapters the academic material on policing, the police organisation and culture, deviance, accountability, commanding operations and police leadership in order to decipher the messages it conveys in relation to system change and future leadership. It is fair to say, however, that we highly value the consent paradigm. Some 185 years on since the consent model began to emerge, it has even become a corner-stone of what is referred to as 'democratic' policing (Manning, 2010). This, in turn, has become the export model of choice for transfer to developing and/or post-conflict societies (Bayley, 2006a). It would be most ironic if this missionary zeal to plant the seed of consent coincided with its abandonment in the host nations. This threatens to be the case with 'paradigm lost' in the Netherlands and is already the case following 'paradigm shift' in the UK. And it appears even to be true for three of the most ostensibly progressive societies in the world – Sweden, Norway and Denmark.

Notes

[1] The contemporary Dutch ME has become well trained, well equipped and highly flexible in tactics and approach; it is much more of a multi-purpose unit, with more specialised personnel and tighter selection. It is deployed in supporting criminal investigations, during disasters, and at sporting occasions and large-scale events.

[2] There were exceptions at the police chief level, with, for quite some time, a preference in some forces for former military officers (Emsley, 2009, p 176).

[3] There have exceptionally been constables or sergeants who have exercised this right, but it is generally accepted that the vast majority adhere to the instructions of superiors, and in disputed cases the judiciary has typically supported those superior in rank (Stenning, 1989).

[4] Until the founding of the Crown Prosecution Service in 1986.

[5] Cricket has traditionally been a sedate sport lasting several days but has been transformed by TV revenues: Twenty20 means a match of 20 overs for each team, lasting a couple of hours and resulting in short, exciting games.

[6] A Police Federation spokesperson refers to this phrase regarding the Met and mentions the cuts, workloads, absenteeism and resignations that make the attainment of these ambitious goals unrealistic (*Guardian*, 24 December 2014).

[7] Reiner (1998) does give an example of being told by a chief constable of direct intervention by Prime Minister Thatcher with regard to the miners' strike of 1984, but he kept quiet about it as he was then conducting his research into chief constables and disclosure would have ended his project.

[8] There is confusion on the 'firing' element: in one case, a chief resigned under pressure from her PCC only to be told afterwards that she should have remained in office, and in another case a chief who was suspended awaiting dismissal appealed and was reinstated.

[9] Both the Labour and Conservative-Liberal Democrat governments in the UK dropped his name as a possible Met Commissioner and Bratton was even paraded around at a Labour Party conference by the then Home Secretary David Blunkett, almost as a warning to British police leaders to perform better or else Bratton might become Britain's 'top cop'.

THREE

Sea of troubles: the nature of policing

The authors wish to stress that of prime importance in shaping the material in this and subsequent chapters is an appreciation of the *uniqueness* of the police organisation. It is this appreciation that in turn will help to inform police education at all levels. This needs to be emphasised from the start and throughout because, since the rise of New Public Management and the widespread reform of public services, there has been a tendency to view the police as simply one of many public service organisations that badly needed to change their ways by adopting the values and practices of private companies (Leishman et al, 2000). There can be little doubt that this approach has had a beneficial influence in certain respects; but it encapsulates a model that does not always fit public service organisations in general and the police organisation in particular.

The nature of policing

This section summarises the highly specific factors that need to be taken into account in relation to the nature of policing which may be viewed as common knowledge in academia. Unfortunately, these factors are not always taken into serious account by politicians and officials when promoting institutional and organisational change. The police agency enjoys exceptional powers as the only 24/7 operational institution – which is uniformed, visible and accessible – with the authority to intervene directly in citizens' lives, deprive them of their freedom or even their lives. An officer's 'authoritative intervention' (Bayley, 1994) in people's affairs is based on the (near) monopoly of violence (Bittner, 1970, 1974). In the UK, this also means primacy over the use of potentially fatal force, including that by the military. This alone makes the policing enterprise unique among public institutions. This key feature makes the interaction between police and citizens highly symbolic, with the police representing the 'state made flesh' in encounters. Crucially, those powers of intervention are most likely to be exercised in first instance by those low in the hierarchy who may have to take vital decisions in relative isolation often at times of danger to themselves and/or others. This is quite unlike most business organisations, although it does have parallels with other 'frontline' social and emergency agencies (Muir, 1977; Lipsky, 1980).

From the first pioneering studies of policing, the police officer emerged not as a law enforcement officer but as a 'peace keeper', using discretion, solving problems and continually assessing situations and people to maintain and restore a highly contextual order. In this craft-like process, the law was just a background prop to be employed at the officer's convenience (Banton, 1964; Bittner, 1967; Rubinstein, 1973). To some, he, and it was predominantly a 'he', was a 'philosopher, friend and guide' (Cumming et al, 1965). Despite the changes since then – including the gender composition of the workforce and use of technology – not that much has altered in that basic, everyday world (Moskos, 2008).[1] Moreover, although the police organisation is capable of mounting large-scale operations that may at times involve thousands of officers, a great deal of its routine functioning is conducted by small groups of officers working in small teams in relative autonomy, employing considerable discretion and geared to specialist duties or to the local delivery of everyday policing services.

The primary functions of police systems have tended to crystallise around order maintenance, crime control and investigations, and providing assistance in emergencies. A persistently recurring theme throughout the history of policing, however, is that some stakeholders and police officers maintain that crime control forms the 'core business' of policing to the near exclusion of other functions, including some of the 'social' tasks mentioned later in this chapter. Yet the evidence is simply overwhelming that the police impact on crime is highly limited. This is conveyed with convincing clarity by a number of authors, including Skogan and Frydl (2004, p 247), who, in an exhaustive overview, state: '… there is often little research evidence about what works under what circumstances. One reason for the lack of evidence is the complexity and ambiguity of police strategies.' There is a wealth of data on this topic indicating that police can have an influence on certain crimes under certain circumstances. But some 50 studies indicate that they do not spend most of their time on crime-related activities (Brodeur, 2010); that some crimes are particularly difficult to detect and investigate; and that the origins of crime are largely beyond the capabilities of the police to influence them (Reiner, 2010). What also has to be taken into consideration is that not all crimes are reported, as victimisation surveys consistently reveal; that not all reported crime is formally recorded; that not all recorded crime is followed by an investigation; that not all investigations are pursued by prosecuting agencies; that not all investigations lead to a court case; and that only a tiny fraction of crimes that are calculated to have taken place or have been reported and processed, ever reach a sanction in court or a custodial sentence.

The crudely simplistic assignment from certain politicians to cut crime has to be assessed in the light of this. In practice, an overemphasis on 'cutting crime' may lead to various forms of data manipulation, including massively 'cooking the books' with intimidation from above to reach targets as happened in New York (Eterno and Silverman, 2012). Of importance is that 'crime' is a heterogeneous concept containing a wide range of offences and an equally wide differential as to the likelihood of an offence being reported, processed and 'solved' (Reiner, 2007). Some street offences have a minimal chance of being solved, while certain crimes of violence have a high chance. All of this has long been known among those working and researching in the criminal justice area, commencing with Wilson (1968, 1975) and Reiss (1971). But this, together with the fact that crime has been falling for some time in many Western countries, does not seem to have penetrated the consciousness of many politicians and the wider society, who appear to be locked into a form of collective, wilful disbelief (Tonry, 2004; Zimring, 2007). In Scotland, for example, crime is at a historic 33-year low point.

A key factor in solving many common crimes, moreover, is swift information from the public, which in turn depends on the level of trust that the public has in the police. People may be mesmerised by the hyper-modern techniques of glossy police procedural dramas like the 'CSI' series on TV, but the reality is that most common crime is solved if the suspect is caught at the scene or there is accurate information from the victim or eye-witnesses about the identity or a description of the suspect. If that is not forthcoming within a few hours, the chances of solving the crime are almost nil. Forensics, moreover, plays a very small role in solving most volume crime, but may be a significant factor in prosecutions, in obtaining guilty pleas and in court cases. The system is essentially lubricated by quick, accurate information and by confessions (Brodeur, 2010).[2] In short, high trust in the police means more legitimacy, leading to more cooperation and information with potentially more crimes solved. A key factor, then, is the trust of the public, and consent to be policed; without those, the police will struggle to function effectively.

It is plain, however, that in certain societies the public has low or no trust at all in the police. For instance, you would never turn to the police at a time of need in those societies with a weak, corrupt or failing state, where the police are part of the problem. There is no better illustration of this than the abysmal conduct of some officers of the Indian police in reaction to several widely publicised cases of gang rape and murder against 'Westernised' young women in 2012 and later (*New York Times*, 2012). By any standards, their response was incompetent, unprofessional, callous and blatantly discriminatory. The consequence is that people do not go to the police with a problem in countries such as this, and neither do they approach the police with information about crimes because they simply cannot trust them. Hinton (2006, p 1) gives the example of a violent abduction of a young man in Buenos Aires witnessed by several people who contacted the police. The ensuing ransom hand-over was bungled and the young man murdered. This became a well-publicised case leading to public outrage about the failure of the police to handle the situation, forcing the authorities to mount an investigation, which revealed that the police were in collusion with the kidnapping rings that paid them not to react to such calls. In Latin American countries, it may not only be pointless, but also dangerous, for eye witnesses to a crime to contact the police (Hinton and Newburn, 2009).[3]

Crime control and prevention are, and always have been, key features of policing, but police organisations have accumulated a diversity of other functions. Some early forces in the US had a dual function as fire-fighters or street cleaners (Miller, 1977). And following the founding of the Metropolitan Police, constables 'regulated traffic, ensured that pavements were unimpeded, kept a watchful eye for unsafe buildings and burning chimneys, licensed street sellers and cabs, administered first-aid at accidents and drove ambulances, administered aspects of the Poor Law, and supervised the prevention of disease among farm animals', and later took on school attendance duties (Emsley, 1996, pp 3, 83). Colonial forces have manned customs and borders and conducted censuses, and some militarised police agencies have gone into combat as counter-insurgency units in war situations, as in South Africa (Ellis, 1988). Police agencies may also be involved in dealing with disasters and civil emergencies, carrying out traffic-related duties, registering 'aliens', administering various forms of licensing, and controlling 'morals' or 'vice' (gambling, prostitution, pornography, homosexuality). They may also assist other agencies in various ways, for example by escorting bailiffs, dealing with juveniles, attending sporting events, investigating work-related deaths and accidents, and accompanying white-collar crime investigators in raiding business premises. In the UK, the police have traditionally been granted 'primacy' in dealing with disasters and civil emergencies whereas in many societies that is the task of the fire and rescue service and/or a specialised emergency response agency. There is also the area of 'high policing' with regard to crimes against the state and the gathering of political intelligence, mentioned above, which is often overlooked in overviews of police functions (Brodeur, 1983; Porter, 1987; Meershoek, 2011). This came to prominence in 2013 following revelations by whistleblowers Bradley (now Chelsea) Manning and Edward Snowden about the massive surveillance operations carried by Western countries, primarily the US, on close allies of the US and millions of ordinary civilians. These revelations were earlier made by Julian Assange, who disseminated vast amounts of classified information on the internet through WikiLeaks.

What emerges strongly from the accumulated evidence, moreover, is that police perform a gamut of 'social' tasks, largely in response to requests from the public and mainly through phone calls (Punch and Naylor, 1973). A number of studies have consistently shown that most calls to the police are not crime-related, but concerned with a varied swathe of problems and comprising requests for, or offers of, information. Bittner (1970, p 22) stated this unequivocally some time ago and referred to these non-crime activities as 'peace keeping'. These peace-keeping or 'social' tasks include helping elderly people who live alone, informing people of a sudden death, transporting emergency medicines, tracing missing persons, providing temporary accommodation, dispensing marital advice during domestic disputes and aiding those with mental health problems. This made the police a 'secret social service' (Punch, 1979b). This insight was something of a revelation at the time Punch and others wrote on this theme, but a visit to the website of a contemporary British, or Dutch, force will reveal considerable attention to social tasks and vulnerable groups. This is in shrill contrast to the 'cut crime' proponents. At times, then, police function as gate-keepers for other services or as the back-stop for the inadequacies or non-availability of professional agencies. This is particularly the case in the area of mental health, especially since the former asylums began to close down in the 1960s. Those with mental health problems are supposed to receive care in the community, but where this is deficient, or non-existent, they often end up in hostels or on the street. Some may also suffer from drug or alcohol addiction, and are vulnerable to situations that result in public disturbances or criminal offences, where they may pose a danger to themselves or others (Bittner, 1970; Peay, 2010). In such situations, they are most likely to first encounter a police officer rather than a mental health professional. When a professional is unavailable, the police may have to detain someone who has committed no offence and whom they are not qualified to help.

This area of social and peace-keeping tasks is related to the degree of accessibility of the police and the measure of willingness to help those requesting assistance. The arrival of public and private telephones, and, more recently, mobile phones, has greatly increased the public's accessibility to the police. It is clear that some calls are not matters for the police – and many forces have become astute at filtering them – but it is not always possible in advance to know how an incident will play out. A call ostensibly related to a 'social' intervention may end in an arrest for an offence, perhaps involving violence against or by the police. An initial 'crime'-related call may lead to a social welfare solution or an on-the-spot resolution requiring no further action. Outcomes in policing are not always determined by the nature of the call, but are influenced by the development of the interaction between those involved (Manning, 1997). Moreover, the institutional definition of 'social' calls may alter over time. With the realisation that much violence takes place in the home and that those who are most vulnerable, typically women and children, may be subject to serial victimisation, the police response has shifted to active intervention to protect victims by removing offenders from the scene and sometimes pressing criminal charges. Charges are often brought by the police as a matter of policy, even when the victim is unwilling to do so, although this position has come under critical review in recent years (Bowling, 2006). An important aspect of all interactions between the police with the public is that a satisfactory outcome for the victim may result in an increased willingness to cooperate with the police in the future. Likewise, a poor response, or no response at all, may confirm a negative stereotype of the police, leading to unwillingness to cooperate. It could be said, rather crudely, that some evidence indicates that people are positive about the police until they have to interact with them (Fitzgerald et al, 2002). There are a number of reasons why such contacts engender friction or disappointment and these are related to a lack of a service mentality among officers, and to a feeling among citizens that they have not been treated according to elementary norms of fairness, politeness and procedural justice.

Policing is further strongly tied to major emergency response with the possibility of a serious incident suddenly emerging where, and when, least expected. This could be related to a public order situation (a riot), a disaster (involving a train, aeroplane, ship, fire or industrial accident), a natural emergency (storm, flooding, earthquake), a major criminal investigation (children missing under suspicious circumstances, serial killings or a terrorist attack), a major road accident, or a shooting spree involving multiple victims and/or police officers (as victims or as those responsible for causing casualties). This need for an instantaneous response plainly places severe demands on the leadership, personnel and resources of a police force (Waddington, 1991, 1994). High demands can be placed on the organisation, particularly in major or capital cities, with regard to large-scale, pre-planned events and operations. There is a planning and 'logistical' side to this, with some forces becoming expert at such arrangements, but there is also a permanent risk factor in terms of a potential disaster or people using a mass occasion for an attack (ACPO, 2010). Many of the tasks and functions in policing have increasingly led to domestic and international multi-agency cooperation. Police and other agencies routinely communicate and cooperate with colleagues in other countries over cases involving drugs, smuggling, pornography, people trafficking, piracy, counterfeiting and cybercrime (Sheptycki, 2000; Bowling and Sheptycki, 2012). This may include bilateral cooperation – as between Germany and the Netherlands on policing their border area – and more widely through the UN, Council of Europe, Interpol, Europol, Eurojust, Cross Channel Intelligence Conference, Drug Enforcement Agency and professional meetings including those of the International Association of Chiefs of Police (Nadelmann, 1993; Mawby, 1999; Andreas and Nadelmann, 2006).

What also has to be taken into consideration is that policing has long been associated with abuse of power, discrimination, excess violence and corruption (Newburn, 1999; Punch, 2009). Particular cases, as with the murder of Stephen Lawrence in 1993 and the subsequent accusation of 'institutional racism' against the Metropolitan Police from a high-level commission of inquiry (Macpherson, 1999), have had a long-lasting and significant impact on policing in London and in the UK with regard to hate crime and the differential police response to it. Sensitive cases exposed by the media, such as those involving discrimination, undue force and corruption (Sherman, 1978), may have serious consequences for the police at both the institutional and personal level, including official inquiries, court cases and the enforced removal of senior staff implicated in the scandal either because of active involvement or professional neglect (O'Hara, 2005: Savage, 2007a). Crucially, policing is intimately related to civil and human rights (Crawshaw et al, 2006), with issues of integrity, transparency and accountability vital to its legitimacy and credibility in a healthy democracy (Kleinig, 1996; Neyroud and Beckley, 2001).

This material conveys, then, that policing involves a wide range of functions and tasks and that it is not only difficult but also distorting to airbrush these out by focusing on one particular facet. In this light, the police organisation can be seen as a complex service agency with a broad mandate and a wide spectrum of functions and tasks, while its legitimacy through accountability forms a revealing litmus test of a healthy democratic society. The implication of this is that police leaders face multiple challenges internally and externally and that their work is complex, shifting and demanding. They interact with multiple stakeholders in constant negotiation over mission, mandate, duties, tasks and accountability. Finally, there are common elements between the police agency and other types of organisation but, in a fundamental sense, policing is not just exceptional but unique. There is a tendency for political and police reformers to overlook this discomforting fact.

Police organisation

When 'modern' police forces were created from the end of the 18th century onwards, they were mostly military in structure and fell under direct political control. Before then, policing was mostly conducted by a patchwork of citizen initiatives, diverse local officials and private agencies, so that policing was rarely institutionalised in a publicly financed, formally constituted organisation. What changed this was the rise of the central state in parts of Europe. In the UK, there was a fear of the central state and a preference for a decentralised model, something that was even more evident in the US, with its messy patchwork of agencies mainly under local or community control that spawned some 18,000 police forces at the local, county, state and federal levels (Brodeur, 2010).[4] In contrast, Continental European police chiefs were rarely at liberty to exercise independent policies and were formally subordinate to local and central non-police personnel for policy and even to ministerial authority for operational decisions. Following the military model, moreover, there was usually separate entry and training for officers and for other ranks. This was partly related to social hierarchy and educational level, and partly to keeping senior staff insulated from the primary processes, with the dangers of becoming too intimate with the lower ranks and of becoming exposed to corruption. Senior officers typically owed their appointments to political connections, were socialised to accept directions from above and not to show too much initiative. The lower ranks faced a caste system whereby they were led by those who had not experienced the primary processes of policing while they themselves could never rise to officer status. There almost certainly would have been both a weak if not absent notion of accountability and of a concept of service to the public together with a near insurmountable gulf between 'officers and other ranks'. There should not be too much of a rosy view that British policing was traditionally all that different from this, despite having everyone start as constable.

The formal structure of British police forces was still partly military and stratified with various ranks from constable to chief constable; promotion was slow and only for the few; and those promoted to higher rank were expected to divorce themselves from the lower ranks. Furthermore, basic training involved much marching and drill – in living memory patrol officers were marched from the station to their posts in some cities – and it was an offence to 'needlessly' converse with a member of the public. The formal culture was, then, largely that of a defensive, rule-bound bureaucracy, with an emphasis on rigid discipline and sanctions for petty digressions (Manning, 1977). Sir Robert Mark (a renowned Commissioner of the Metropolitan Police in the 1970s) wrote of his early days in policing in the late 1930s:

> The Manchester force was dominated by a philosophy not unlike that of [Queen] Victoria's army. There was no suggestion of leadership by example. Seniors battened on and bullied juniors and the force as a whole did the same to that part of the public not able effectively to look after itself ... the system was harsh, unimaginative, unintelligent and ruthless. (Mark, 1978, p 20)

Supervisory officers would spy on the patrol officers and there were heavy sanctions, including dismissal, for digressions. To a certain extent, the discipline represented a highly authoritarian culture typical of the times. It was doubtless necessary in the early decades of British policing because it took some years to develop a disciplined and reliable workforce. However, that pattern of authoritarian organisations with strict discipline based on extensive regulations that were tightly enforced from above persisted; this tended to elicit solidarity in the lower ranks with inventive rule bending. But even in recent decades, there was typically deference to the experienced constables, discouragement of independent thought and an expectation of near 'blind obedience' to superiors (Paddick, 2008, p 14).[5] This rigid, hierarchical and unthinking system was at odds with the idea of policing both as a craft whereby the lower ranks exercise discretion and as a profession with senior officers espousing independent ideas.

Indeed, there emerges from many accounts a near universal feature of police organisations which is the gulf between the lower and higher ranks. Related to this was the traditional problem – how to supervise and even locate the lower personnel (Holdaway, 1983). For controlling the patrol officers in the early years, the typical answer was to arrange fixed beats, to meet the sergeant at specified intervals, and, in a later period, to phone the duty sergeant. But patrol officers have cunningly invented ways to evade or manipulate control; for example, they would find attractive 'watering holes' on their beat to ameliorate the monotony of patrol (Emsley, 2009).[6] This was even more true of detectives, who, before the days of radio and even afterwards, could effectively 'disappear' and work, or not work, with high autonomy. It has been said of the Dutch police that it comprised 50,000 'one person companies' (*eenmansbedrijven*), indicating that, beneath the veneer of organisational control, individual officers were still largely going their own way (Kees van der Vijver, personal communication).

This raises a pivotal issue with regard both to organisational control and leadership (Punch, 2003). This is that the structure and culture of police work leads to autonomy at the base of the organisation, to subverting control and to the ability to undermine policies and instructions from above. It also poses a dilemma for senior officers: if they put too much emphasis on overt control, they may frustrate, if not alienate, the lower ranks and encounter resistance. Indeed, it could be maintained that the history of policing conveys that many attempts to alter and reform policing have been thwarted by non-compliance of the lower ranks. This has been particularly the case in the US, which has a tradition of militant and conservative, if not reactionary, police unions (Walker, 2005; Skogan, 2008).[7] Another crucial feature of the police organisation is that it comprises essentially two organisations, or organisational modes, in one; these function in different ways at different times (Punch and Markham, 2000). First, there is the devolved organisation of daily routine, with many diverse units carrying out their work with various degrees of autonomy and cooperation in a 'loosely coupled system'. In this sphere, there is usually a distinct informal status hierarchy, much rivalry and a fervent determination not to cooperate or share information. Second, there is the organisation in emergency response mode, which requires a double institutional shift to a 'tightly coupled system'. Faced with a serious emergency, a sort of 'shadow' organisation has to shift instantaneously into 'command and control' mode (in British jargon) with a classical pyramid structure, a hierarchy of authority and centralised control. Simultaneously, the organisation has to mobilise an extensive range of emergency services and stakeholders, including central and local government, perhaps the military, the media, other police forces and intelligence agencies abroad, and regulatory and transport authorities. The evidence is that police organisations can rise to the occasion and perform well if not superbly, as in the Met's response in aiding relatives, friends and acquaintances of victims and missing persons following the 2004 Asian tsunami (Paddick, 2008, p 238). But they can also, under trying circumstances, fail abysmally. This happened at the Heizel Stadium disaster in Belgium in 1985 when 39 spectators died and 600 were injured as a result of fighting on the terraces, with spectators trying to escape and in the tumult getting crushed when a wall collapsed ('t Hart and Pijnenburg, 1989). Lack of coordination and communication between diverse police units and a 'control' mindset geared to preventing a pitch invasion meant that the seriousness of the situation was underestimated and the subsequent emergency response lamentable.[8] It is obvious that the required double shift into emergency response mode will place immediate demands on the quality of leadership, preparations and training, resources and infrastructure, the ability to cooperate with other agencies and the skills of officers at every level. Such occasions, as emphasised in the following chapter and throughout the remainder of the book, are a test of leadership at the top but also at other levels from high to low and between police and other agencies.

Police occupational culture

In pondering the features associated with police organisation, control, paradigms and reform, it is essential to take into account the tenets of police occupational culture (Schein, 1985; Young, 1991). Again, there is the proviso that research on this topic has been dominated by Anglo-American academics, so we know far more about it in a few Western societies than in many other societies (O'Neill et al, 2007). However, those tenets, going on the existing material, appear to be resilient and near universal, and they can form a barrier to change when they influence actual behaviour of officers that is at odds with organisational rules and values. Even in an 'enlightened' force in Australia with a reform agenda, a renewed training programme and more diverse and well-educated recruits than earlier cohorts, there was evidence that the newcomers – who were not uncritical of certain practices – began within a matter of time to conform to the values and conduct embedded in the traditional culture (Chan, 2003). That reflects that the culture is difficult to alter and that it is rooted in the nature of the work, which is often seen as a dull, but also, at times, dirty and dangerous, and largely unrecognised and unrewarded by the institution. For most front-line officers, moreover, their close colleagues in their team or unit are the essential reference point, so that solidarity with them enforces conformity to stereotypical views and practices (Loftus, 2009). The 'cop code' also reflects the views that other ranks hold of senior officers and the qualities deemed essential for those holding high rank. These archetypal tenets are not always attractive and may come across as sour and somewhat negative, but they are prevalent in the literature and they may well reflect collective norms that do not necessarily translate into conduct. Indeed, there may well be an element of idealism beneath the cynical surface and the extent to which different units express the occupational culture in words and deeds is likely to vary. The fundaments of police culture are generally held to rest on the following:

- *Sense of mission*: policing is seen as a vocation, if not a noble mission, and as performing valuable work not fully appreciated by outsiders.
- *Danger and sacrifice*: the awareness of potential danger is embedded in the culture; there are specific areas and assignments associated with danger; and danger is unpredictable and may arise at unexpected moments.
- *Solidarity*: the nature of the work, operating in uncertain situations of potential conflict, generates strong solidarity. In the 'cop code', officers must always back up partners and respond rapidly when an officer is in trouble; anyone who 'bottles out' is derided, if not excluded (Reuss-Ianni, 1983).
- *Rule of silence*: a domain assumption is that officers will follow the rule of silence, that is, they will not speak ill of their colleagues (Kleinig, 1996, p 67). Breaking the code elicits strong informal sanctions such as threats, ostracism, damage to personal property, malicious rumour and even violence. Internal and external investigations of police misconduct in the US and elsewhere have often faced the 'blue wall', whereby officers refuse to testify or to incriminate colleagues, and have also been known to intimidate investigators, threaten to retaliate, and interfere with evidence.
- *Cynicism*: officers encounter the seedy and disreputable side of society and are exposed to human frailty and suffering related to drink, drugs, violence, sexual abuse and poverty; their work may appear pointless and lead to cynicism. This cynicism may mask an underlying motivation to gain results, act as an occupational thick skin or even indicate an underlying concern and commitment (Manning, 1977, p 119).

- *Hedonism*: officers may demonstrate a propensity or tolerance for drinking, drugs and sex, both on and off duty. There may be a tendency to drive fast in patrol cars in races and dares, and to participate in wild parties, pranks, sexual escapades and other forms of 'backstage' behaviour.
- *Machismo*: policing has predominantly been a male occupation and there are accounts of a prevailing strong masculine ethos with bullying, sexism, harassment and intolerance. Certain roles encourage a strongly masculine ethos, for example those in special detective units, SWAT and firearms squads. Macho behaviour may lead to aggressive incidents; for example, off-duty officers have been known to get drunk, trash hotels and get into fights (Hopkins-Burke, 2004, p 2). It is also posited that the perceived feminisation of policing has produced the following attitude among the British police studied by Loftus (2009, p 188): 'The crime-fighter mentality, defensive solidarity and masculine ethos found expression within a resentful posture of white, heterosexual, male officers who considered themselves as challenged, beleaguered and unrecognised'.
- *Pragmatism*: the culture may support an anti-theoretical view that practical knowledge gained on the streets is the key to police craftsmanship; that 'theoretical' knowledge and formal learning is suspect; and that innovation and change are characteristics to be resented (Skolnick, 1966; Lee and Punch, 2006).
- *Taking it easy/work avoidance*: some features of police culture replicate the truculent views of blue-collar, industrial workers about not working too hard and resenting 'rate-busters'. Some officers seek 'cushy' roles within the force – in a band, sport or indoor job – and avoid patrol and other duties.[9]
- *Social isolation*: the nature of the work, hostility from the community, shift-work and so on, may lead to social isolation, with officers preferring to socialise with colleagues outside of work, thus contributing to negative feelings about outsiders, and a sense that only a fellow officer can truly understand 'what it is really like'. In some communities, officers are seen as pariahs (Manning, 1977, p 134) and in some forces they are housed together in police accommodation or barracks, so that work, social life and housing combine to make an 'occupational community'.
- *Suspicion*: continual exposure to danger, and frequent interaction with untrustworthy and disreputable individuals, may impregnate officers with an inherent suspiciousness, with the result that they look out for 'symbolic assailants' (Skolnick, 1966), discount the accounts and motives of suspects and reverse the assumption of

innocence with the supposition that suspects are guilty until proven innocent.

- *Dichotomous thinking*: this divides the world into simplistic, rigid categories based on a dichotomy between good and evil, rough and respectable, trustworthy and untrustworthy, 'them and us' – with an accompanying battery of negative epithets for 'them' ('assholes', 'scum', 'animals' and 'toe-rags'; Van Maanen, 1978).
- *Excitement/action and 'real' police work*: routine work is disparaged with a predilection for action involving the chase, the scuffle and the arrest, culminating in delivering the prisoner to the station with accolades for a good arrest. 'Real' police work is held to be crime fighting and 'catching crooks', while other tasks are denigrated as 'shit work'.
- *Rough justice/just deserts*: there are informal norms about distributing 'rough justice', for example, against suspects who flee arrest and/or resist arrest, abuse officers and their families, attack a female officer, refuse to be subdued in custody, spit at an officer, threaten officers with retaliation, and so on. These views can rationalise gratuitous violence and 'dirty tricks' on the part of officers, including using fake statements, planting of evidence and committing perjury in order to get a conviction against a suspect because 'he deserved it'.
- *Moral/political conservatism*: police officers usually come from relatively conventional backgrounds (Reiner, 1978), but the occupational identity can shape a 'conservative' view of the world, favouring stability, order and a tough approach to crime with antagonistic stereotypes of certain societal groups.
- *Ducking and diving*: the culture is often posited on the view that the work requires cutting corners and bending rules, with the result that officers learn to bend rules without perceiving this to be illicit (Young, 1991). Those skilful at rule bending may be revered and they may elicit respect from colleagues for being cunning, artful 'duckers and divers'. Such manipulation and fabrication may become routine and be seen as legitimate to garner a desired outcome.

The stereotype that emerges from this compilation of the darker underpinnings of police culture and practice may seem unduly negative. Yet it is the case that in a survey commissioned by the Metropolitan Police in the early 1980s there were reports of sexism, racism, drinking on duty, bribery and persistent rule bending (Smith and Gray, 1985). That was 30 years ago and thus may be held to be unrepresentative, but some undercover reporting has in recent years exposed deviant and racist conduct in several British forces (Paddick, 2008, pp 218-19;

Brunger, 2013). Furthermore, the archetypical detective in film and TV series is invariably idiosyncratic, displays contempt for formal rules and superiors, uses violence or dubious methods and follows non-routine procedures to solve the case. This mostly also holds true for the increasing number of female leads in police series, so the stereotype largely overrides gender. The cultural message conveyed by popular fiction is that police have to bend or break the law in order to enforce the law (Brodeur, 2010).

Perhaps two factors are worthy of particular attention. First, although the expression of the culture may not necessarily dictate behaviour, it is plain that almost universally officers define 'real' police work as 'catching crooks' – even when there is little crime and very few crooks to catch. There is, then, an affinity with those in the wider society who prioritise crime fighting as the core business of policing. Second, and again almost universally, there is scepticism about senior staff that has traditionally been prevalent in male-dominated environments such as the army and factory work, whereby knowledge and experience of the primary processes was and is considered essential to understanding the nature of the tasks to be done. This is partly related in some systems to a hierarchy based on class and education that creates a caste system where the lower personnel can never expect to be promoted above a certain level and the higher personnel will never share the experience of the primary processes. In the military, for example, the ordinary soldier's perspective is based on scepticism about officers with no experience of real combat who are incapable of 'leading from the front'. These tenets are understandable because the quality of the officer can determine life or death. Indeed, in the most proactive units – paratroopers and special forces – officers with little experience and poor leadership are usually not tolerated (Asher, 2008). Although the consequences of poor leadership in policing are not as dramatic as in armed conflict, there is a powerful underlying notion that you have to have 'front-line' experience and to have shared the primary processes, and earned membership, in order to be capable of directing the lower ranks (Bittner, 1970). Yet even in the Anglo-American systems with one entry point and promotion through the ranks, that rift between the lower and higher orders remains. This issue will resurface throughout this publication, with the key factor being to what extent senior officers should experience the primary processes and what leadership style they should adopt in response to the tenets of the occupational culture.

Deviance, corruption and the 'enemy within'

Throughout the history of policing – in diverse ways and to varying extents in different societies – there have been periodic scandals, suggesting that not all was under control or was under the wrong sort of control. To a large degree, 'leadership' and 'management' are intrinsically associated with the notion of control of the organisation. Yet there is rich evidence of some measure of deviance in all organisations – sometimes evading efforts at control even in the most restricted environments such as prisons – which conveys that social order in organisations is often problematic and negotiated (Shearing, 1981; Manning, 1997). It is particularly ironic, and damaging, if deviance is exposed among law enforcers when their conduct undermines the mandate and reputation of their own organisation (Marx, 1988). But the stark reality is that there have been repeated episodes in policing of corruption, excessive force, manipulation of evidence, lying in court, 'stitching up' suspects (falsifying statements, confessions and evidence to get a conviction, sometimes against innocent persons) and conspiracies to cover up police deviance. This is plainly a serious problem of internal control for police leaders, assuming they are not themselves involved in, or colluding with, the deviance. Hence, while senior officers may be fixated predominantly on the external threat of corrupting elements, they also have to be aware of the 'enemy within', that is, their own personnel whom they may trust fully. For the policing literature conveys strong evidence of widespread and even systematic deviation from rules and laws by officers (Dixon, 1999; Newburn, 1999). There is reference to internal disciplinary offences, and criminal offences such as use of excessive violence, abuse of human rights, burglary and perjury, while in some societies the police have been known to become involved in political violence, assassinations, drug trafficking, abductions and torture.

'Corruption' as a broad label referring to police abuse of power needs, then, to be viewed as an inherent and universal facet of policing; it is not simply the product of 'bad apples', but is at times the product of 'bad orchards' (Punch, 2003; Holmes, 2014). Indeed, the spectrum of police corruption, with officers seriously abusing the trust bestowed on them to engage in grave offences against citizens, suspects and criminals, can only lead to the conclusion that this is a matter of 'crime by cop'. Police may collude with external groups such as politicians and/or organised criminals to engage in serious crime but most research attention has examined practices that are largely internal to the police organisation and fall into four main categories.

- *Grass eating*, which involves the passive acceptance of perks such as free meals and gifts. This type of low-level corruption may involve some implicit reciprocation, such as turning a blind eye to minor offences, and it may be widespread and viewed as perfectly acceptable.
- *Meat eating*, whereby proactive, corrupt entrepreneurs regulate 'graft' by effectively licensing criminal and legitimate enterprises, demanding money and cooperating with certain criminal groups. Generally this will be found within detective units with close links to organised crime and the police are plainly the regulators of the corruption.
- *Noble cause corruption*, which represents activities where officers rationalise that to secure a conviction they 'must' bend the rules; such activities are driven by a determination to achieve results. In such cases, officers have been known to falsify statements, interfere with evidence, pressurise suspects to give false confessions and lie in court. In high-profile cases, such behaviour is often justified by the intense pressure on officers to secure a conviction, but there is evidence that deviant techniques are widely employed in routine cases, particularly in respect of vulnerable suspects.
- *Super-predatory behaviour*, which relates to the criminal behaviour of officers who engage in gratuitous violence, stealing drugs from suspects and recycling them, burglary and theft at crime scenes, selling criminal cases to other officers, sexual offences, collusion with criminals and even murder. They have become organised criminals within the police organisation, which provides them with the cover for their illicit activities.

'*Birds*' are a further category of officer who, in contrast to those who fall into the four main groupings, distance themselves from deviant behaviour and manage to stay out of corrupt practices. They tend to be forgotten, yet they are an interesting group, because they 'fly above' corrupt or corruptive practices. A NYPD officer before the Knapp Commission (1972) spoke of the 'birds' who glided above without looking down and without taking part: 'The birds just fly up high. They don't eat anything either because they are honest or because they don't have any good opportunities' (Punch, 2009, p 21). These officers doubtless had reasons for consciously or instinctively keeping their hands clean and consciences unsullied; perhaps it was from moral or religious convictions or sensitivity to long-term career prospects. Of interest is that female officers do not typically get involved in corrupt practices for several reasons, including exclusion from male-dominated circles and self-exclusion in not wishing to get into trouble. They perhaps feel they have to work harder than men to prove themselves and do not wish to risk their career and reputation (Punch, 2009).

In short, police corruption takes many forms, is a recurring and tenacious element in policing, and can be highly pernicious. Furthermore, revelations about corrupt practices can have considerable implications within and beyond the police organisation (Sherman, 1978). This does not mean that all forms of corruption are necessarily found in all forces and at all times. In the Netherlands, for instance, the dominant form is noble cause corruption – with the ends justifying the means to gain a result – and the other forms are less evident (Punch, 2009). All the forms described have been reported in the US, while extreme police deviance, such as systemic corruption and even police death squads, can be found in a number of non-Western societies (Belur, 2010). The accumulated evidence, moreover, indicates that corruption cannot be dismissed as individualistic 'human failure' or as episodic because it can be engrained and systemic, and it is not just a matter for the lower ranks or for detectives. In UK policing, for instance, there has been a string of serious accusations within the past 10-15 years against chief officers (Hales et al, 2015). In one case a new chief constable found that his deputy had been accused of sexual harassment. As a result, the deputy was suspended and stood trial, but was acquitted and subsequently left the force (Blair, 2009, p 95). Further, in a near unprecedented case, the deputy and chief constable of one force were arrested on suspicion of corruption and the chief was dismissed; this was the first such case in 35 years (Brunger, 2013). Then a senior officer in the Metropolitan Police, who had been seen as a champion of minority ethnic groups in policing, was sentenced to four years' imprisonment: he had made a false 999 emergency call leading to a wrongful arrest and was jailed for misconduct and attempting to pervert the course of justice (Brunger, 2013). In another case involving the Metropolitan Police, both a commissioner and an assistant commissioner resigned over allegedly close relations with the media that were said to have had an influence on decision making within the force. This was related to various inquiries into the role of Rupert Murdoch's News Corp; the devious methods of journalists, including mobile-phone and computer hacking; the possible bribery of police officers by journalists; and members of the media having intimate and inappropriate contacts with politicians and senior police officers (Leveson Report, 2012).

Inevitably, the subject of corruption raises painful issues for police, but these cannot be denied or ignored. If police agencies claim to be in the business of public service, policing by consent, tackling crime, creating security and of establishing 'client-friendly' relations with the public, they cannot abuse people's rights, physically and psychologically assault them, distort evidence or collude with criminals. And chiefs cannot resort to the defence of 'that sort of thing doesn't happen here', because the research evidence graphically illustrates that policing and corruption are inseparable. This does not mean that corruption is universal, but it does mean that it is always an occupational hazard threatening a possible institutional crisis. Thus it must remain a persistent concern for police leaders, forcing them to consider how they can prevent deviance and corruption within their organisation and how they will cope with the internal and external fall-out if corruption is exposed. For if policing is essentially about the rule of law, due process, respect for citizens' rights, professional ethics, transparency, oversight and accountability, the police chief faced with scandal has to explain how corruption could have taken place on his or her watch – implying that he or she, or a predecessor, was not fully in control of the organisation. At such critical moments, the police force and its leadership are called to account, and accountability is a core task for the police institution, for its leaders and indeed for all its personnel. As stated by the Patten Commission on Policing in Northern Ireland (1999, p 22): 'Accountability should run through the bloodstream of the whole body of a police service.'

Accountability

Policing as a vital institution in Western, democratic society is formally based on respect for the rule of law, adherence to due process and, above all, accountability. Given the unique powers of the police agency and its far-reaching responsibilities for a wide and diffuse range of tasks, as outlined earlier, it simply has to be held accountable for its actions and be institutionally geared towards accountability. This is especially the case given what was said earlier about police deviance and corruption where officers evade responsibility and undermine accountability, leading in some cases to grave miscarriages of justice (Walker and Starmer, 1999). The message is, then, that the police organisation should not react opportunistically, defensively or blindly to the controversial matters that on occasion confront it, but rather should anticipate, think through and embrace a culture of accountability (Markham and Punch, 2007a, 2007b). Moreover, this should happen at two levels – the institutional and the operational. Accountability is a broad and diffuse concept related to formal obligations within a democracy, and to notions of good governance, transparency of policies and conduct towards the public and other stakeholders, and internally generated norms and standards of professional accountability. In this sense, the police organisation and its personnel are primarily accountable on two main fronts: *politically and institutionally* for their policies and conduct towards authorities in a legally elected (central and local) government; and *legally*, with both individual officers and collectives of officers in a group, unit or force being answerable to the law, oversight agencies and the courts both nationally and within Europe (as with human rights – Crawshaw et al, 2007).

Furthermore, alongside these fundamental and overriding commitments, the police can be said to be accountable to the following stakeholders in various ways and at various times:

- to central and local government for an efficient managerial administration, levels of quality and a healthy and controllable financial and budgetary administration. The rise of New Public Management, which began in the 1980s with the simplistic 'management by objectives' mantra, led in the UK to an escalating emphasis on managerial accountability (Jones and Newburn, 2007);
- to parliamentary commissions and to specific judicial and public commissions of inquiry;
- to external independent investigatory agencies with regard to complaints and possible abuses of power, including in the UK to the IPCC for England and Wales and Police Ombudsman for Northern Ireland, and in the Netherlands to the National Police Internal Investigation Department (*Rijksrecherche*);
- to their own organisation through a system of internal justice and subsequently in a court of law (raising the prospect of 'double jeopardy');
- to civil liberties and human rights groups and other monitoring agencies;
- to delegations of foreign politicians and officials;
- to the media (providing regular updates on policy and procedure, holding briefings and conferences, and employing social media are now held to be routine and essential features of communicating in the public arena); and, last but not least,
- to the public and to communities.

British policing, as mentioned earlier, was traditionally geared to 'policing by consent' and this feature was developed in forces adopting community policing and problem-oriented policing. Part of that consent process is taking account of, and being willing to be accountable to, local communities. Some even see this as a move from latent consent to 'active cooperation' with the community; this was, until recently, strongly evident in Dutch policing. The importance of the consent paradigm was evident during the brokering of peace in Northern Ireland, when the police were criticised for lack of accountability during the 'Troubles'.

> In a democracy, policing, in order to be effective, must be based on consent across the community. The community recognises the legitimacy of the policing task, confers authority on police personnel in carrying out their role in policing and actively supports them. *Consent is not unconditional, but depends on proper accountability, and the police should be accountable in two senses – the 'subordinate or obedient' sense and the 'explanatory and cooperative' sense.* (Patten Report, 1999, p 43; emphasis added)

The latter distinction in the Patten Report, viewed by some as the gold standard on accountability, is most important. The 'explanatory and cooperative' sense was more typical of British policing until the first decade of this century, and of practice in the Netherlands from the 1970s to the 1990s, albeit within a formal setting of 'subordinate or obedient' accountability to the mayor and public prosecutor. There is, moreover, a third way in which answerability may be viewed that is based on a contractual, calculative accountability linked to delivery of performance with an implicit or explicit factor of tenure or reward being dependent on results. But it could be argued that there has been a shift in recent years in both countries towards the 'subordinate or obedient' mode, at times mixed with the 'contractual' mode. There is a wider issue here, which is that a law enforcement agency can never have complete autonomy and has to be convincingly accountable for its actions. In that sense, the traditional operational autonomy of British chiefs and forces has always been contingent on it being used in a legal and accountable manner. States and governments will always retain the prerogative of intervening and redefining the relationship of an agency to its political masters. And at the institutional level – between individual forces or police systems and local and/or central authorities – there may well be variations over time of the formal and/or informal terms of the accountability relationship. In that relationship there is the structure of accountability as well as the culture of accountability in relation to the values that help or hinder its functioning.

In the Netherlands, for example, the formation of the National Police with a single chief answerable directly to a minister has been a sea-change in accountability for Dutch policing. The 10 regional unit chiefs are still accountable to the mayor and public prosecutor in the local 'triangle' for local enforcement, but they are now primarily accountable to the First Chief Commissioner in The Hague for all central and management issues and also directly subordinate to him, as they are no longer police chiefs of a region but of a 'unit' within the National Police. In the UK since 2012, there has been an elected official, the Police and Crime Commissioner, who oversees the policies of police chiefs and who can hire or even dismiss them. This is a major innovation in British police governance and the first time that chiefs have been directly accountable to a single elected official at the local level. The exception was with the Met, which answered institutionally to the Home Secretary. In recent years, as mentioned earlier, the Mayor, through the Greater London Authority, has claimed the right to appoint, and dismiss, the Commissioner, and also the PCC for the Metropolitan Police is now located within MOPAC in City Hall. There is also an increased tendency to call police officers to public account before the parliamentary Commission for Home Affairs. Furthermore, the UK media have become increasingly assertive in recent years, with an emphasis on investigative reporting, sometimes using devious methods, and pursuing running cases with vigour, persistence and ample resources. They also have a tendency to focus on historical cases that reflect poorly on particular forces or specific individuals so that officers can never know when a past case might be resurrected and come back to haunt them. The Hillsborough football disaster of 1989 is an example of this, with fresh evidence emerging after more than 20 years of a police cover-up (see Chapter Four), and the revelations about covert surveillance of the Lawrence family following Stephen Lawrence's murder some 20 years ago were touched on in Chapter One. Technology such as CCTV, designed to prevent crime and identify criminals, may help expose police deviance and misconduct, but above all it is the rise of social media that has heralded a new era of 'hyper-accountability' or 'sousveillance' (Goldsmith, 2010). The rise in popularity of smart-phones with cameras and camcorders means that passers-by can photograph or film almost any public incident involving police and post the files on the internet without delay or censorship. It takes just one selective image seen by thousands if not millions of internet users to determine public perception of police conduct in a controversial incident (Goldsmith, 2013).

The implication of these tendencies in both the UK and the Netherlands is, then, a clear shift towards both tighter compliance to formal oversight agencies and stakeholders – with the 'subordinate or obedient' mode in the ascendancy – and instant accountability when images are disseminated almost instantaneously through social media. With regard to the latter, damaging material may be spread inadvertently by officers themselves, or by family or friends, or deliberately for a variety of reasons. In the UK, with the removal of fixed tenure of employment and the advent of limited, renewable contracts, there is also a tendency towards calculative accountability, which is doubtless found elsewhere. In short, there is an increasing emphasis structurally on diverse forms of accountability with multiple stakeholders in various arenas. For when the police are involved in a controversial incident, the public and others, including police officers themselves as employees, have the right to full and transparent accountability based on sound governance. The police organisation, and police leaders, have, as an essential matter of professional ethics and enlightened self-interest, to implement and support a culture and practice of proactive and positive accountability. This strongly reinforces Patten's adage that there needs to be a culture of accountability running through the 'bloodstream' of a police service that permeates managerial accountability both at the institutional level and at the operational level. The institutional culture should enshrine accountability as a core institutional value in relation to leadership decisions and police conduct.

Conclusion

This chapter has conveyed that time and time again the available evidence from over half a century of police research consistently emphasises that while the police organisation appears to be powerful in certain respects, it nevertheless cannot have a major impact on crime. This is because the origins of crime lie outside its control; it is, then, distorting to make crime control the sole priority because police perform many other tasks, and an undue accent on tackling crime may alienate the public. The public is more concerned with a sense of safety and security than with crime itself and also with being treated properly by police when they interact with them. Of pivotal concern is that there is trust in the police, leading to compliance, cooperation and provision of information. Furthermore, this chapter has highlighted that the police organisation is essentially two organisations in one, and has outlined the subsequent demands this places on the quality of leadership at all levels of the organisation. Moreover, negative features of police occupational culture and the occurrence of deviance within the organisation place strong demands on the required 'moral strength' of police leadership. Given the highly symbolic significance of policing, moreover, accountability necessarily takes centre stage, including operational accountability with regard to commanding operations. Regardless of the specific choices made when it comes to preferred leadership, dealing with major incidents in an effective, just and accountable manner has to be an integral part of police leadership. In essence, accountability is as much, if not more, about culture and values than about structure and formal obligations.

Notes

[1] Moskos (2008) attended the police academy and worked as a patrol officer for a year in Baltimore for his PhD at Harvard. In some respects, his account reveals that not that much has changed in US front-line policing since the early ethnographies of policing in the 1960s and 1970s.

[2] At one time in the UK, a proportion of these came from prisoners already convicted and who were prepared to 'cough' to other offences that would not affect their sentence and helped the detective's clear-up rate. These were known as 'TICs' for 'taken into consideration'.

[3] In a case in Brazil, police officers entered a hospital to murder a young eye-witness in his bed whom they had earlier wounded when he had seen them engaged in an illegal shooting related to police involvement in drug dealing (Mercedes Hinton, presentation at the LSE, 2008).

[4] In some early US forces, officers did not want to wear uniforms or carry firearms as they saw themselves as primarily citizens for the preservation of order and the peace in the US tradition of 'delegated vigilantism' (Miller, 1977; Klockars, 1985).

[5] A former NYPD officer (O'Donnell, 2007) writes that many police departments are 'lousy places to work'. He writes of 'bullying, humiliating and dictatorial behaviour' and 'cops often feel belittled and infantilized by their bosses. Giant reservoirs of criticism can be unleashed at any time, while praise is rare.' A paradox is that 'outsiders believe cops are near-omnipotent; in fact, internally cops are made to feel powerless'.

[6] What first disturbed Serpico as an eager rookie cop in New York – who later in the 1970s blew the whistle on corruption – was that many fellow officers were avoiding work and 'cooping' at night: they slept in warm spots out of the cold with folding beds and alarm clocks to wake them so they could phone the duty sergeant at the allotted time as if they were really on duty (Maas, 1974, pp 54-5).

[7] In the US, there has, for instance, been implacable opposition from police representatives against external oversight; the Police Patrolmens' Benevolent Association has not only virulently objected to civilian oversight, but has also mounted legal actions against special commissions to investigate police corruption, such as the Knapp and Mollen Commissions in New York (Punch, 2009).

[8] It beggars belief that the match was still played.

[9] To large extent in the UK, the practice of taking part in police sport and bands during working hours has disappeared as a traditional avenue for 'easing' behaviour (Holdaway, 1979); 'value for money' regimes have led to an emphasis on no-frills productivity, so that these activities have shifted outside of work time or have disappeared entirely.

FOUR

When matters become 'really real': commanding operations

> ... there is no need for an ACPO officer to have had any operational experience at all. (Barham, 2010, p 12)

This chapter examines a range of major incidents that have required different responses from police leaders. The aim is to convey the variety of situations that forces and officers may encounter and to demonstrate that all incidents are a matter of judgement, risk analysis and an appropriate response. Each area could be dealt with extensively, but here the aim is simply to illustrate briefly the challenges that arise in policing that need to be dealt with by officers on the basis of training and experience and that require them to exercise a number of competences. Running though the examples, moreover, are the underlying insights that officers, at all levels, never know what they might encounter; that in reacting to a spontaneous incident organisational structure and leadership style have to alter instantly; and that there will always be a demand for internal and external accountability. Incidents are potentially a learning experience but may also early on – or even a great deal later – become a matter of dispute, recrimination and apportioning blame.

The topic of sudden intrusive reality in policing, the potential immensity and unexpectedness of certain major incidents and the choice of appropriate institutional and individual response can be illustrated by the shooting down of the Malaysian aircraft MH17, allegedly by a rocket, while flying over Ukraine in July 2014.[1] This disaster has been a traumatic experience for the Netherlands as it involved a civilian airliner carrying many Dutch passengers flying in approved air space and being hit by a missile launched as part of a conflict within the Ukraine with possible Russian involvement. Such a scenario was completely unforeseen as far as the Dutch authorities and police were concerned. Police officers, members of the *Marechaussee* and other officials had to respond instantly and were suddenly confronted with the largest criminal investigation in Dutch history, with the task of determining the cause of the deaths of the 196 Dutch citizens on board and the audit trail leading to those criminally responsible. Hundreds of police officers – including the specialist Disaster Identification Team – started working on the case in cooperation with multiple agencies from across the globe. Officers had to fly at short notice in an Air Force Hercules to Ukraine, confer with multiple stakeholders, negotiate access to the crash site and – in an armed conflict situation – visit the vast crime scene where their priority was the recovery of bodies and possessions. This is a daunting task with multiple facets that will involve many agencies over a long period of time. It also has a strong values element, with officers required to liaise with the victims and their families and friends with dignity and compassion as well as offering more mundane, practical support. Of the essence during this exceptional operation has been, and will continue to be, the various forms of leadership in diverse arenas and at different times necessary to guide the mission in all its facets in a highly professional manner.

Clearly this is an extreme case, of which the 9/11 attacks in the US are the ultimate example. Of course, most policing is about a range of incidents of varying seriousness of the type that can be anticipated or has occurred and been addressed frequently in the past, leading to a reservoir of experience and of planning for such events. But in all emergency incidents at whatever level, there are balances to be made and, while much can be achieved in advance, officers are often confronted with new situations or unexpected developments during an operation that require flexibility of response. This illustrates the challenging nature of leadership in policing, which should not be underestimated and which requires a strong and profound institutional commitment to resources, skills and learning for leadership. The selected cases described here are also introduced as potential material in experiential learning programmes designed to shape senior officer competences. Such cases emphasise the range and diversity of incidents as well as the complexity of factors to be taken into account by police leaders who have to prepare and manage teams, units or branches within a force. This further raises the issue of the importance of preparing for operations, conducting them successfully and learning from them. There is battery of activities and skills involved, including risk assessment; preparation and resources; selecting, motivating and directing personnel when assembling a team with the appropriate expertise for specific events; briefing, record keeping, debriefing and post-incident evaluation; handling internal and external communications, given that the media are especially demanding and intrusive in high-profile incidents; dealing with diverse authorities, other forces and stakeholders at home and at times also abroad; and keeping within the law, remaining accountable and staying within budget. To crown all that is the need to remain flexible throughout the decision-making process, and adapt to unfolding events with their inherent shifting risks, new information and windows of opportunity. This is a demanding list, but these factors are essential in thinking about preparations for tackling major incidents and shaping and testing leadership competences.

Major incidents and leadership

Sieges

A sudden siege situation may occur when criminals or terrorists are disturbed during criminal activity, take refuge in a building and spontaneously hold a number of people hostage. Another scenario is when someone who is psychotic, or emotionally wrought up, or under the influence of drink or drugs – or a combination of these – holds family members or others hostage and threatens them with violence. These can be especially taxing incidents as the suspect may be someone with no criminal past and no history of violence but who remains immune to communications and negotiation while continuing to pose a threat to those held hostage as well as to members of the emergency services. In extreme cases, a politically motivated group may take over a building, school, hospital, train, ship or plane and hold people hostage in the pursuit of political ends, sometimes threatening to kill hostages or even blow up the siege site. Examples in the Netherlands include the occupation of the Indonesian ambassador's residence in Wassenaar (1970) and the Indonesian Consulate in Amsterdam (1975); the occupation of a primary school in Bovensmilde (1977); and the seizing of two trains (at Wijster in 1975 and De Punt in 1977). All of these concerned militant groups of young South Malaccans striving for an independent homeland in Indonesia. There were fatalities among the hostages in several of the sieges, but no fatalities among the hostage takers until the second train siege when six of the eight hostage takers and two hostages were killed during an assault by the military. The ultimate decision as to how to handle all these cases was taken at government level and it is clear that the then government was most reluctant to use force and, especially with the train sieges, believed in prolonged negotiation (referred to by some as the 'Dutch approach'; Bootsma, 2001).[2] This succeeded in the first train siege when, despite three fatalities among the hostages, a surrender was negotiated. In the second train siege – which lasted no fewer than 20 days – there were no fatalities throughout the siege until negotiations with the group broke down and the decision was taken to mount an assault involving overwhelming firepower (Rosenthal, 1989a).

In the UK, there have been three skyjackings of aircraft entering UK air space leading to siege situations at Stansted Airport that were handled by the Essex Police; all three ended without bloodshed. Incidents such as these require preparation and training with other services and special forces so that the hijacked plane can be directed to the designated airport and to a suitable location on the airfield. There will also be much inter-agency consultation regarding a swathe of matters. These include preparing for the possibility of an assault by the military with the risk of casualties (there were around 200 people on board the Sudanese plane in the 1996 skyjacking at Stansted); identifying any survivors and/or victims; providing accommodation for survivors; liaising with embassies regarding foreign hostages and hostage takers; deciding when to close down the airport; and, not unimportant, supplying refreshments for the people inside the plane, the police and other emergency personnel. There may be other complications, as in the case of the Stansted skyjacking involving an Afghan Airlines plane in 2000, when some 80 passengers immediately requested political asylum following their rescue. Finally, after such incidents, a major criminal investigation has to be mounted. Negotiations with the hostage takers play a crucial role in this type of incident, and this has become a specialised role in policing, while communication with the embassies of the foreign countries is also highly important in cases where foreign nationalities, property and diplomatic premises are involved. Given the magnitude of certain decisions, such as responding to a hostage taker's political demands, the government is likely to be involved. Clearly these are often difficult, costly and stressful cases where the potential victims are innocent bystanders caught up in the drama – as with the young school children in Bovensmilde – and they place a heavy burden on all involved during, as well as after, the siege.[3]

In the UK, during the renowned Iranian Embassy siege (1980), a daring rescue by the Special Air Services Regiment (SAS) took place under the glare of TV cameras. The embassy had been taken over by members of an Iranian Arab minority group who were demanding autonomy for their region, the release of prisoners in Iran and a free passage out of the UK. The government refused to meet their demands and following the death of a hostage, the Metropolitan Commissioner requested the intervention of the SAS. Through the military aid to the civil power (MACP) protocol, the police may request military assistance via the Home Secretary; it is clear that the Prime Minister, Margaret Thatcher, was also asked for her consent in this case. This would have been necessary because forcefully entering an embassy, taken to be sovereign territory, infringes protocols in the Geneva Conventions. Thatcher took the line that one should never negotiate with terrorists and approved an assault. The operation would also have been discussed at the Cabinet Office Briefing Room A (COBRA), which is the Whitehall crisis facility comprising top government officials and representatives of relevant agencies. Military deployment does not alter the legal situation regarding use of force; the police retain primacy, but the military has the right to use force for the duration of its operation (in the case of the embassy siege, about an hour). SAS soldiers entered the building, shot all but one of the hostage takers and rescued all but one of the hostages who was killed by the hostage takers; the perpetrators also wounded two other hostages during the rescue (Firman and Pearson, 2011).

The police had a wide range of issues to deal with during the operation, including cordoning off the affected area in the middle of London; securing the site with an inner cordon of armed officers; controlling the extensive and at times intrusive media; performing covert surveillance of the embassy premises and the interactions and conversations inside; providing medical support for casualties; and consulting with the government and military about the rescue operation and the terms of the SAS role under MACP. Of considerable importance were the police officers' negotiations with the hostage takers, which was clearly demanding, stressful and emotional. The negotiators endeavoured to build a relationship with those they were speaking to and sought a peaceful solution, but remained outside of the operational decision to mount an assault, which is standard procedure. However, the phone line inside the embassy remained open when the rescue took place, and the negotiators could hear the people they had been speaking to for several days being shot. It was highly emotional for them and tears were shed (BBC Radio, 2009). The then Met Commissioner made it clear that once the government would not accede to the hostage takers' demands, which was a clear political decision taken after consultation with the Islamic Republic of Iran, the operation was fully in his hands, except for the short time when he formally handed over responsibility for the assault and rescue part of the operation to the SAS (McNee, 1983). This autonomy, assuming his account is fully accurate, would almost certainly not be the case in many other jurisdictions where operational decisions would have been taken at ministerial or prime ministerial level. Like several of the other categories to be covered in this chapter, sieges can be extremely challenging, involving political and sometimes international dimensions, major risks with the possibility of high numbers of casualties, a long time-frame and considerable use of resources, including personnel. Leadership may be tested to the utmost and requires dealing with a range of stakeholders; directing a large number of officers with diverse skills; negotiating the role of the military; and having to make the tough choices that go with a senior command role. This will be a major thread running through all the cases discussed here.

Terrorism

The Netherlands has not faced any prolonged and persistent terrorist campaigns, although there have been sporadic series of incidents involving South Malaccans in the 1970s (referred to earlier), some probable IRA shootings,[4] and armed confrontations with German Red Army Fraction members and with a domestic jihadist group (Buruma, 2006; Cramphorn and Punch, 2007). The UK, by contrast, has had to face some 30 years of turbulence in Northern Ireland and elsewhere during the 'Troubles' (1968-98). Some 3,600 people were killed during this time – including around 300 RUC officers and more than 600 military personnel – and there were bombings, shootings, abductions and sabotage within the UK, Ireland and on the Continent (Geraghty, 2000). Much of the conflict was fought out in Northern Ireland, but there were also shootings and bombings on the mainland with attacks in London, Birmingham, Manchester and elsewhere with much loss of life and immense damage. There was an attack on the hotel in Brighton hosting the Conservative Party Conference (1984) with a delayed action bomb that nearly killed Prime Minister Thatcher and members of her Cabinet; mortar bombs were fired into the garden of No 10 Downing Street when the Cabinet was meeting there (1991); a MP was blown up in his car within the Houses of Parliament (1979); and a number of bombs exploded in London and elsewhere causing casualties and much damage. In short, the UK police had to deal with the longstanding threat of 'domestic' terrorist activity, a range of incidents involving many victims and suspects, and a long stream of criminal investigations.

The devastating attacks of 9/11 in the US were a wake-up call to Western societies that they were vulnerable to attack by militant Muslim jihadists from abroad. The London bombings of July 2005 (referred to as '7/7'), however, came from within and involved young men of Asian background who appeared to be perfectly integrated into British society but who had become radicalised to the extent that they were prepared to become suicide bombers. The London bombings on three underground trains and one bus left around 700 people injured and 56 deaths (including the bombers), the biggest loss of life through violence in the capital since WWII: the explosions paralysed London's entire transport system for a time. Attention turned to potential 'home-grown' aspiring jihadists especially after another attempt was made shortly afterwards on the transport system by four suicide bombers, who all failed. In the search for the four suspects an innocent man was shot dead on an underground train by Met firearms officers (see the section on firearms later in this chapter). This was a scenario that no-one had ever considered and these events formed the greatest operational challenge since WWII, according to the Commissioner (Blair, 2009).

The UK had earlier been affected by external terrorism of a different but massive sort. The explosion in an American jumbo jet above Lockerbie in Scotland (1988) created one of the largest and most horrendous crime scenes in history, with 259 bodies and wreckage spread over a vast area. There were also 11 fatalities on the ground when wreckage fell on nearby houses causing much damage. Within hours the then smallest force in the UK was overwhelmed by government officials and technical experts, extra emergency services, airline executives, secret service agents and the national and international national media, all streaming into the small and ravaged community of Lockerbie while distraught relatives – the victims comprised 21 nationalities – desperately sought information. Given the height and speed of the disintegrating plane, the bodies, body parts and over 10,000 pieces of plane wreckage were widely dispersed and had to be recovered from a large area – a gruesome and painstaking task. When it emerged that the likely cause of the plane's disintegration was an explosion, the possibility of terrorist involvement was raised and security services from several countries, especially the US, were summoned. An immense forensic operation was mounted, requiring many body bags, a temporary mortuary, multiple autopsies and specialised undertakers, along with a combined effort between police and other services to aid the victims' families and support the shocked community. The shell of the plane was reconstructed as much as possible and kept at a Civil Aviation Authority hangar at Farnborough as evidence for subsequent criminal trials. There followed a massive and prolonged criminal investigation formally conducted by the Dumfries and Galloway police, leading to the prosecution of two Libyans suspected of being the perpetrators of the bombing. The case, 25 years on, continues to attract speculation and is still not closed.[5] It is plain that Lockerbie, the London attacks of 2005 and the 30-year IRA campaign – as with terrorist activity in other societies – takes policing into the realm of 'high' policing and counter-insurgency, involving political and international dimensions, inter-agency cooperation and the balancing of risks and rights. As with the MH17 case in Ukraine, there is not only a need for an immediate response but also a long trail of subsequent investigation, and sometimes criminal trials continuing for years if not decades.

Criminal investigations

Police conduct major criminal investigations into a broad range of serious offences, including terrorism, disasters (if criminal charges are laid as a result of the disaster), cyber-crime, fraud and other business-related offences, hate crime, sexual offences, gun and knife crime, people trafficking, corruption in business or politics, serial murder, organised crime (with domestic and/or foreign gangs), blackmail, drug-related crime, political crimes and so-called 'common' or volume crimes including theft, burglary and assault. Much bulk detective work is dull and routine – for example, typing statements about property or car theft for insurance claims – but major investigations may involve many agencies and multiple suspects. Brodeur (2010, pp 203-4) writes of a high-profile case in Canada with some 36 forces involved and a Hell's Angels trial where there were over 30 defendants. Another case in Canada cost no less than $70 million. Particular cases can, then, not only be especially complex and expensive but also most stressful for the personnel involved.

One such example is the 'Amsterdam vice' case, which started when a man in the US was arrested in 2010 for possession of child pornography. Through Interpol some of the material was traced to the Netherlands and, after a photo of one of the very young victims was shown on TV, the child was recognised. This in turn led investigators to a day-care centre in Amsterdam. Subsequently, Robert M. was arrested.[6] M., originally from a Baltic country, had been working in three day-care centres in Amsterdam and had advertised himself on the internet as a childminder. He often took a camera with him to work and was at times alone with babies and toddlers. He confessed to abusing 83 young children from the age of three weeks to talking age. He had taken photos and films of the abuse that, with the aid of his Dutch husband, he placed on internet sites. He was found to be in possession of nearly 50,000 photographs and 4,000 movies of a pornographic nature. There were around 500 parents whose children were at the establishments, who had to be informed and asked if they would watch the material to identify if their child was involved. This was incredibly stressful and some refused. But a particularly shocking aspect of the case was the existence of extensive global networks of child pornography sites, some run on a commercial basis, including – as in this case – babies just a few weeks old being abused and photographed. M. has since been convicted and jailed, as has his husband (Sterling, 2012). The case caused immense concern among many parents with young children in Amsterdam. It involved police liaising with many different agencies to support the parents and continually communicating with the public along with the mayor and officials at City Hall. It also showed that transnational policing can be greatly helped by the digital investigative networks of Interpol which led fairly swiftly to an arrest. Dutch detectives, and police elsewhere, now routinely scan such sites looking for leads to crimes with foreign connections and other global child pornography rings; indeed, the Robert M. case led to 43 arrests abroad. Not surprisingly, this disturbing case caused some of the officers working on it to experience psychological and emotional difficulties as a result of having to spend days on end viewing the graphic and harrowing material displaying serious crimes against the most vulnerable and defenceless members of our society.

Violence against vulnerable individuals was also a feature of the highly demanding criminal investigation in 2002 into the disappearance of two young girls in Soham (Cambridgeshire), who were later found murdered. This unleashed the most intense media attention and the small, provincial force was almost overwhelmed, with the press focusing on the abilities of the force's detective department, the force's willingness to cooperate with other forces and its information-sharing processes. For some people, both without and within the police, this case was symbolic of the need for regional or national units, of the limited competency levels of some senior and chief officers and of weaknesses in communicating information between forces. It emerged that if information had been sent to Cambridgeshire Police from another force about the criminal record of the subsequent offender, who worked in the school the girls attended, he would have been identified, and the bodies located, much earlier. As it was, the families and the community were kept in a state of hope and fear for longer than was necessary. As the suspect worked in education, a post requiring automatic screening for any past offences of a sexual nature, he should have been identified during the job application process, but it emerged that he had used an assumed name; inquiries early in the investigation could easily have uncovered this.

This high-profile case raising intense emotions led to severe public criticism of both forces and a public inquiry (Bichard Report, 2004). The chief constable of the force that had not passed on information on the suspect's previous record of sexual assaults was subsequently held responsible for this failure and suspended. This indicates how an investigation can have a major impact on a force and leave a long trail of institutional and personal consequences. Investigations can be complex, extended and involving many personnel and require sound and consistent leadership with a relay of supervisory staff. There are many facets involved but in particularly harrowing cases – as in the Amsterdam vice case – there can be the issue of duty of care, and of leadership being sufficiently alert to this dimension of stress among the personnel.

Firearms and shootings

Firearms are the ultimate expression of the use of force by police officers, and when they are drawn they are always potentially fatal. There are the issues of firearms use by criminals and others, shooting sprees/massacres, and firearms use by the police themselves: these in turn lead to a range of possible scenarios. Of importance, moreover, is the law and policy in specific countries on the police use of firearms as potentially fatal force, official guidelines, choice of weaponry and ammunition, training and command structures. One key matter is whether or not police are routinely armed; most forces do arm all officers but several countries – including Ireland, Norway and New Zealand – do not, along with the UK except for Northern Ireland (Punch, 2011). This means that unarmed officers are vulnerable when faced with armed opponents – and being defenceless may die as a result. For instance, in one case in Manchester in 2012, two female officers answered a call and were shot dead; they were lured to the scene and ambushed by a man who shot them and also threw a hand-grenade (*Telegraph*, 18 August 2012). But even armed officers taken by surprise may have no time to defend themselves, while a lone officer may have his or her weapon taken and used against him or her, as happened in Baflo (the Netherlands) in 2011 with fatal consequences. In such cases, the response focuses on getting medical treatment to the scene and the search for an armed and dangerous suspect or suspects. Clearly, it may take more time to mobilise an immediate armed response in a largely unarmed force. This will also hold for the time needed to mobilise a specialist armed response to a major incident. This was the case at shootings at Hungerford and Dunblane in the UK in 1987 and 1996 respectively (North, 2000; Punch, 2011), and, most acutely, at a mass shooting in Norway in 2011, during which Anders Breivik shot dead 69 mainly young people and wounded 110. This was on a small island with almost no escape, except by swimming, and it is a feature of such shooting sprees that they typically take place without warning in undefended and confined places. There is almost never a police unit on the spot, and the first responders typically face a heavily armed opponent who is determined to carry on firing.

In a provincial town in the Netherlands, Alphen aan den Rijn, in 2011, a young man with a mental health history entered a shopping mall early on a Saturday morning when it was still fairly quiet. He was equipped with several weapons – a semi-automatic rifle and two hand-guns – and opened fire using over 100 rounds, killing six people and wounding 17 before shooting himself. A note in his car warned of explosives in the mall and two other malls. The first to respond was a patrol car and the officers would have been instructed not to engage the suspect – who had considerable fire power and was clearly prepared to kill – but to pass on information about the ongoing risk and casualties and to wait for reinforcements. Once it was clear that the danger was over, the deployment would have moved to removing casualties, securing the site for forensics and scene of crime officers, informing relatives and communicating with the local community and the media. The local authority 'triangle' – mayor, public prosecutor and police chief – took the lead in this process.

The implication in cases such as this is that forces have to develop the ability to respond rapidly to shooting incidents, with a command structure ready to back up vulnerable front-line officers and with specialist units ready to be deployed for serious incidents. In the Norway massacre, it is understandable that in an unarmed force it took time to mobilise a specialist unit, but speed would have helped to minimise the tragedy, especially as Breivik surrendered immediately. An escalating situation would have been had he taken hostages and fought it out with the police with the likelihood of more casualties among the hostages, perhaps with the use of explosives which he had employed earlier in Oslo to devastating effect. This type of scenario raises similar challenges to siege situations, where the perpetrators take hostages and are prepared to use violence – as in the IRA Balcombe Street siege in London in 1975. Here the tough decision is whether or not to force an entry in a rescue attempt and risk the lives of the assault team and the hostages. In another case, an attempt to break into an apartment in The Hague in 2004, where two armed members of a Muslim jihadist group (the *Hofstad* group) were holed up, was met with a hand-grenade attack that wounded three officers. And in Spain a jihadist group suspected of involvement in the Madrid bombings

(2004) blew up the apartment they were in when police tried to force an entry, killing an officer.

To a degree, the elements to be taken into account at the command level are generic and have parallels with the scenarios discussed earlier in the chapter. But there is also the need for specialised leadership roles in these situations, with expertise in dealing with cases involving firearms. The command structure regarding firearms can be in place prior to raids on premises with suspects thought to be, or known to be, armed; for pre-planned operations against an anticipated armed attack on a bank or money transport van; and when escorting dangerous suspects. What has to be taken into account is that firearms use is always potentially fatal so there is a permanent high-risk factor; that officers miss their target most of the time (with the risk of ricochets hitting bystanders); and that there is a psychological factor involved in such scenarios whereby a combination of stress and confusion can foster mistakes (Klinger, 2004). However well prepared and well trained an armed unit is, there can at times be a combination of factors – including visual and aural misperception, misinterpretation of information and communication problems – that can lead to the wrong decision being taken. There is an irreducible element that in high-pressure situations requiring split-second decisions things will go wrong – and at times badly wrong. Given that mistakes can be fatal for suspects or officers, there can be a long trail of incriminations, investigations and court cases if operations are mismanaged. In the Netherlands, for example, an officer was called to an incident at a railway station in The Hague in 2012 where a man was threatened by someone who said he had a firearm. When challenged, the suspect ran away and the officer fired a shot at his legs, but hit him in the neck, which proved to be fatal. The officer had felt threatened, but the suspect had not produced a firearm and was running away from him. The officer was initially prosecuted for manslaughter, and later for murder, but was acquitted. However, the case caused a great deal of consternation and there have since been threats against the officer and demonstrations protesting about the failure to convict.[7] Such emotional reactions, with wide community unrest, frequently follow such shootings of young unarmed males, especially when they are from a minority background, as we have seen recently in the US and UK.

With regard to shootings, attention has begun to turn from individual liability to responsibility at the organisational level. In the UK, for example, an armed raid on an apartment complex in Sussex in 1998 to arrest a suspected drug dealer who was possibly armed was poorly planned, led and executed. Not only was the suspect not present, but an innocent man, naked and unarmed, was shot dead by an officer. The officer concerned was prosecuted for murder, but acquitted; at his trial, however, the judge made it clear that others in the police hierarchy should have been called to account in court. Subsequently, the Crown Prosecution Service prosecuted a Sussex superintendent and two inspectors on other charges, with the prosecution blaming inadequate training and 'the organisational state' of the Sussex police force, but the case folded in court. Nevertheless, the 'blame trail' continued, with two investigations by other forces and pressure from the Home Secretary on the Chief Constable to step down (he retired early). Only after 11 years was a settlement reached with the family, whereby Sussex Police admitted negligence and paid damages.

Then there was the shooting of an innocent man, Jean Charles de Menezes, on an underground train at Stockwell Station by armed Metropolitan Police officers in 2005, which became surrounded with controversy. The day before – and only a few weeks after the devastating 7/7 bombings in London – four suicide bombers had attempted to cause explosions on the London transport system. All four attempts failed. Immediately an intense search was mounted for the four suspects, who might try again, might have accomplices and might be relying on a bomb manufacturer. This was a high-pressure moment and a combination of ensuing factors – relating to command structure, ambiguity in communications and operational misunderstandings – led to an innocent man being shot with hollow-point bullets at point-blank range; this can only mean death. There followed an investigation by the Independent Police Complaints Commission (IPCC, 2007); an extensive inquest, with the key officers concerned called as witnesses and cross-examined; and a prosecution of the Metropolitan Police under health and safety law, which led to a conviction and fine (Punch, 2011). The circumstances here were exceptional and the pressures extreme, but the subsequent plethora of investigations and inquiries placed the Metropolitan Police organisation – its procedures and practices – under a critical microscope. This indicates that, while individual responsibility remains the legal cornerstone in police shootings in the UK, attention is increasingly being turned on the organisational component of accountability.[8] Use of fatal force in policing is a highly charged issue, as a mistake or what is viewed as such – for example, shooting dead an unarmed youngster or killing a suspect who could have been apprehended without fatal force – may lead to major riots (as has happened in London, Paris and Ferguson, Missouri), prolonged community unrest, the long-term souring of relationships between police and citizenry, extended hostile media campaigns and criminal and/or civil court cases.

Public order/security

Policing and public order can involve large-scale, peaceful events and demonstrations, gatherings with a clear risk of disturbances, demonstrations where two conflicting groups have to be kept from clashing; and spontaneous riots triggered by some inflammatory incident (Waddington, 1991, 1994, 2007; HMIC, 2011).[9] National and VIP security may also have a public order element. Capital and major cities are often required to host presidential or royal visits, international meetings (involving, for example, the UN, EU, G20, World Trade Organization and other global agencies), large-scale sporting occasions (such as the Olympic Games, and various World and European Championships), national celebrations and party political conventions where there is both a security element and the potential for political demonstrations (Manning, 2008). For instance, at international financial meetings in Seattle (1999), Gothenburg (2001) and Genoa (2001), vicious street battles broke out between police and anti-globalists whose express intention was to provoke violent confrontation.

A massive security operation was launched for the 2012 London Olympic Games, especially since a terrorist incident was considered in the risk analysis to be a highly realistic threat. Planning started years in advance and there was extensive security in place throughout the Games. There was a warship moored in the River Thames (largely as a communications centre), armed patrols on the river, anti-aircraft rockets on the roofs of buildings, fighter jets and special forces on standby, armed police in attendance from all over the country, and thousands of military, transport police and private security personnel engaged in security at airports, on public transport and at the various Olympic sites throughout the event, including at the Paralympic Games. A similarly vast security operation was mounted in the Netherlands for the Nuclear Security Summit (NSS) in March 2014 in The Hague, with some 60 heads of state attending, including President Obama, along with some 5,000 delegates and 3,000 journalists. US presidential visits are always accompanied by a huge security entourage that arrives weeks in advance to scour all buildings and routes related to the visit. The NSS required, therefore, an all-out effort by more than 25,000 personnel from the National Police, military and Dutch security services along with other domestic and foreign agencies. Nothing was left to chance and there were consequences for traffic, railways and airports, with warships patrolling the coast, an Airborne Warning and Control System plane and F16 fighter jets permanently in the air, attack helicopters and special forces on standby and anti-aircraft batteries on instant alert. Fortunately, both events passed off without serious incident. Such events are beyond the experience of most officers in most forces but, again, they illustrate the potential for officers to be involved in huge operations that involve long-term planning, extensive logistics, support from other forces nationally and in some cases internationally, complex and prolonged inter-agency consultation and negotiation, and constant evaluation of risk and threat.

But it is the case that capitals in particular but also some other cities regularly attract large-scale demonstrations and a range of other events which more often than not pass without major incidents. While such events can be extensively planned for in advance and may almost become routine, officers still have to cope with them effectively during an intense, concentrated period that always involves a risk potential. At the more mundane level, it may be that routine events approached with complacency become a hazard when matters unexpectedly unravel, and the poor handling of such incidents may reveal underlying fault-lines that have not been addressed (O'Hara, 2005). In the Netherlands, for instance, in 2009 a large annual beach party at Hook of Holland that had gone smoothly for several years and was not deemed a risk, got completely out of hand (Muller et al, 2009). Thousands more people turned up than was expected and lax private security failed to prevent far too many people entering the terrain without any form of control. A relatively small number of officers in standard uniform were on duty and there was no reserve available close by from the Mobile Unit. This was despite the fact that it was known that a group of trouble-makers, who had a background in football-related violence in Rotterdam and who had turned to disrupting mass events, were planning to attend. This group ascertained that the police presence was minimal, and proceeded to incite fights and surround isolated officers, who drew their weapons; some of the crowd then turned against officers coming to the aid of their beleaguered colleagues. A mass confrontation developed, with members of the crowd mounting coordinated assaults on the police, and some ringleaders shouting that the officers had no back-up and would not dare to shoot. The situation culminated in officers resorting to their firearms, causing one fatality. Some officers were out of ammunition from constantly firing warning shots – 76 bullets were fired, which is quite exceptional in the Netherlands – mobile phone batteries became flat, communicating by radio proved difficult and officers stated afterwards that they were convinced their lives were in danger. Most had never encountered anything as intense and threatening before, and some required counselling (van Iersel, 2010). The command centre did not react adequately and there was a breakdown in communications. Eventually, a number of experienced constables and sergeants took charge of several groups of officers, and, with the help of a mounted unit close by that charged into the crowd and helped to break it up, they soon brought the situation under control. In the absence of command, the officers themselves spontaneously reorganised, with formal and informal leaders taking control and restoring order. This disturbance, which might well have led to more casualties, exposed a wider institutional failure to heed warning intelligence about known trouble-makers, to arrange confident operational leadership of the appropriate level and to provide back-up in case of need (van Iersel, 2010).

Certain violent groups, like the one involved in the Hook of Holland incident, are clever in their use of tactics, well prepared for confrontation and ready to use violence. This has been the case with a number of activist movements in the Netherlands. The prevalent progressivism of the 1970s and 1980s also carried a militant, radical element, including squatters who strongly defended squatted premises when faced with eviction and who could mobilise large numbers of supporters to demonstrate at the same time (housing shortage had long been an emotive issue). In 1975, there were serious riots in the Nieuwmarkt area of Amsterdam, as a protest against the demolition of houses for the construction of an underground railway. When some squats were forcibly entered, with the police using armoured cars to break down heavily reinforced doors and firing tear gas into the building, officers were pelted from above with paint, bricks and other debris, while the assembled mass of rioters threw all sorts of missiles at the police lines. A large crowd of sympathisers fought the police solidly for the entire day; they hurled pieces of cobblestones – easily pulled up and broken into pieces – at the riot squad, which responded with charges on foot or with horses, tear gas and water cannon. As the skirmishes ebbed and flowed, there were casualties on both sides. Then, in 1980, in anticipation of the clearance of a squat, an inner-city Amsterdam street was barricaded by squatters, blocking off traffic. To the horror of many inhabitants, army tanks rumbled through streets for the first time since WWII and demolished the barricades, which had been set alight by the squatters. Also in 1980, at the inauguration of Princes Beatrix as queen in the New Church in Amsterdam, squatters with others started a major riot that stretched the police to their limit. There were vicious battles throughout the inner-city area, and the fighting was so intense that it almost reached the Royal Palace where the new queen was about to be presented to the public (Rosenthal, 1989b). Police officers have since said that if the demonstrators had broken through that final cordon, live bullets would have been fired.

Another example of an ostensibly peaceful gathering that ended in violence is the 2013 Boston marathon. Routine precautions were put in place, but it was deemed a low-risk event, and the bombings near the finish line were totally unexpected. There were three deaths and some 260 people injured in the attacks. However, there was a considerable police presence, and by all accounts the emergency response, followed by the manhunt for the suspects, led by Bill Evans of the Boston Police, was exemplary. Having run in the race, Evans calmly took control: he has since become the Boston Police Commissioner (Andersen, 2014). Another cruel reminder of the vulnerability of such recreational events to high casualties emerged at the Love Parade in Duisburg in Germany in 2010. This was viewed as a 'fun' occasion that had attracted vast crowds in the past with few serious incidents. But the occasion suddenly turned into a grave emergency when too many people tried to enter a confined space, resulting in 21 deaths and some 500 injuries. Not only did the authorities underestimate the number of people who would turn up – as well as the areas of potential risk on the festival terrain – but also the emergency services seemed incapable of intervening in the tragedy evolving before their eyes. Some of those involved in managing and regulating the event have since faced legal proceedings.

Especially demanding are demonstrations where two widely conflicting and militant groups have to be kept apart to avoid a pitched battle, say an anti-fascist movement and an extreme right-wing group. In East London, for example, a large police presence of around 3,000 officers was required in 2013 when a few hundred members of the right-wing, nationalist English Defence League (EDL) marched provocatively through a largely Muslim area, protesting about the spreading Muslim influence in British society. The EDL had to be kept apart from about 7,000 Unite Against Fascism members and others, some of whom tried to break the police cordon in order to attack the EDL group (*Independent*, 8 September 2013). Here the police had to hold the line to prevent a disturbance getting out of hand with the two antagonistic groups clashing. Some level of disturbance was anticipated in this case, yet, in the absence of a judicial injunction preventing the march, both groups had a right to demonstrate and in a sense the police were upholding that legal right by holding the line between them.

That was a one-off demonstration, but there also campaigns lasting weeks if not months, conducted by well-organised and determined groups, such as animal rights and environmental activists. The former have been known to mount long, threatening campaigns against laboratories, or facilities at pharmaceutical companies and universities that employ live animals in experiments. Environmentalists can be equally resourceful and skilful in their efforts to oppose developments perceived to have a detrimental impact on the countryside and/or on the environment, from new motorways and airport extensions, to green-site building projects or nuclear facilities. Both entail a major commitment and huge budget for policing those premises over a long period of time. In Germany, for instance, the periodic transport of nuclear waste by train has become a trigger for regular protests, during which some 16,000 police officers in riot gear, equipped with water-cannon, tear-gas and armoured vehicles, fight constant battles with sometimes more than 20,000 determined demonstrators in an effort to move the train towards its destination. The police are placed in the predicament of defending the two sets of rights at stake: the right to demonstrate and the right of companies and services to transport goods.

Another emotive issue in the UK in the mid-1990s concerned the export of live animals to countries with less stringent animal welfare practices than the UK. This emotional cause united people of all ages and from across the political spectrum and led to large demonstrations at ports and airfields. One such demonstration led to a fatality when a female protester was crushed by a lorry. Animal rights activists were involved in leading the demonstrations and blockades, but the protests were largely a result of grass-roots movements attracting ordinary citizens, many of whom had never demonstrated before. A small port in Essex at Brightlingsea reached by a winding country road was used in 1995 for exporting live animals. There were widespread protests from people from all walks of life, including the inhabitants of the town, who found they could easily delay the lorries in the narrow streets by using a variety of obstruction tactics (Markham and Punch, 2004). The police had to balance the rights of both parties involved, taking into account that some of the protesters were local residents who would still be living in the area when the campaign was over. There was also the issue of safety; with many people attempting to surround large vehicles in confined spaces, the convoys sometimes had to be diverted to avoid danger. On one occasion, the police had managed to push aside the crowds of protesters to the point where the vehicles had almost reached their destination, and the police allowed them to drive on despite a local time ban on heavy traffic. This decision was taken precisely because it would have been unsafe to turn the lorries at that spot. The breaking of the ban by the police was contested in court, but upheld by the judge, who accepted the argument about safety, with the senior officer in charge of the operation taking accountability for the operation and appearing in court (Markham, 1999). Here at Brightlingsea the police were facing primarily their own citizens whom they would have to police after the demonstrations were over. Throughout, then, the operational decision-making had to balance continually this factor, with much attention paid to communicating with local residents, while there were two fundamental and legal rights at stake along with the issue of safety.

This conveys that 'public order' policing is not just police facing a particular group on a single occasion leading either to no difficulties or to some form of clash. Single-issue politics may galvanise large groups of ordinary citizens, who may never have demonstrated before, to protest over a controversial plan – say, the construction of a motorway through an area of outstanding natural beauty – and engage in a determined campaign of resistance for months, if not years. One notable such incident occurred in the Netherlands at Amelisweerd, an attractive wooded estate outside Utrecht, where determined demonstrators – and smart activists mounting legal procedures – held up the building of a motorway right through the estate for several years. This was in the late 1970s and early 1980s, when hundreds of action groups often found a sympathetic ear among progressive politicians and even the judiciary (Verbij, 2005). The police had continually in that period to deal with militant groups of squatters, animal rights activists, environmentalists, and, in particular, groups opposing the Vietnam War, nuclear armament and US dominance in world affairs. These movements could sometimes rely on massive public support: opposition to NATO's plan to station cruise missiles in the Netherlands, for instance, led to protest marches with 400,000 demonstrators in Amsterdam (1981) and over 500,000 in The Hague (1983). Both marches were overwhelmingly peaceful. The militancy of groups and the size of demonstrations has diminished since then in the Netherlands and the police have become more sophisticated in their assessment of risk and in employing a variety of tactics to match the situation.

Officers may also be called on to police industrial disputes where aggrieved workers may carry out picketing and other activities for a considerable period of time. Particularly explosive are situations where strikers try physically to prevent non-strikers from going to work and the police have to intervene. In the UK in 1984 this was one element in a massive and often violent confrontation between striking coal miners and cohorts of police officers. These pitched battles occurred during a period of months and required police support from almost all over the country (Adeney and Lloyd, 1986).[10] Other occupational groups facing wage cuts, plant closures, redundancies or other economic measures – a major issue since the 2008 economic crisis – have also been known to take to the streets, with truck drivers blocking motorways and farmers spreading milk, vegetables – or manure – over the streets or using live animals in the protest.

But probably the most demanding public order situations are the spontaneous ones, where an incident or series of events sparks off widespread rioting that is not anticipated. There are numerous examples of this, including in Amsterdam (1966), London (1981 and 2011) and Paris (2005). In August 2011, police shot dead a man in North London whom they thought was armed but which turned out not to be the case. The initially peaceful protests that followed rapidly developed into violent confrontation between protestors and police, followed by serious rioting in other parts of London and in other cities. Police vehicles were destroyed, buildings and buses were set alight, and shops were looted. Five people died in the violence, some £200 million worth of damage occurred, around 200 officers were injured and over 3,000 arrests were made. There were several explanations for the riots, including racism (the man shot by police was black), widespread youth unemployment, frustration at cutbacks in facilities in deprived areas, resentment of selective police 'stop-and-search' tactics and the hedonism of rioting and looting (LSE, 2011; Newburn, 2015). The speed of communication between groups of rioters and people in other areas was enhanced by use of the social media, although, ironically, this also worked to the advantage of police in tracing suspects, victims and witnesses. This was the most serious rioting in the UK (outside of Northern Ireland) in years. The police were taken by surprise and their response was heavily criticised for being too slow. So any immediate response to a major public disturbance that requires a sudden shift in organisational mode and the mobilisation of thousands of officers may also result in the police being subjected to intense media exposure, political questioning and an array of investigations for some time afterwards. Like other forms of policing, the maintenance of public order may be routine, without incident and gaining wide approval, but may equally lead to a trail of recrimination, public scrutiny, court cases and civil claims.[11]

Disasters/civil emergencies

Police are crucial in responding to disasters and civil emergencies. Indeed, in the UK, as mentioned earlier, the police have 'primacy' in dealing with such situations, whereas elsewhere they are the responsibility of the fire service and/or a specialised emergency agency. Disasters include plane, train and shipping accidents, industrial accidents – including on-site or in-transit explosions and toxic emissions that threaten the environment, drinking water and the population in the affected area – and terrorist incidents where explosions lead to high casualties and/or major physical damage. Serious civil emergencies, and the accompanying police response, tend to receive less attention than these more dramatic disasters. But storms and widespread flooding, which have affected many countries around the world in recent years, may also cause considerable danger, high casualties and widespread dislocation over a prolonged period of time (for example, mass evacuation, loss of power, and the disruption of transport and economic activity). The Netherlands, for instance, was subject to periodic flooding – on a catastrophic scale in 1953 and again on a large scale in 1995 – and in late 2013 and early 2014 extensive flooding in the UK caused enormous damage and disruption. Floods require a major inter-agency effort in anticipation of, and especially during, the emergency. The massive outbreak of foot-and-mouth disease in the UK in 2001, which resulted in the extermination of some 10 million cattle and sheep, was an example of a civil emergency where the task was so great that the Army was brought in to assist the police. It became a national emergency demanding a nationwide effort by police, Army and other agencies under the central direction of the Prime Minister and Cabinet through COBRA in Whitehall.

The Netherlands has also had to confront several national disasters, including the El Al plane crash (1992); the Turkish Airlines crash close to Schiphol (2009, resulting in nine deaths and 86 injured); an explosion and fire at an industrial complex (Chemipack in Moerdijk, 2011); a fire in a crowded café with many youthful casualties (Volendam, 2001); and several train crashes. A massive explosion in 2000 at a fireworks depot in Enschede (in the East of the country) illustrates the danger inherent in locating industrial plants in densely populated areas. In this incident, around 800 kilograms of fireworks were set alight. The area devastated by the explosion looked as if it had been hit by several bombs, with some streets completely flattened. Twenty-three people were killed (including four firefighters) and 947 injured; 400 homes were destroyed and 1,500 damaged; and some 1,000 people were made homeless. No one had ever envisaged this scenario as the depot was regulated and inspected, and the fireworks were dispersed in deep bunkers so that an explosion would be contained. Somehow a fire started and the bunker doors were open; what was not supposed ever to happen in fact happened. The result was devastating for the community and daunting in the extreme for the police and emergency services (Vuyk, 2010).

A disaster where terrorism was immediately seen as a possibility, given that this involved an Israeli carrier, was the El Al cargo plane crash on a block of flats in Amsterdam in 1992. The Boeing 747 had just taken off from Schiphol Airport when two motors fell off one wing. On attempting to return for an emergency landing, the pilots lost control of the plane, which was fully loaded with fuel and cargo. It crashed into an apartment block in Amsterdam South-East, resulting in an explosion that killed over 40 people and a huge fire (Dekker, 1994). There were challenges posed by the immediate emergency response – involving at one stage 300 firefighters and other emergency personnel and about 500 police officers – but a particular difficulty lay in identifying the victims amid the wreckage of an aeroplane deeply embedded in a collapsed building that had been swept by an intense blaze. This was a particularly gruesome task carried out by a special unit, the Disaster Identification Team, which was under political pressure to complete the work swiftly.[12] This was partly related to the fact that a number of illegal immigrants and unregistered home owners lived in the flats so there was considerable confusion about the number and the identity of the victims. The crash occurred on a quiet Sunday afternoon around meal-time, and it required individual officers and the entire police force to change gear instantly to cope with a mega-incident where terrorist-related sabotage was a distinct possibility from the start. But this turned out not to be the case.[13] The disaster had to be dealt with at the domestic level, under the direction of the mayor, but also at the international level with Israeli and US security services, air accident investigators, Boeing and El Al. It was also a case where the mayor played a directing, visible role, which is usual in the Netherlands where he or she had regional responsibility for disaster management.

In the 1980s in the UK, there was a spate of disasters that drew police attention to coping with such challenging incidents. The Management of Disasters and Civil Emergencies (MODACE) course at Bramshill Police College dealt with the range of incidents that police may encounter. Two in particular – Zeebrugge (Belgium) in 1987, where a British ship capsized with 193 fatalities, and the Hillsborough Stadium Disaster in 1989 when 96 people died in a crush due to overcrowding at a football match – are examined here. Of importance in extracting lessons from these events is to think of three phases – pre-disaster (planning and training), during the disaster (actual response) and post-disaster (learning, inquiries and court cases, which can take years if not decades, and counselling for personnel). Specific lessons may be drawn from specific events, but a general insight, as evidenced by the examples here, is that a disaster should always be viewed *a priori* as a crime scene. Also of great significance is the role and functioning of senior officers in leadership roles. This is examined later in this chapter.

Capsizing of the 'Herald of Free Enterprise' at Zeebrugge

In 1987 at Zeebrugge in Belgium, the cross-channel ferry *Herald of Free Enterprise* capsized just outside the harbour in the evening in calm conditions (Punch, 1996). This was a British ship, carrying mostly British passengers, but it lay in Belgian territorial waters. However, Kent Police were granted primacy, and were faced with nearly 200 dead (many still in the wreck), a large number of survivors in Belgian hospitals and other accommodation, intense media interest and a stream of requests from relatives and friends for information and help. Kent officers also had to cooperate with a foreign police force with very different procedures and command structures from the British ones. The wreck lay on its side in shallow water and it was evident that the bow doors were open; this immediately raised speculation about the cause of the accident. But the ship had to be recovered, the bodies had to be removed, a maritime accident court of inquiry had to be held and an inquest had to be opened. An official inquiry into the accident was scathing about the management of Townsend Thorensen, the operating company, and the lack of attention to safety on board. Yet the Department of Transport decided not to prosecute for gross negligence. Later, however, the inquest to establish the cause of death brought in a verdict of 'unlawful death', which consequently required Kent Police to commence a criminal investigation. Only then, months after the accident, did the police mount the criminal investigation. No-one had thought of examining the ship as the scene of crime, but long after the event, hundreds of people had to be interviewed and the decision-making within Townsend-Thorensen had to be investigated to prepare a case of 'corporate manslaughter'. The prosecution case was not successful but the Zeebrugge incident exuded a strong message to police forces to think in terms of 'liability' from day one and to treat every disaster, apart from natural ones, as a potential scene of crime. This reinforces the importance of police primacy in disaster management in the UK, as a civil agency for major emergencies might not be so inclined to pursue criminal liability as with the initial regulatory response to the *Herald* case.

Hillsborough Stadium disaster

The Hillsborough Stadium disaster was a truly appalling incident that reflects poorly on the police and continues to reverberate to this day. It forms a valuable lesson in conveying that not getting it 'right' in advance, and not having effective leadership in place to cope with the circumstances while they unfold, may leave a bitter legacy of pain and distress for those people affected and form a long path of opprobrium for those who failed and for their organisation. The incident – an important football match (a semi-final of the FA Cup) played at the Hillsborough Stadium in Sheffield in 1989 – led to the deaths of 96 mostly young people, who nearly all died from asphyxiation when they were crushed in the crowd. Although the South Yorkshire Police (SYP) had considerable experience with major football games, there was a series of failures in preparing adequately for the game (Scraton, 1999). Then on the day of the match between Liverpool and Nottingham Forest, a large number of mainly Liverpool fans were massing at the turnstiles at the end of the ground designated for them. Some of the spectator bays at that end were already crowded, but there was no filtering of the crowd and no monitoring of overcrowding. As the pressure outside mounted prior to kick-off, a police officer, fearing a dangerous situation was developing at the gates, asked for permission for several gates to be opened to relieve the pressure. This led to a sudden surge of fans, who, without guidance from stewards, rushed for the nearest pens, which were already over-filled. A crush resulted, in which many young fans at the front were pushed up against the perimeter fence. At that time, stadiums in the UK had fences to prevent a pitch invasion by 'hooligans' and, fearing such a scenario, the police were slow to open the small gates in the fence. When it started to become clear that a major disaster was unfolding, many spectators had already died or were unconscious. The emergency medical response then proved confused and inadequate.

For survivors and relatives, there followed harrowing scenes at hospitals and the temporary morgue where the dead were laid out. Many fans later complained that they were brusquely interviewed, almost as if they were suspects; that the communication of information was poor and insensitive; that the identification process was harsh if not brutal; and that relations with the police were often strained. An important factor emerged about the command structure in that it had effectively collapsed. The 'silver' commander (see later in this chapter) was in the police control box in the stadium, but there was poor communication between him and the officer in charge outside of the stadium as well as with the supervisory officers inside. The latter were drawn in to aiding their officers on the pitch by helping them to pull out the injured from the stands and get medical help for them. There was a breakdown in communication, and as a result the rescue effort was poorly coordinated. In notes penned shortly afterwards, it was clear that front-line officers felt left down by their senior officers. One wrote: 'Sergeants and inspectors seemed to be milling around and direct radio control seemed to be lost. There did not appear to be any leadership' (Hillsborough Report, 2012). There was a 'gold' commander sitting in the stands – and hence not in a gold command centre – but by the time he intervened, it was already too late.

There is much to be learned from Hillsborough as a disaster case study, but here the emphasis is largely on the post-disaster phase. For this emotive event has fostered a continuing stream of inquiries and other responses, including books and several powerful television programmes. Importantly, there was a police inquiry by another force, West Midlands Police (WMP), which placed most blame on the Liverpool fans, who were said to have turned up late in a state of intoxication, to have caused the crush at the gates forcing them to be opened, to have stolen from the victims and later to have abused the police trying to help people escape from the stand.[14] This was accompanied by a degree of demonisation of the Liverpool fans in parts of the media. There followed a long series of inquiries and developments over the next two decades. There was an inquest, and a public inquiry into the disaster (Taylor Report, 1989); this was quite critical of the police, who paid damages without accepting liability. There was also a judicial review ordered by the Home Secretary, and the prosecution of two officers, which failed to result in convictions. But the parents of the victims, relatives, friends and survivors clearly felt that responsibility had not been apportioned and, in particular, that they had never been adequately informed about the underlying causes and exact circumstances of their relatives' deaths. They were aided by two well-organised interest groups of parents and supporters that were relentless in not giving up on seeking the truth. They were much helped by the supportive advocacy of Scraton (1999) and by his influential academic research and publications.

A turning-point came in recognising this unrelenting effort when the Labour government in 2009 allowed a new inquiry that would have access to all the relevant data. The report of the Independent Panel on Hillsborough[15] was published in 2012 after extensive interviewing and research, delving into an archive of some 450,000 documents. It exposed multiple failures before and during the event and stated:

'As a result, rescue and recovery efforts were affected by lack of leadership, coordination, prioritisation of casualties and equipment.' It estimated that possibly some 40 wounded could have been saved if proper procedures had been immediately followed. But most damning was that South Yorkshire Police responded in defensive mode at the highest level by blaming the victims, avoiding liability, doctoring the 'recollections' of officers and pressurising them to change statements. Furthermore, a South Yorkshire Police officer, a federation (police 'union') member and an MP allegedly planted negative and false information to the media through a news agency. After publication of the Panel's report in 2012 there followed an apology in Parliament by the Prime Minister David Cameron; a new inquest was ordered; the IPCC started an investigation into possible offences by police officers; and a criminal investigation ('Operation Resolve' under a Chief Constable) was launched into possible offences by police officers and others. The officer in charge of the police control box on that day nearly 25 years ago is again (in early 2015) facing critical questioning and may possibly be prosecuted for a second time.

Hillsborough is, then, the prime example of a disaster that harshly exposed the police, and others, regarding deficiencies in all three segments of the 'chain' – pre-disaster, disaster, and post-disaster. The system failed in that the South Yorkshire Police, Ambulance Service, Football Association and Sheffield United club owners collectively did not heed warnings and did not keep to guidelines. The case especially reveals that the trail of a disaster may extend for many years and may haunt the reputation of a police force and some of its officers, including in this case senior officers who had been promoted to high rank in other forces.[16] The new inquest opened early in 2014, some 25 years after the disaster. It is likely to take at least a year and be penetrating and persistent about the circumstances surrounding the deaths. A very strong message emerging from this appalling and sad story is the importance of conducting the planning in advance thoroughly, getting the command structure right, putting in competent and reliable people and, above all, building in accountability that would not allow the defensive disinformation and manipulation that took place in the Hillsborough case. In particular, there was a serious failure of leadership at the operational and institutional levels.

All the cases described draw attention to the complexity of serious incident management and the need for grooming officers for leadership roles, as well as for having a philosophy, structure and training for command role. For this, the authors will turn for example to the command models employed in Britain and the Netherlands.

Command and control in British policing

Command and control – taking control of, and displaying leadership, in operations – is a core activity in policing. The model developed and widely used throughout the UK initially emerged in the 1970s and 1980s with regard to public order. It was deemed necessary to have a crystal clear command structure for large-scale planned operations and for unfolding incidents. There was also the realisation that the first person on the scene of any incident – which could be a major incident, disaster or serious conflict situation – was likely to be a constable or sergeant. This became particularly acute from the late 1960s and early 1970s onwards with the prolonged threat from the IRA and the increasing use of firearms by criminals, for it was obvious that in potentially dangerous situations involving a firearm, the first officers to respond would almost certainly be unarmed. This led to the development of the armed response vehicle (ARV) to get armed officers to the scene to support their unarmed colleagues. ARVs were in use in the 1970s but they were nationally implemented after the Hungerford massacre of 1987 (Punch, 2011, pp 35-7). The policy became that those on the front line who suddenly faced an incident of any sort, but especially one with a risk element, would receive swift support – from an ARV in the case of threat from firearms – which in turn would be able to hand over accountability to readily available senior officers. Here we shall examine the model of command and control, which implies that the police service must have a readily available system that grooms officers for leadership roles at various levels, producing confident, competent, tested (certified) leaders who can take control of incidents. In the UK, this system is based on three operational levels – gold (strategy), silver (tactics) and bronze (implementation). Compared with the French-Continental model, as reflected in police command and control in the Netherlands, British officers are generally granted more operational autonomy, but are consequently subject to more accountability.

Command structure

This model is based on clarity of roles and an adherence to the threefold division of responsibilities during operations. It assumes that senior officers who take the gold role have taken the 'Gold Commanders course' and may have taken other specialist courses – say on public order, firearms, siege management or investigations – at the gold level. The model functions as follows. Gold sets the strategy for the operation and oversees and monitors it, but the operation is clearly run by silver, and bronze works to silver's orders. There is only one gold for a specific operation, but there can be several silvers and bronzes; this is likely to be the case in large-scale, pre-planned operations in several localities where the roles are fixed in advance (for example, large-scale public order situations, or anticipated flooding, at several locations). There are profiles with specified competences for all three leadership roles, with training available. The endeavour is to groom officers at all three levels and set a standard whereby most chief officers are competent to fill the gold role. There is usually a protocol setting out which level of incident will be dealt with by which rank, and in some forces it is determined that gold functions will be carried out by chief officers. But it may well be that on occasion gold holds a lower rank to silver; the system is role-specific and not based on rank. It has proved possible, however, for some chief officers to gain high rank without strong operational experience – they may have gained expertise in other areas such as ICT, strategy, personnel, training, traffic or as a staff officer – yet they may assume the gold function because of rank without taking the Gold Commanders Course. In an ideal world, this should not happen.

It is clear, moreover, that generalists have a better chance of promotion than specialists and that this strongly applies to those who have spent most of their career in the detective branch who often do not make it to chief officer rank. But it means that many chief officers have never led a major investigation. Furthermore, the competences of senior officers are rarely tested on promotion. On some occasions, this has been painfully exposed and some chief officers have been removed from gold responsibility for poor performance. Indeed, in one force, senior officers who could be called out for command roles were put through a decision-making test, and around a third failed. There followed interviews as to whether or not they wanted to continue in that role or wanted to take actions to bring them up to speed on operational practices and responsibilities. This indicates that it is necessary to evaluate personnel periodically to assess their skills and motivation and not simply assume that they have both. This may entail asking some officers to stand down from their role and helping others to gain confidence and expertise.

Implementation

This is how the command system is (ideally) implemented according to the information received from our UK respondents.

- All senior officers will work on a 24-hour availability schedule. There will always be a gold commander available on a 24/7 roster who is in uniform with a driver and a car which is a mobile communication centre with a loggist to record decisions and communications. This practice has become enshrined in major incident training where the adage is always have a loggist: 'a trusted junior officer records what you do and say as it happens, *in preparation for the enquiry that will inevitably follow*' (Paddick, 2008, p 97; emphasis added). For all command roles, it is assumed that the officer is well rested, in good physical condition and has not consumed alcohol prior to coming on duty.

- For a number of situations, there is an ACPO manual setting out what needs to be done and who needs to be contacted. This is a substantial document, and one task of the loggist is to make sure that the guidelines in the manual are followed so that details or contacts are not overlooked. During the MODACE course at Bramshill, for example, the presenters of actual cases they had been involved in all emphasised that they had made mistakes or overlooked important matters. The loggist can help to prevent that happening by having the manual at hand for consultation.

- Gold sets the strategy, and stands above the operation and carries accountability for an operation internally and externally. A log will be started that contains all decisions, correspondence and visual material. Briefings and debriefings may be visually recorded, as may the actual incident. This record is essential for providing accountability. Gold usually operates at a distance, with an oversight, monitoring and facilitating function – say, by contacting other agencies or mobilising support – and may or may not visit the scene. A typically active gold may always want to visit the scene. That may be useful and even vital in some cases, but his or her presence may distort the command structure if he or she cannot resist interfering in silver's tasks or a weak silver defers to an over-assertive gold.

- Maintaining clarity of roles and functions is of the essence and the intention is that gold does not interfere with silver's functioning unless the strategy is clearly not being implemented or a serious error is being made. There will be a gold command centre with restricted access to ensure a measure of tranquillity and preservation of data; this can be at police headquarters, elsewhere or in a properly equipped vehicle.

- There will always be a number of silver commanders available 24/7 who are in uniform and out on the roads ready to operate with a car which is a mobile communication centre, with a driver and loggist.[17] There will be a silver command centre in pre-planned or prolonged operations with restricted access but typically with more support personnel and more on-going, busy communications traffic than a gold command centre.

- Among junior supervisory personnel performing shiftwork or other duties there will be bronze commanders instantly available, while for set-piece operations bronze commanders may be mobilised in advance.

- The choice of gold, silver and bronze personnel may be related to the nature of the incident or operation in question and the respective qualifications and experience of the officers available. It is advisable to have settled teams for certain operations on the understanding that people with matched expertise who have worked together on other occasions will enhance the cooperation between them.

Operational philosophy

Underpinning this model is the following philosophy (Punch and Markham, 2000; Markham and Punch, 2004). The police service as a professional organisation is responsible for producing confident and competent leaders who have been tested for the three levels; this implies that not all officers are suitable or qualified for command roles. The police service is responsible for front-line officers in vulnerable or risky situations and as such will provide cover as an institutional and moral imperative. These presumptions can only lead to the realisation that a service that does not have an effective command system in operation is not fit for purpose. Further, officers who are not competent in operational roles should be taken off operational duties, but given the opportunity to return to those duties if they prove capable of retraining to the required level of competency. A service that has an effective system in place should not have to fear external scrutiny because it has done all it can to conduct operations responsibly and can with confidence face stakeholders, regulators and inquiries with a complete operational log. This means that the police service should set competency profiles for leadership roles, should design courses to provide the necessary skills and should test those competences at regular intervals. This requires determined and consistent institutional investment and an uncompromising position on setting and maintaining standards – as happens in other professions. The pay-off is the confidence of the public in the police; the commitment of the lower ranks when directed and supported by capable senior staff; and the reassurance among leaders throughout the organisation that they are capable of delivering the performance expected of them.

This model, with its accompanying philosophy, is meant to be implemented throughout the UK and is strongly reflected in the ACPO *Guidance on command and control* (ACPO, 2009). It may well be that there are varying interpretations of it in some forces and with certain chief officers, and that in practice, under particular circumstances, it is not operated adequately. Two key elements – testing for competences and tying this to promotion for chief officers with the likelihood of removal from operational policing if they are not competent – may not be widespread in the service. The assumption that gold is ultimately accountable for the operation may also not always be followed and will be dependent on circumstances. The model is built on clarity of roles and responsibilities, but, like all systems, it depends on the quality and competences of those operating it for it to be implemented effectively. It has, however, proved to be a viable model throughout the UK for pre-planned, unfolding and major incidents.

Command and control in Dutch policing

As in the UK, the Netherlands has a specific command and control structure for major incidents. This structure – the staff large-scale and special operations (SGBO) – is mobilised if the regular organisational structure is considered insufficient. Again, as in the UK, this is used both for unforeseen incidents as for planned, large-scale operations. Obviously, the structure becomes more elaborate the greater the seriousness and the higher the potential impact of 'incidents'. There are protocols for who deals with what and when on a scale of one to five – with national government involvement at five. This section will describe the model as it relates to local public order. The very different governance structure in the Netherlands, in which the mayor and the public prosecutor are involved in directing policing, has led to an alternative command and control structure and philosophy to the UK. In practice, the policing of many recurring and routine, operational events and incidents will be conducted with considerable autonomy, but on specified occasions or with major incidents the 'triangle' will take the lead, with the mayor responsible for public order and the public prosecutor for criminal investigations. The mayor in the Netherlands is not elected but is – as are the public prosecutor and chief of police – appointed by the Crown, and he or she effectively becomes a non-partisan government official with considerable powers. This means that when there is a serious incident, the triangle is primarily responsible for the operation and not the police leadership. At such times, this policy, and the decision-making triangle of mayor, public prosecutor and chief of police, will be activated, and, while primacy may be given to the police chief because of his or her expertise, formally the mayor is in charge for those cases defined as 'public order'. The mayor may also mobilise support from other agencies and will communicate with diverse authorities at the local, regional and central levels. In many cases, the triangle becomes a 'pentagon' when the chief of the fire service and a designated representative of the regional health services will join the others. The coordination between the different organisations is viewed as most important. So, next to the triangle, there is also a 'collective interface' comprising the operational representatives of the three (or five) aforementioned organisations.

To a certain extent, the triangle functions as the equivalent of gold in the UK. Then, roughly equivalent to the British silver, is the general commander responsible for a particular police operation. This is routinely an experienced officer at the commissioner (*commissaris*) level (comparable to a British superintendent or ACC). The SGBO model works with predesigned processes – from gathering and disseminating information to maintaining community relations – that are implemented by experts from within the police organisation who are under the command of the general commander. In relatively local public order incidents, the triangle will prove sufficient without going outside the unit's region for police assistance or higher for governmental support. There are clear advantages to having these three officials primed to cooperate and coordinate in a formalised structure. But two of them are professionals in their respective areas whereas one is a government official with a wide mandate who may have at first little previous experience of policing or public order. Generally, the mayors of the large cities are experienced and well qualified, but that is not always the case elsewhere. The impact this can have on a public order situation and police deployment is illustrated by an incident in Haren (a small town in the northern province of Groningen) that is referred to as the Dutch 'Project X' or 'Facebook Party'.

Project X

On 6 September 2012, a teenager in Haren sent out an invitation to her 16th birthday party to her friends via Facebook. Some of them invited friends of their own, which created an unforeseen snowball effect leading to 16,000 responses within a day. The youngster removed the invitation, but it had been picked up in a number of other countries and was further spread through social media so that by 21 September there were some 250,000 invitees – with 30,000 claiming they would attend – and around 400,000 messages on Twitter referring to 'Project X, Haren'. The mayor and police chief prepared for a stream of visitors, but forbade parties. Initially, only a few hundred people turned up, but soon thousands were arriving. At first, matters were festive but later in the evening disturbances broke out, with cars, bikes and shops being damaged. The Mobile Unit was employed but soon required reinforcements from other provinces; eventually, around 500 officers were mobilised, there were 34 arrests, 51 people were injured, including 15 police officers, and the total damage was estimated at over one million euros. An investigation into the disturbance came to the conclusion that the authorities had not coped well with the developing situation, had not provided alternative attractions for those who might turn up, and did not have a clear strategy for a possible disturbance so that police officers felt they had not received adequate instructions. There was an underestimation of the scale of the likely turnout of visitors and, in particular, the mayor had waited too long to call for reinforcements (Cohen Commission, 2013). The mayor subsequently resigned.

The key to the affair was a complete lack of understanding of the influence of the social media and a failure to prepare adequately; above all, the triangle, led by the mayor, had failed badly in judgement and decision making. In a small, quiet town far from the bustling cities, the capability of the authorities was not adequate to meet the challenge of this serious incident. The affair attracted immense media interest at home and abroad, and strengthened the belief in some quarters in more centralisation for policing, as local control was seen as having been too limited and inexperienced as well as too complacent.

That local authority reliance on the triangle is still very much a reflection of the Continental model of civilian and judicial control of public policing. If things go seriously wrong, the police chief might take the accountability but in other circumstances it could well be the mayor. This means not only that a Dutch police chief formally has two bosses above him or her, but also that, in certain circumstances, the mayor rather than the police chief is held accountable for an incident gone wrong – as in Haren. But to a degree, this has started to change; now the situation is that the Minister of Security and Justice has ministerial responsibility for the National Police as well as being force manager, which considerably increases his or her power and greatly reinforces the centralism of the new model.

The precise division of responsibilities is still in a state of flux, but with a sense that the triangle will deal more with fairly local matters and that authority in dealing with major incidents will increasingly lie at the national level, with possibly ministerial involvement or oversight. In the case of Haren, where the local 'triangle' was formally responsible and accountable, the minister himself was questioned in Parliament about the competence of the responsible police chief. The minister defended 'his' police, although the authority for that operation was plainly local and not central. This was symbolically revealing about the functioning of the new structure, as not only was Parliament trying to hold the minister accountable for a local operation, but the minister was effectively drawing accountability for aspects of it to the ministerial level, and this went against the agreed division of accountability in the new system. It illustrates that the move to a national force under a single minster who is also the force manager carries with it a creeping centralisation of both control and authority, whereas for 200 years the structure and culture in Dutch policing was designed to keep them apart. This is still supposed to be the case within the new, local 'units', according to the legislation (Police Law, 2012).

Conclusion

This chapter conveys that many spontaneous and unexpected incidents, as well as pre-planned events that suddenly go wrong, are typically accompanied by initial chaos and confusion, problems with communications and, almost certainly, mistakes. Moreover, most police officers are never confronted with a disaster or major incident and those that are may only see one in their career. It is an instant learning experience with a rapid learning curve, but how a senior officer responds in those critical moments under intense pressure may well be subject to media and judicial scrutiny for years to come. This may have consequences for his or her reputation and career and for the legitimacy and liability of a police force. That it is why it is vital to get matters right as much as possible before something demanding happens.

Probably most other police systems will have something rather like the British command and control structure which is both nationally implemented and also used by the other emergency services. It is employed here for comparison with the Netherlands and elsewhere. In the 'non-system' of the US, with its devolved structure and 18,000 agencies – many of which have less than 30 officers (Manning, 2010, p 112) – there is no equivalent of ACPO and HMIC for promoting national policy, no Bramshill or College of Policing for national education and no uniform system for command and control. The larger US forces in the major cities employ something similar but perhaps not as explicitly as the British gold–silver–bronze model (David Bayley, personal communication). Indeed, there is no national leadership programme in the US and police leaders there can take diverse courses at a variety of academic or practitioner institutes, including the FBI Academy. Such programmes tend to be fairly instrumental courses of limited duration with little attention to the subject of strategic and command leadership. Select senior officers may attend the Kennedy School/National Institute of Justice *Executive Session on Policing and Public Safety* at Harvard University, while the Police Executive Research Forum offers the *Senior Management Institute for Police* at Boston University. Leadership development and command systems in the US are, then, highly dependent on individual states, cities or police departments.

Finally, the chapter has dealt with the challenges for leadership arising in a selection of major incidents – when 'matters are really real'. The examples used were not exercises or simulations but highly demanding events – where at times the stakes were high – that needed to be dealt with instantly, competently, confidently and with concern for values and for accountability. Here the emphasis has been on what really happened and what this conveys about what is required of leaders in the most challenging of circumstances. This may appear daunting in the extreme, but it is of the essence in policing that one never knows – at the micro or indeed 'mega' level – what one may encounter. Along with this uncertainty is the necessity for swift institutional deployment into 'command mode', as incidents do not always come neatly packaged and fitting within established scenarios. This assumes a capacity at all levels for dealing with a range of incidents where leadership, and at times a significant shift in leadership style, is simply essential.

Notes

[1] *Rapport van eerste bevindingen: Crash van Malaysia Airlines Boeing 777-2000 vlucht MH17*, the initial report into the crash by the Investigatory Board for Safety in The Hague, September 2014.

[2] In 1974, four members of the Japanese Red Army took the French ambassador and some of his personnel captive, wounding two police officers in the process. Their demands were met after five days and they departed with a sum of money and a free passage, having secured the release of a Red Army member from a French cell.

[3] The skyjacking of an Afghan airliner that landed at Stansted in 2000 led to an Essex Police bill of about £ 3.6 million for the four-day police operation and subsequent work including an investigation (*Guardian*, 17 February 2000).

[4] In 1979, the UK ambassador and his butler were shot dead in The Hague, presumably by the IRA. In 1990, the IRA was thought to be responsible for shooting dead two Australian tourists by mistake in Roermond, thinking they were British soldiers. Members of the Active Service Unit of the IRA thought to be responsible were captured in Belgium and extradited to the Netherlands, but were freed by the Dutch court despite possessing the weapon used in the killing.

[5] Both were members of the Libyan security service and there were suspicions of high government involvement, which made it a most politically sensitive matter at a time when several Western countries were seeking a rapprochement with President Gaddafi. After the fall of Gaddafi, it was alleged that he had personally ordered the attack. Given the continued uncertainty about the guilt of the two suspects, one had his conviction quashed and the other was released from prison on compassionate grounds, a fresh inquiry was launched with the cooperation of the new Libyan government.

[6] The full last name of a suspect is not published in the Netherlands prior to a trial and even when it is later known, the suspect is still often referred to by the capital letter of his or her surname.

[7] This was even more true of a case in London where two police officers shot dead a man whom they thought was armed but was found to be in possession of a table leg. This led to widespread condemnation and bitterness among local communities and in the media. The officers faced a six-year period of no less than 10 separate judicial and civil procedures. At one stage they were arrested, before finally being cleared (Punch, 2011).

[8] This was reinforced in the UK in 2007 by legislation on 'corporate manslaughter' that no longer contains crown immunity for the police.

[9] Given the exceptional situation in Northern Ireland during the Troubles, where there was frequent and intense rioting between pro-republican (Catholic) demonstrators and pro-loyalist (Protestant) demonstrators, as well as between the former and the security forces (RUC and Army) often resulting in much violence and damage – for example, on Bloody Sunday when the military shot dead 14 unarmed demonstrators in a pro-republican march in Derry in 1972 – we shall not deal with this in relation to public order in the UK.

[10] It is generally accepted that there was effectively direct political interference in policing the strike, given that Prime Minister Thatcher was determined to break the power of the trade unions. It is also assumed that some senior officers resented this, with the next generation of chiefs determined not to be used in this fashion. This may explain some of the friction between obdurate chiefs and insistent politicians in the 1990s and beyond.

[11] At the G20 meeting in London in 2009, a Met officer struck a man with a baton and roughly pushed him to the ground. The middle-aged man was not involved in the demonstrations, and was able to walk away, but died shortly afterwards. That one moment of unwarranted assault on someone who was simply in the way was caught on camera and transmitted widely through the mainstream and social media. It led to intense debate about police public order tactics, and the officer concerned faced criminal charges. He was acquitted but dismissed from the force, while the Met apologised to the family and paid compensation. He was a member of the Territorial Support Unit, a specially trained and equipped unit that had attracted criticism for its assertive tactics.

[12] The police Disaster Victim Identification Team has been involved in major incidents at home, including the El Al plane crash in Amsterdam, and abroad for several decades, including during the 2004 Asian Tsunami. In late 2014 and early 2015, it also helped identify nearly all of the MH17 crash victims.

[13] 'The El Al plane crash in Amsterdam and the emergency response', presentation to MBA students, Nyenrode University, 14 December 1992, by Bernard Welten, the operational commander of the Amsterdam Police for the disaster and investigation.

[14] At a MODACE course at Bramshill in 1993, a presentation on Hillsborough was given by the officer from the WMP who had led the investigation and he repeated all those accusations that placed the blame on the Liverpool supporters as if they were established facts.

[15] Formally the 'Report of the Hillsborough Independent Panel', here referred to as the 'Hillsborough Report', 2012.

[16] A SYP officer involved in the 'black propaganda' unit found that Hillsborough dogged his career after he became Chief Constable of Merseyside, where his area of command included Liverpool and where his appointment was unpopular. Later, as Chief Constable of WYP, he resigned, following renewed controversy about his earlier role in the SYP after the publication of the Hillsborough Report (2012).

[17] In 2004, following a shooting with several casualties – two of which proved fatal – there was criticism of the slow response in mobilising the command structure to deal with a firearms incident within the Thames Valley force. As a result, two roving silvers with firearms experience were put on duty with 24/7 cover (IPPC, 2004).

FIVE

Leadership and leadership development

This chapter deals with leadership and leadership development, which are key matters in policing (Adlam and Villiers, 2003). There is an immense literature on leadership of varying quality and in different disciplines, along with a range of popular books, courses and gurus informing people how to become a successful leader. Yet 'leadership' remains one of the fuzziest concepts in social sciences. A leading authority in the area, Manfred Kets de Vries (of INSEAD, the prime European business school), once stated at a conference that no-one really knows what the term means. Indeed, there are, according to Alison and Crego (2008), as many definitions of leadership as there are authors on the subject. It is, then, an infinitely elastic concept that confusingly stretches across diverse disciplines. In Chapter One the authors opted for viewing leadership pragmatically as what is needed given the nature of the police organization and the challenges it faces operationally and institutionally. Following on from that – and illustrated by the examples of serious incident management in Chapter Four – there would seem to be a need for officers who are competent, confident, tried and tested, and, importantly, whose leadership is rooted in the values of an accountable public service within a democracy. Having explored the general leadership material, the second part of this chapter is dedicated to leadership development and how police leaders make it to the top in England and Wales and the Netherlands. The position taken is that a number of leadership styles are required to direct the police organisation and to take charge of operations; that leadership is required *at all levels* throughout the organisation; and that far more attention needs to be paid to shaping leadership development geared to the specific mandate and unique nature of policing and the need for different approaches at different times.

Exploring leadership

In the area of leadership studies, much of the available material is historical, biographical and psychological. It may be based on published profiles and/or interviews with leaders by journalists or academics using structured interviews for research purposes. The subjects are typically successful or controversial politicians, generals or business executives. Discussions on the broad subject of leadership also tend to involve successful military, political, business or social leaders – for example, Hannibal, Margaret Thatcher, Steve Jobs and Gandhi – or legendary sport coaches such as Vince Lombardi or Sir Alex Ferguson. Much has been written about successful military leaders given that they have taken some of the most momentous decisions under extreme circumstances. They may have taken control over thousands of men and require strategic acumen, courage in adversity and great strength of character to cope with the stress and strain of combat (Keegan, 1978). There is too a genre around social entrepreneurs, philanthropic and religious leaders which focuses on personality, positive achievement and how there are generic lessons to be learned from taking these people as role models who are regarded variously as inspiring, constructive and praiseworthy. Not all leaders are viewed in a positive light, however; some contemporary and historical material holds that certain 'born leaders' have caused untold suffering. There is a disturbing pathology of leadership – including Hitler, Stalin, Mao, Idi Amin and Pol Pot.

These are extreme examples, but dysfunctional and even destructive conduct on the part of a leader may have a highly negative impact on any organisation. Indeed, Dixon (1979, p 307) warns us that:

> ... those personality characteristics which take people to the top and establish them as all powerful decision-makers tend to include the very nastiest of human traits – extremes of egocentricity, insincerity, dishonesty, corruptibility, cynicism, and on occasion ruthless murderous hostility towards anyone who threatens their position. Even worse, if that is possible, than the traits which take them to the top are those which they acquire upon arrival – pomposity, paranoia and megalomaniac delusions of grandeur.

Generally, this pathology is not a topic given much attention in professional education, where the emphasis is understandably on developing positive qualities, but it would be inept not to pay it consideration. There is much evidence to warn us that the power that leaders gain at the top of an organisation may have a distorting influence on their behaviour and that this requires serious attention. It might be a good idea for police chiefs to have a copy of the Dixon quote on their desk, for it is an element of power that those at the top can start to abuse that power by manipulating expenses, resorting to nepotism and harassing female subordinates. And on exposure not quite understanding that what they did wrong was wrong. Furthermore, as the leadership qualities of prominent people are usually held to be related primarily to character, or to character linked to context, this seemingly places leadership outside any shaping by training or development courses. This is particularly the case because some successful leaders were unconventional, poor at formal education, resistant to discipline and labelled as future failures until they were given an opportunity to display their innate qualities. But education for formal systems typically cannot focus on the unconventional, outspoken, creative and seemingly poorly performing individual as a potential success later as it is primarily geared to a stereotypical product which fits into established institutions. It appears, then, that not only do you have to be born with leadership qualities but also that you can display them only if the moment and context are right. The deflating message would seem to be that it is impossible to 'bottle' leadership in a formal programme.

There is a considerable social-psychological literature drawing on material in the public domain, questionnaires and laboratory tests for the psychological study of character traits. The empirical base, and its validity and reliability, is not always particularly robust because of sampling difficulties, the elusiveness of some leaders and their determination to manipulate accounts about themselves. What tends to be neglected is structured observation of leaders during their functioning for research purposes. This reflects the wider problem for researchers of gaining access to people in positions of power. These people are often happy, if not more than happy, to talk about how they became successful – somewhat less happy to do so when they have failed – but are reluctant to have a researcher watching them at length who intends to publish his or her findings. Mintzberg (1973) did study managers *in situ* as did Dalton (1959). But Dalton did so covertly which would certainly founder these days, given the stringent ethical guidelines in universities governing research.

This raises a dilemma when speculating about police leaders. We may know who they are and what they think about their work and profession, but we know much less about what they actually do in practice. In the UK, our knowledge in this area is largely thanks to the pioneering work of Reiner (1991) and the valuable contributions of Wall (1998), Savage, Charman and Cope (2000) and, more recently, Caless (2011). Through their work we know a fair amount about British chief constables and chief officers; Wall (1998), for example, traced chief constables from 1836 to 1996. In the Netherlands, all but one of the then 26 police chiefs were interviewed early in the first decade of this century, but many of the influential generation that emerged in the 1970s, and who held office for some time (one for 22 years), have retired in recent years (Boin et al, 2003). A decade is, moreover, a long time in contemporary policing. In the UK, a police chief will probably spend no more than four to five years in office, and in the US it is more likely to be only two years on average. In the UK and the US, some chiefs have written their memoirs, but memoirs are patently not a reliable source as to what actually happened and what the chiefs really said and thought. They may be frustratingly anodyne following imposed or self-censorship, a form of special pleading with the settling of scores or unbridled self-promotion for commercial gain. They may contain interesting snippets about specific operations and investigations, relationships with politicians and interactions within the force – as when Robert Mark (1978), who became a powerful and reforming Met Commissioner in the 1970s, arrived at Scotland Yard[1] only to be told he was not welcome – but in Britain the government and the publisher's lawyers would have screened the text for any infringement of the Official Secrets Act. In the Netherlands some police chiefs have been written about by others on their retirement in terms of their personal biography, professional writings and contribution to policing (Zwart, 2004): but there is simply no tradition of police chiefs penning their memoirs and it would be distinctly frowned upon. In brief, we do not fully know what they do in daily practice in interaction with others, at moments of high tension and when taking routine or crucial decisions of which some are understandably confidential.

This work focuses on a selection of material from the organisational, social-psychological and managerial literature, starting with the indispensable Warren Bennis (Bennis et al, 1997; Bennis, 2003; Bennis and Nanus, 2003) and including Argyris and Schön (1974), Morgan (1986) and Useem (1998). This opens up a huge range of material on management, strategy, change and leadership that cannot be dealt with here. This is of widely varying quality from erudite and research based to some which caters to the managerial market seeking 'quick fix' solutions and magic bullets. One of the mega-selling books in this segment – *Who moved my cheese?* (Johnson, 1998) – is an engaging set of adages but with no foundation in empirical research. Such work may lead to simplistic concepts becoming fashionable – as with 'transactional' and 'transformational' leadership – with little basis for saying when one is more appropriate than other and encouraging a choice for one when they are best seen as flexible options for changing circumstances. One explanation for this insatiable and uncritical demand is that management in business and other organisations is often complex and uncertain, and people are drawn to ready-made formulas for success (Knights and McCabe, 2003). But success cannot be guaranteed and may prove elusive. For instance, in the past decade a number of prestigious firms that were once viewed as cutting-edge corporations, delivering high shareholder value and earning plaudits for their corporate leader, have ended up in abject failure, leading at times to bankruptcy, and the criminal courts followed by the low-security prison. Behind the glittering facade of leading banks, moreover, there was at times failing leadership, unbridled greed, manipulation of data for regulators and shareholders, failure to supervise maverick traders, contempt for the customer and a culture of undue risk which gravely destabilized not only the global financial markets but also entire societies (Lewis, 2010; O'Toole, 2010).

This is a warning that in the climate of change and pressure for results in policing, which is palpable in the middle 2010s, we should be wary of simple, pat formulas for success. The uncomfortable sociological adage is that 'it all depends' on a swathe of contingent factors. Bratton, for instance, preached of his policing style, 'if it works in New York it will work anywhere'. That is palpable nonsense, and yet hundreds flocked to New York to witness the 'miracle' of that city's spectacular fall in crime, and rushed to apply the 'silver bullet' in their respective countries (Punch, 2007).

In contrast, the material presented in this book conveys that policing is a complex matter that is highly contingent on context and culture and is also, by the nature of its work, prone to accident. What works well in one country or force does not necessarily work well in another; and what works now in one force does not necessarily work later on in another force. What this encourages is serious thinking and a built-in critical caution regarding policing, strategy, change and leadership. There is to aid in this process a spectrum of serious academic publications and established universities and institutes that can help to stimulate debate within the profession and be of collective value in setting a direction and managing innovation. After a number of years of service, for instance, police leaders may find that a professional development course – say, an MBA degree focusing on public management – provides not only helpful guidance on managing an organisation but also an opportunity to stand back and reflect on issues of great professional concern. Other academic subjects are also of value but it helps if the programme is full time so that the officers get outside the police culture for a period and mix with a variety of people with widely diverse occupational backgrounds and experiences who have other ideas about solving particular problems (Lee and Punch, 2006). Such a degree is of value for its knowledge component, but also for providing a network that can be drawn on later in a professional capacity. In general, most standard courses do not deal in any depth with leadership, although there is a range of business and management institutes and commercial enterprises that do so. Some of these construct 'how to do' courses, often of an 'outward bound' nature. This is usually combined in degree courses and executive programmes with acquiring academic knowledge in the functional areas of management which usefully combines leadership with organisational change and development rather than viewing the former in isolation.

In leadership courses at the prestigious Wharton School (University of Pennsylvania), for example, Professor Michael Useem in the Center for Leadership and Change Management uses mountaineering and other testing environments both for group training and for reflection on leadership roles and values. There are a series of exercises for MBA, executive and agency-specific programmes involving a 'wrenching' experience, with intensive team work and physical commitment – such as climbing in Patagonia, Alaska or the Himalayas – combined with interpreting the relevance of the experience on returning to the workplace (Michael Useem, personal communication). Behind such courses is the idea of removing people from a structured environment and placing them in a challenging context with few resources; emphasising the need for engaging in group activity in order to solve problems; shaking participants from formal roles in their normal organisational hierarchy to encourage situational leadership; and encouraging innovative thinking to solve the challenges faced. Furthermore, from teaching and researching in this area Useem (2011) has developed a 'check-list' – drawing on research, examples from the functioning of airline pilots and surgeons and using extensive interviews – which serves as a valuable reminder of essential factors before and after entering the decision-making process for leaders in a range of institutions. This depends on it being employed as a shared tool to be held up to adjudicate everyone's performance including the top executive or official. It can act as a check-list prior to action but also as a template in post-incident evaluations. Although the Wharton School is largely geared to the business world, its programmes draw on the expertise of leaders who have faced catastrophic risk situations – including the Chilean mine rescue and 9/11, through the experience of a New York Fire Department chief who was first on the scene after the terrorist attacks on the World Trade Center in Manhattan. The various groups of students and executives also visit battlefields, including Gettysburg, and examine decision making though the dilemmas confronting military leaders, the options they faced and the decisions they took. A strong theme in all these scenarios is leaders displaying high personal courage and determination along with the ability to galvanise a team in achieving high if not extraordinary performance under extreme circumstances. In other cases relating to contemporary successes in business and other organisations the emphasis is on the leader's personality, unconventional ideas, accepting and presenting challenges, innovation, empowering teams and also gaining an impressive collective goal. To a degree that applies more to business than public management.

Leadership programmes and exercises can, then, be useful in transmitting skills and raising consciousness on the dilemmas of leadership in stressful situations but there is also the factor of 'transfer'. Can those skills and insights employed by executives in business organisations be transferred to those facing quite other sorts of challenges, and do they 'deteriorate' over time without periodic retraining? For in tough situations people typically resort to underlying responses unless the practices have become engrained through repetition. A team in the Formula One pits can only service a racing car within seconds if it trains, trains and then trains some more; it cannot carry a weak link in the team and has to learn from the times when, despite its dedication, things still go wrong. This is particularly relevant to policing and other emergency service organisations, and to the military, where it is not so much a question of 'will I ever meet such a challenge?' but more often one of 'when, how often and how large will the challenge be?'. The armed forces are a special case because the training is strongly and constantly based on leadership at the various levels and is often conducted nowadays in a highly astute manner using a wealth of academic expertise. It typically begins with the abrasive boot-camp experience with much physical pressure and discomfort accompanied by verbal abuse – as graphically portrayed in the 1987 Kubrick film *Full Metal Jacket* – but extends to a range of programmes and exercises throughout the military career. Unlike the police, however, the basic military mandate is to enter combat where armed forces will inflict as much physical and psychological damage as to make the enemy desist and, if necessary, destroy it (Keegan, 1978). It is also inherent in warfare that a unit going into action takes casualties; that some personnel may even be viewed as expendable; and that there may be 'collateral damage' among non-combatants. That is why the British Army trained officers to function two levels above and two below them in rank in order to be able adjust to the sudden loss of leaders on the battlefield. Furthermore, combatants enjoy immunity from prosecution for violence used against other combatants, but not civilians or prisoners of war, in international armed conflicts under international law. This means they are schooled in a totally different culture, and mindset on deployment and use of force, compared to the individual and institutional accountability of civil police based on restraint, minimal force and answering to the courts. Furthermore, battle provides an urgent and instant test of leadership competency where rank and length of service may not be that important and where swift promotions, and demotions, can take place (Beevor, 2009). In the intensity of early aerial warfare in Britain in WWII, young pilots, with an average age of 20, could gain intense, rapid experience and develop the personal authority to be swiftly promoted to squadron leader or even wing commander, and were considered old at 25 (Hastings, 2011).

Modern armies have, of course, become increasingly flexible and multi-faceted, but military personnel are fundamentally a different social animal from the police, which clearly does not preclude the police learning from the military. For instance, the British SAS, an elite special forces unit, has a powerful culture of self-discipline, low hierarchy, group decision making and the critical questioning of assignments while officers in command of operations have to have credibility through having 'done the business' (Asher, 2008). This is related to the fact that the SAS gets the toughest assignments with the highest risks, so that success, and survival, are dependent on getting it right; it cannot afford any weakness in the four-man 'bricks' (primary operational units) that form the basis of its operations and which do not tolerate a less than competent superior officer. Although it is formally a regiment in the British Army, the SAS was founded by mavericks outside of the establishment and does not follow the hierarchy and rituals of conventional units. Its working structure and culture is geared to performance above rank and formality. While special forces might not be everybody's role model, the way they function does have useful implications for training and for the functioning of police in command and control mode.

Implications for police leadership

Under high-pressure circumstances, then, there should not be a mentality of blindly following – and giving – orders, and there should always be critical post-incident evaluation of *all* those involved. This implies that those at the top of the police organisation must have a close understanding and strong affinity with those conducting the essential and demanding tasks lower down. How that is gained – for instance, by direct experience in a range of operational roles over a significant period of time or through lateral entry from other backgrounds and experiences – is a key issue. That issue is in turn intrinsically related to the reality that senior leadership in policing – which can be at the system, force or diverse command level – cannot be detached from emergency response. Senior police officers are not the same as managers scrutinising financial spreadsheets in the executive suite atop the corporate skyscraper. Not surprisingly, some of these top managers prove to be inept in the face of a real crisis, as has been evident in many corporate disasters, including the BP oil spill in the Gulf of Mexico in 2010 (Useem, 2011). Rather, policing is intimately related to coping with emergencies, along with the other emergency services, requiring varied responses at different levels to diverse problems or threats, including life or death matters, and where accountability is a given. Leadership and group dynamics in emergency response mode can range from the small team (Flin, 1996) to the large-scale response with inter-agency cooperation at major or mega-incidents. The latter would include the London bombings of 2005, where there was an emergency plan in place backed up by prior multi-agency exercises drawing on the experience of the 30 years of threat from the IRA. In the US, however, 9/11 went way beyond any worst-case scenario that anyone had ever considered. This included the destruction of the emergency response centre located in one of the Twin Towers in Manhattan and the death of 300 firefighters.

It could be argued that practitioners should learn to think beyond the worst case to an even worse case, but many small players in quiet places would probably think that futile, as the likelihood of such an event occurring is remote. But, as evidenced by the 9/11 terrorist attacks, a police force never knows what may hit it. There are numerous examples of forces having to deal with the unexpected. In the Netherlands, one such incident occurred in 2009 during celebrations for the Queen's birthday. This event is traditionally marked by a public holiday, with the monarch and members of the royal family visiting towns, and communities organising street markets, entertainments and a range of other festive activities. It is an informal occasion with the royals strolling through the streets and some younger members of the royal family taking part in games or dances. There is always a security presence, but the event is viewed as a pleasant national occasion and normally passes off without incident. In 2009 in Apeldoorn, however, a man drove his car at high speed through the safety barrier, knocked down 17 people and careened across a square narrowly missing the open bus carrying the royals. The car almost knocked down a police officer, crashed into a pillar and the driver was mortally injured. There were seven other fatalities and 10 people were injured, including a police officer. Suddenly, out of the blue, a joyful day was transformed and this will have altered police and security thinking about such festive events.

Another such unexpected event occurred in the UK in 1987 in the peaceful, rural town of Hungerford, where a man with several fire-arms shot and killed 17 people, including an unarmed police officer and himself. Like many shooting sprees, this one happened in a defenceless community with almost no immediate police response available. It was devastating for the people of Hungerford, traumatic for the police force concerned (Thames Valley) and a wake-up call for British policing (Punch, 2011). It was, then, a major incident that had to be dealt with immediately at the local level but had a significant impact on public opinion, legislation and even national police practice.

At such exceptional moments, the police force involved is almost swamped and has to adjust and learn rapidly. Its leadership at all levels will be stretched to the limit, although through prior agreement reinforcements can be called upon, and inevitably mistakes will be made. It is the responsibility of the police organisation to provide first responders with training through courses and inter-agency exercises to ensure that every unit or region is prepared to some degree for the eventuality of such spontaneous incidents. And incidents such as the ones described earlier convey that policing – which is mostly routine and often dull to the point of utter boredom – always entails the possibility of something major if not exceptional emerging out of the blue in places, and at times, where it is least expected. Officers may think 'nothing much ever happens here' but these and other horrendous events did happen somewhere: and they happened in ordinary forces in ordinary places and had to be dealt with by ordinary officers – who sometimes performed in an extraordinary manner but who sometimes failed conspicuously. This means that both the policing system and individual leaders have to develop a built-in consciousness of risk during routine events and of the likelihood, however remote, of a major incident occurring on their watch.

One important facet related to this is the awareness that under sudden stress and unusual situations people – and 'systems' – can fail. There is an exemplary analysis by Weick (1990) of system failure regarding the crash in Tenerife of two jumbo jets on the runway in 1977 that illustrates how a number of unexpected events led to a distortion in communication that proved fatal. This failure may be tied to the individual, group or system levels raising issues of incompetence, negligence, liability, institutional flaws, poor communication, technological complexity or lack of leadership. Indeed, failures in leadership are often instrumental in military disasters (Dixon, 1979) and in police operations that go seriously awry, as at Waco in Texas in 1993 (O'Hara, 2005). Another truly appalling case amounting to system failure was the Dutroux scandal in Belgium, when a convicted rapist was released early from prison and went on to abduct, abuse and murder young girls whom he was hoping to sell into international paedophile rings. It not only exposed the failure of the state to protect its citizens and dramatically conveyed incompetence, corruption and institutional failure in the police and judicial systems, but also fostered a nationwide, grassroots demand to reform the 'rotten' political system (Punch, 2005). This in turn keeps us aware that the police and other emergency organisations are capable of high achievement but also of poor performance that sometimes amounts to system failure, and that the quality of leadership may be instrumental in both.

The major psychological pitfalls and distortions in decision making, and often an element in system failure, are especially linked to mechanisms such as group think, tunnel vision, cognitive dissonance and the 'Abilene Paradox' (Dixon, 1979; Alison and Crego, 2008). The concept of group think was developed by Janis (1972) when examining military blunders; it occurs when a group gets locked into a collective position that no individual wants to challenge and that overestimates the group's capabilities and underestimates the enemy and level of threat. A psychological concept related to group think is that of 'tunnel vision', when, say, detectives become determined to achieve a result in a case, become fixated on a particular suspect as the prime offender and filter out any evidence or signals to the contrary, thus shaping the investigation to ensure the conviction of that 'offender'. This can lead to grave miscarriages of justice, with innocent people being jailed – sometimes for very long periods – or even executed. Cognitive dissonance refers to a situation whereby an individual holds a strong belief, which, when challenged, fosters not only a rejection of the challenge but also strengthens the belief. The 'Abilene Paradox' is used to describe a benign form of group think, where people end up going to Abilene (Texas), a place none of the individuals actually wanted to go to: but no one wanted to disrupt what they thought the others wanted. So everyone in the group is locked into a decision based on what they think the others want and goes along with this without ascertaining the real wishes of each member. Clearly, it is not easy always to be conscious of these distorting group processes and dig oneself or the group out of them.

What can exacerbate these distortions is a fixation on ends, pressure for results, lack of firm leadership and, above all, group think driven by unrestrained autocratic conduct. These processes may be found in all organisations but have been well documented in the military when the stakes are high, the culture is authoritarian and the rank structure is dominant (Dixon, 1979). But to a degree, policing also shows tendencies to group think, linked to consciousness of rank, fear of mistakes, inertia and risk avoidance, or a blind determination to achieve results (Alison and Crego, 2008). This again illustrates that behaviour in organisations and groups is not always rational and may be skewed by overly dominant leadership (Watson, 1994). Indeed, Kets de Vries and Miller (1984) have used psycho–analytical insights to dissect the 'neurotic' element in organisations, and Kets de Vries (1995), himself an analyst, has illuminated the perverse personalities of some top executives. This reminds us that there is always a negative side to organisational life and to leadership within it. Ostensibly organisations are rationally structured and function in an orderly manner according to the formal rules, but much research in organisations, and often personal experience, informs us that this is not always the case and that, at times, the distortions can be pathological and fatal.

Finally, undaunted by the discouraging range of leadership material and the chronic fuzziness of the subject, the view here has been limited to the consequences for police leadership and leadership training. But there is also a clear argument that if policing is being redefined in ways that will fundamentally influence it in the decades to come, then that evidently demands 'leadership' with strategic vision at the highest level but also operationally at all levels. And given the nature of policing – which touches on some of the most sensitive issues relating to the relationship between the citizen and the state – the authors have in mind the image of the 'reflective practitioner', referring to the classic book by Donald Schön (1983), *The reflective practitioner: How professionals think in action.* One can imagine how some right-wing politicians and the cynical editors of certain newspapers might react to the term 'reflective' when applied to the police, a term they may well consider derisive in this context. But if there is one occupation that requires reflection as a *sine qua non* of leadership, it is policing (Rowson and Lindley, 2012; Robinson and Smith, 2014).

Developing police leaders

Most police systems have been through a number of management cycles since interest in this area started to make inroads into public services in the 1980s. Many senior officers have undertaken degrees, executive programmes and courses related to management of public services, and have been involved in organisational and management development programmes. It is a positive thing that they have been encouraged to think about strategy, finance, public relations and human resource management. They will probably have read, or read of, the dominant management gurus of the past four decades – Drucker, Mintzberg, Morgan, Senger, Chomsky, Porter, Kanter, Peters, Handy and Hofstede – while some will have attended (expensive) seminars with them. Most of these gurus were, or are, American, typically worked at leading university business schools or management institutes, wrote bestsellers, developed prestigious executive programmes and advised leading companies and even governments. To a considerable extent, their ideas and proposals grew out of the changing global economy in the 1970s and 1980s and the challenge from new Asian economies, particularly Japan. There was an emphasis on change, innovation, institutional flexibility, speed of response to shifting markets, product quality and dynamic leadership. Many large Western firms were seen as sluggish and bureaucratic and badly in need of a shake-up while there were new-style ICT firms developing with an emphasis on knowledge, speed to market, customer support and global image.

Insights and practices from this complex and shifting managerial movement started to become applied to public services. This imbibing of management ideas and techniques was sorely needed in policing, given the shifting and increasingly demanding political and fiscal climate from the mid-1980s onwards, but it is debatable as to what extent all facets of the business model and its leadership requirements are applicable to public services in general and policing in particular. Indeed, it is not as if management ideas are somehow neutral, universally applicable and conveniently packaged by some criminal justice DIY store, with off-the-shelf solutions.

There are two prime strands derived from the early schools of scientific management and human relations management. The former was built around the individual, pressure to produce related to rewards and quantifiable results: and 'Taylorisation', referring to the pioneer of Scientific Management Frederick 'Speedy' Taylor, became a tool of tough management determined to get the maximum effort from its workforce through 'time and motion studies'. In contrast, the human relations school focused on the group, on informal leaders, on group motivation to produce or to limit production and on the relationship between the firm and its management (Watson, 1994). Both draw on alternative views about human behaviour related to motivation, rewards and productivity; and, although both have been constantly refined and redefined – and management studies and practices have advanced considerably – the two underlying views are broadly discernible in management philosophies and policies today. On the one hand, there are bottom-line companies geared to high profits for low costs; and on the other hand, there are companies that believe in investing in the workforce and working conditions to enhance productivity. For instance, some companies no longer speak of human resource management, because people are not resources but 'assets' that one invests in, and some firms are sceptical of quick fixes. Such views are most likely to be found in flexible, innovative sectors that rely on a return from investing in their personnel (Mintzberg, 1989; Knights and McCabe, 2003). Next to these two strands, however, has come the dominant and ideologically driven neoliberal paradigm.

This was first propagated by US President Ronald Reagan and UK Prime Minister Margaret Thatcher, and it espoused political and economic policies that argued for the primacy of markets within the capitalist system, cuts in public spending and a tougher approach to crime. A central pillar of neoliberal thought was that private enterprise was well managed and preferable to public services, which were poorly managed; the answer was to transfer managerial practices – rooted in market forces, competition and consumer choice – from the former to the latter. Along with this, there has been the expansion of the private sector both in public service provision and criminal justice. There are now large numbers of uniformed security guards and information analysis personnel working for private security companies; governments increasingly employ private security as do some police forces; and private prisons have been established (first in the US and later in the UK). This indicates that the state is willing to contract out segments of the criminal justice system that were previously the monopoly of state agencies (Stenning, 2000). This pressure – accentuated by the impact of intense competition from the new economies since the 1980s and latterly by the 2008 global economic crisis – has resulted in job losses, deindustrialisation, deskilling and stringent cuts in government spending. The impact on public services has been significant, with changes in employment contracts, increased flexibility in the workforce, pressure to produce, reclassification of tasks and payment by results.

To a degree, the ideas of scientific management have returned to the contemporary workplace with a vengeance. This has not gone without debate about the applicability of a neoliberal-driven New Public Management in public services, and, given their social mandate and the disputed concept of 'markets' in services, an argument for returning to public value. It could be maintained that turning senior police officers into managers, or 'corporate executives', has come at a price – that price being the distance between the corporate world and the complex, messy world of operational policing where things are 'really real'. It would be unwise to rush to the other extreme – as police systems are wont to do – and opt for an undue accent on practical, 'operational' policing. Given what has been said in previous chapters, it is clear that the authors favour a balance personified in the 'reflective practitioner'.

In short, the theme running throughout this material is that societal changes and the dominance of neoliberal ideas and policies represent a threat to what may be considered 'healthy' policing rooted in the values of a democratic society, of service delivery (in the wide sense *including crime control*) and of respecting rights. Moreover, there is a need for a substantial effort and response from the policing profession in general and from police leaders in particular to combat this threat. Behind this response should be the conviction that 'leadership' is clearly essential to policing *and can be developed*. Further, it is the responsibility of the system to arrange and supervise that development. In other words, leadership development has to be seen in terms of the nature of policing, of the police organisation and of the context in which the policing takes place. It has generic elements but has to be closely geared to the roles and functions within a specific organisational setting; it is not merely a matter of developing individual leadership skills but also of *enhancing institutional capacity*.

The initial focus of the Dutch leadership project is on the senior ranks, but with the intention to cover leadership training at all levels in the next few years. This does not neglect the highly particular feature of policing, namely that its frontline structure, and mandate as first responder to diverse emergencies and crimes, means that *officers lower in the formal hierarchy make some of the most important decisions*. They initially face some of the most demanding situations before reinforcements and senior staff arrive. It could be said that much policing, whether routine or in response to an emergency, relies heavily on the quality of the sergeants – meaning the primary supervisory ranks (Van Maanen, 1983). Leadership in policing is, then, not something solely associated with the formal leaders in the upper hierarchy, but is also vitally necessary at other levels in the police organisation (HMIC, 2008). This views leadership as a collectively determined and learned set of skills geared to the specific institutional purposes of policing. This in turn requires setting competences and developing them in learning trajectories. Furthermore, as outlined earlier in this chapter, policing is seen as a *unique* service with exceptional duties, functions and powers, which needs to embrace the fundamental responsibility of accounting to government, oversight agencies, the media and the public. The focus is, then, on that persistent pressure on senior officers to display both leadership and its corollary – accountability. These two elements are intertwined and inseparable; police leaders should not only lead but should also stand to account for their actions as head of a responsible public service in a democracy.

The discussion here is confined primarily to the leadership element, while recognising the equal importance of accountability. Indeed, leadership cannot be seen as merely an instrumental attribute that can be routinely injected through a standard course; that may well be of value but of the essence is that leadership is intimately related to the philosophy or paradigm of policing in use and the socio-political governance structure within which it is embedded. The authors, for example, work with the conviction that in a democracy based on the rule of law, police leaders should be professional and accountable and that all officers should deliver a service to citizens whose demands they see as legitimate and whose rights they respect. It is debatable as to how many police systems are founded on this paradigm, which is most likely to be found in more liberal Western democracies. Drawing on the material in previous chapters, one may, then, perceive the multiple and conflicting requirements for police leaders to think strategically, to handle a baffling range of stakeholders, to cope with increasingly diverse personnel, to maintain performance standards, especially in crime control, and yet prove capable, with competence and confidence, of handling major operations. Those two qualities of competence and confidence are vital and interrelated: competence generates confidence and confidence reinforces competence. An officer with low competence and poor confidence – or worse, unjustified overconfidence masking low competence – is a liability. And that is not an individual matter but is the collective responsibility of the system. Yet throughout the 50 or so years of police research there has been near universal carping by the lower ranks, as well as by others, about the standards of leadership.

This widely held feeling about senior officers lacking leadership qualities and operational acumen is prevalent in many societies, is a staple complaint of those lower in the hierarchy and is standard in depictions of police in films and TV series. On the screen – and in police canteens and watering holes – police chiefs are typically portrayed as 'well-meaning buffoons … career opportunists … political weasels' (Caless, 2011, p 7). They are seemingly divorced from the reality of front-line policing, and are seen to bureaucratically restrict initiative and slyly avoid accountability. This is a recurring theme, from Dirty Harry to Sarah Lund, and reached its apotheosis in the brilliant and insightful TV series *The Wire*. Only occasionally have there been efforts within TV series to portray the world of leading officers fairly realistically, with the characters in *Chief* (a male officer) and *The Commander* and *Prime Suspect* (both female senior officers) being positive British examples (Brown and Heidensohn, 2012). In many respects, however, this negative popular and occupational image needs to be contrasted with the fact that most Western police organisations have made significant strides in a number of respects in the past few decades. They have become more effective and technically sophisticated in crime control and prevention; more 'customer-oriented' and aware of victims' needs; more geared to multi-agency cooperation; more conscious of diversity in the workforce; and more linked to transnational policing networks. Some forces have impressive websites and make useful information readily available through diverse media, and many are more open to the press and more transparent to oversight.[2] In general, then, most senior officers are probably better trained and equipped in dealing with the management, stakeholder and standard media commitments that adhere to their office than in the past. Yet some commentators maintain that these positive developments have been bought at a fourfold price that impinges both on policing in general and on police leaders in particular.

First, there is an argument that the fixation on externally imposed performance standards and on the powerful and increasingly intrusive media has fostered short-term, reactive, incident-oriented behaviour. Even forces with an image of strategic sophistication seem prone to abandoning reflection and instantly chasing after the latest incident, newest hype or the morning's headline. Second, there is the contention that demands on senior staff to be well-rounded and multi-skilled has led to a new elite who can be dubbed 'strategy cops', distant from the reality of 'street cops'. Reuss-Ianni (1983) first drew attention to the potentially conflicting interests of 'street cops' and 'management cops' in New York in the late 1970s. However, it is argued that nowadays the middle ranks have become the management cops and above them are the 'strategy cops' and that the 'gap' between the various layers has become wider. Third, there has arisen criticism from politicians and the media – and even within policing itself – that this highly developed, often well-educated and even 'liberal' elite has focused too much on diverse aims and diffuse tasks at the cost of crime fighting and public order (Punch, 2007). These are seen by many stakeholders – including politicians, segments of the public and the media, and the carriers of the resilient police culture – as the 'core business' of policing, which is being neglected. Powerful groups inside and outside the police – notably the detective branch and prosecution service – who felt threatened or disadvantaged by this liberal, plural policing model lobby for a return to 'real' policing whenever there is a moral panic about transnational organised crime or criticism of the police for failing in high-profile criminal cases. And fourth, the accumulated influence of pressure to produce, competition for posts and insecurity in the face of major change is said to have fostered a degree of egoistical resolve to look after 'number one' among senior officers and to have made them somewhat risk averse.

These matters are worrying, given the need for the entire organisation to shift operational style instantly to meet sudden challenges such as disasters, civil emergencies, shooting sprees, sieges, abductions, terrorist attacks and complex investigations. Such situations will stretch their response capacity and leadership qualities, as they require officers instantly to change roles, especially leadership roles, at all levels (Punch and Markham 2000). This also applies to much of the routine functioning of police where a situation can suddenly escalate as with domestic violence incidents or at late night entertainment locations. Yet there is the persistently nagging theme that due to those multiple, conflicting pressures and rapid, complex developments, the operational cutting-edge of leadership at the top level has been dulled. How many chief officers have run a complex criminal investigation; how many have held command at a large and rapidly shifting major public order event; and how many have led a major firearms incident? These three types of scenario allow us to identify three functional areas of police leadership, as outlined in Chapter One: institutional leadership; concern leadership; and incident leadership. In England and Wales, aspiring senior officers are tested in these three areas at the Police National Assessment Centre (PNAC). Taking this to its logical conclusion, and attempting to identify the single most urgent issue demanding swift attention in police leadership, we pose the following question: how can one shape strategic vision and managerial ability, and maintain a philosophy and ethic of an accountable public service, while at the same time enhancing institutional leadership and operational competence?

Making it to the top in England and Wales

As a starting point for considering the police hierarchy in England and Wales, we focus on research by Caless (2011). Of the 218 police chiefs from the 43 police forces, Caless interviewed 85 top officers and collated questionnaire responses from nine. Since then there has been the introduction of PCCs which has changed the ground rules of police governance with a potential loss of operational autonomy. The issues raised here are: how do they reach chief officer rank and what is their level of (operational) competence? But first let us take a look at who these chief officers are and what they think about their work through the research of Caless (2011). Most are white males; the women who make it to chief officer do not normally get positions in the larger urban forces, suggesting there is a 'blue glass ceiling'. There are five female chief constables, seven deputy chief constables and 23 assistant chief constables: at 16% of chief officers women are clearly under-represented. The 'top cops' all tend to be workaholics, putting in 70-75 hours a week. Most are highly committed to policing; are uncomplimentary about the police authorities that appoint and supervise them; are critical of Her Majesty's Inspectorate of Constabulary (HMIC), which evaluates forces; and are fairly scathing about politicians, especially the Home Secretary (Theresa May), and the Cameron-led coalition government. They are most negative about the Home Office – referred to as the 'Dream Factory' with its officials on 'Planet Loony' – which, they intimate, turns direction at every puff of wind, leading to ad hoc proposals that are difficult if not impossible to implement. A major concern was the then impending election of Police and Crime Commissioners, which would put civilians in charge of policing and of the appointment of the police chief. The then serving chief officers feared that this would sound the end of operational autonomy. In general, the research respondents are frank, critical and even somewhat bitter. One reviewer of Caless's book found them to be 'demoralized, pessimistic and distrustful not only of those politicians to whom they are accountable, but also of the media, the public and their peers' (Stenning, 2015, p 58).

There is a clear hierarchy among forces – as in all policing systems – and some of the chief officers including chief constables hope to move to one of the leading forces, particularly the Met, but also Merseyside, West Yorkshire and West Midlands, as well as the Police Service of Northern Ireland and forces in Scotland. As the Caless interviews were anonymous, the research respondents were able to speak freely about other chief officers, and it is clear there is a great deal of competition, rivalry and mutual antipathy among them, with some openly critical of colleagues' levels of competency. Most see themselves primarily as 'managers/executives' – with one stating, 'I prefer the term "senior executive leader" to describe my role' (Caless, 2011, p 109) – but of a special public service organisation, with some feeling that a manager from outside could do 80% of their job. Indeed, a number do not oppose lateral entry, which the government was proposing at the time of the interviews, and, in fact, several forces have recruited civilians to senior positions with chief officer titles. They have no executive powers, however, and primarily perform financial, staff and human resources functions; some forces refer to them as 'directors'. Most respondents joined the police with little thought of getting to the top – although some were ambitious for high office from day one – and it was usually a colleague higher up the hierarchy who took notice of them, 'tapped them on the shoulder' and indicated they were potential chief officer material. To a degree, patronage from above remains highly important. Equally true is that a promising candidate may not be supported until a change at the top brings in a senior officer who acknowledges his or her potential and encourages their application. Nearly all chief officers have a university degree – gained either prior to entry or during their service – and many have two degrees (Lee and Punch, 2006). This is partly related to the fact that although policing has traditionally not been perceived as a graduate career, efforts have been made in recent years to recruit university graduates; moreover, a second degree is now seen as valuable, if not essential, for promotion.

Although everyone in British policing starts at the level of constable, there have been efforts since the 1970s – and earlier in the 1930s with the Trenchard Scheme[3] – to provide accelerated promotion for promising candidates. For example, the High Potential Development Scheme (HPDS) has emerged in recent years. About half of those who apply, and applicants may only do so with a chief's recommendation, do not make it through the selection process. The successful applicants undertake a module-based course at Warwick University or at a police establishment that is strongly geared to public services management. These high potential candidates can nowadays move fairly quickly through the ranks to chief superintendent; one even made it to chief constable in 15 years. Before achieving chief officer rank, they may have run a major investigatory or specialised unit, had an important staff function, or had responsibility for a district with a budget of over £35 million and some 1,000 personnel, which is larger than some of the former Dutch regional forces and about the size of some of the smaller UK forces (Paddick, 2008, p 130). Some may prefer to stay at the chief superintendent level for career or personal/family reasons. For instance, a chief constable has to have had prior experience in two forces, which means many applying for chief officer rank have to face the possibility of moving home, perhaps several times. Sometimes a move to an assistant chief constable post may be only temporary, as the person is simply waiting for the next career move; these officers are known as 'butterflies'. Those with almost exclusive experience as a detective may not want to return to uniformed work, while it is known that few career detectives make it to the top. Others may baulk at the cost of housing elsewhere if they move, the career consequences for a working partner and/or at the implications for their children's education. All those who want to aim for chief officer level must take the Strategic Command Course (SCC) at Bramshill Police Staff College (up until 2015); without attending the SCC an aspiring chief simply cannot become a chief officer.

The College of Policing is responsible for a new initiative that aims to reform police training and development. The new college became operational in early 2013 but it is not yet clear what new form senior officer training and development will take; meanwhile, a review of leadership development is under way. In order to attend the SSC, candidates have to take an 'extended interview' at PNAC for which there are three chances; after a third failure there is no chance of becoming a chief officer. The assessment is generally perceived to be tough and demanding; about 50% get through, a number are encouraged to reapply and reapplying for the remainder is left open. There has, however, been no objective evaluation of PNAC's merits in selecting chief officers (Caless, 2011). The SCC was originally a six-month residential course, but nowadays it is delivered in module form. At one stage, the SCC was delivered partly at Bramshill and partly at Cambridge University; at Cambridge, the officers could gain a Diploma in Applied Criminology within one year or a Master's in two years. The Cambridge option has now become voluntary.

It is fairly clear that much of the non-specialist training and development throughout the service is classroom-based and increasingly geared to educational qualifications. The academic reading required for the SCC, for instance, is considerable; those with a more academic orientation clearly have an advantage, but maturity and motivation could compensate for that after the culture shock of moving from hands-on management to reflective, knowledge-based, analytical discourse. The SCC also has the important function of taking officers who are typically deeply engaged in local management in one branch of policing, and giving them exposure to macro issues and an opportunity to reflect more widely on policing and society in general. It further ties officers into a useful national network of colleagues – and competitors – for their further career. Participants in the Caless research (2011) were nearly all complimentary about the SCC, which they say gave them time and space to appreciate the larger picture. As one respondent put it:

> 'It was great, it really was. Here you were, freed from the daily hassle and away from all the pressures … and able to think of what to do and more importantly, whether there are other ways to do it. We met chiefs who are legends and some household names from industry. Where else could I do that? The discussions we used to have about operational resilience would get quite heated and there were lots of different points of view. It was stimulating but also bloody hard work.' (Caless, 2011, p 67)

Going on the experience of one of the authors of this work, who taught on the SSC, and others who have been involved in the programme, it was noticeable that those with a more academic background tended to thrive at Cambridge, while others had difficulty with the assignments and discussions. Some were edgy, defensive and even aggressive because they were suddenly under scrutiny and were wary of receiving a poor evaluation. This was related to the fact that they usually had large egos, had previously achieved a great deal in policing terms but now were being exposed to other, demanding criteria and their performance on these was seen as vital to their further career. Officers who had previously been highly successful in their field could feel insecure at the thought of performing poorly with the threat of subsequent damage to their reputation, and some were quite abrasive after receiving poor grades in assignments (not unlike some undergraduates). It is important to note in interpreting this behaviour that during the Bramshill module, SCC participants were in uniform, and were observed in their formal roles by representatives of the Home Office. At Cambridge, in contrast, they behaved and dressed more like students, and the atmosphere was casual and relaxed. It was widely assumed that those observing them would be influential in guiding the better candidates to the more 'important' forces: although appointments were primarily the responsibility of the local police authorities there were suspicions of the selection processes being lubricated from Whitehall. Indeed, Paddick (2008, p 243) strongly asserts that the Home Secretary exerts his or her influence over *all* promotions, and could appoint the Met Commissioner and Deputy Commissioner. The selection for the top Met position seems mostly to have occurred without a serious procedure or critical questioning and in one case 'without anything recognisable as an interview' (Blair, 2009, p 101). Towards the end of the SCC, aspiring chief officers start applying to forces and subsequently do the round of interviews. Of the Caless respondents, one was accepted after the first interview – an exceptional occurrence – and some after three or four interviews; one applicant underwent 17 interviews before gaining a post. Some chief officers interviewed by Caless were convinced that a number of appointments were 'inside jobs'. Success often depended on satisfying the particular interests of the local authority, but nearly all the respondents were eventually appointed to chief officer (only one or two were unsuccessful). Throughout their career as chief officer, they could draw on continuous professional development for support. In all, it remained the case that support from one's own chief constable was crucial to success.

The formal key points, then, for 'getting to the top' in England and Wales are as follows.

- All officers start as constables and begin to work their way through the ranks after two years;
- some progress rapidly and some are selected as high potentials through HPDS or other channels (the Met has its own *Emerging Leaders Scheme*);
- those wishing to become a chief officer must be assessed at PNAC, and have three chances to pass. If they fail to get through, they will never be promoted to chief officer;
- aspiring chief officers must also pass the SCC; hence all chief officers have been through the selection procedure and have completed the same course. Passing the SCC effectively guarantees promotion to chief officer but a few did not get promoted (Caless, 2011).

On paper, this looks impressive as it requires jumping a number of apparently challenging hurdles while at each stage there is selection and the chance of failure. Nevertheless, there is talk that some get promotion by carefully managing their C.V. – developing broadly based experience and not staying too long in criminal investigations – and building up credit with their superiors, say by acting as 'staff officer' to a chief constable. Moreover, those who do reach chief officer rank are not always effective; there are reports of chiefs looking down on their peers, for example, and there have been cases where chief officers have failed conspicuously at critical moments. A particular claim is that some officers have 'slid up' the hierarchy despite having little operational experience. This has implications for the role of chief officers in the 'command and control' function and for reinforcing the sceptical views of the lower ranks. Yet it remains the case that the UK police service has in recent decades built up a wealth of experience in key professional areas such as public order, counter-terrorism, disaster management, risk assessment, diplomatic protection, the handling of large-scale sporting events, inter-agency cooperation and major criminal investigations. Formally no one can tell a police chief what to do and, with over 40 of them (in England and Wales), this does not always guarantee coordination and harmony regarding policy, practice and coordination. Taking that into account ACPO has done a great deal to support and develop training, operational manuals and exercises to generate a measure of unanimity in police practice, and this task was continued together with the former National Police Improvement Agency (NPIA) and to a certain extent the HMIC (Savage et al, 2000). Several of these guidelines are of a high order, including those on risk assessment, use of firearms and 'command and control'.

The quality, then, of many British specialist senior officers is indisputably high. A leading expert on policing was in 'awe of their skills' (Jonathan Crego, personal communication). This may not, however, be true of all chief officers. One respondent in the Caless research candidly admitted that he had been promoted as a 'manager' and not as a leader, and, like many chiefs in other countries, was sceptical about the level of leadership training he had received:

> 'It has changed on the surface, I think, with greater media savvy and more evident skills in handling the public appearance of policing, but I don't think that leadership has changed fundamentally. It is still absolutely bloody awful, basically, and most people who get to the top, including me, get there because they can manage, not because they can lead. I think leadership in the policing is in its infancy and it has got to develop if it is ever to be taken seriously. At the moment it is all "froth and bubbles".' (British chief officer; Caless, 2011, p 116)

Making it to the top in the Netherlands

When Boin and colleagues (2003) interviewed all but one of the 26 Dutch police chiefs in office early in the first decade of the 20th century, there were 25 regional chiefs and one chief of the KLPD compared with the 165 chiefs before 1993. The authors commented:

'We talked to motivated, often still fairly ambitious, and, without exception proud people. We were told time and again that being a [Dutch] police chief is the best profession around' (Boin et al, 2003, p 238). Most were from fairly conventional if not conservative, middle-class backgrounds; some had a close relative in the police or in public service, all were white and all but one were male. Nearly all were in their fifties and had become police chief in their forties, and several had been long in office – one for 19 and another for 22 years. They had spent most of their working life in policing, and they would have known one another intimately and for a long time. Some had spent most of their career in one force; this was especially true of the large forces – principally Amsterdam, Rotterdam, Utrecht and The Hague – which only recruited chiefs internally or from those who had served previously in the force. It was quite pointless, one chief said, for an 'outsider' to apply to Amsterdam. The larger forces also produced a disproportionate number of the regional chiefs.

This reflected two prominent features of Dutch society. One is the dominance of the *Randstad* – the Western conglomeration of major cities – economically, politically, socially, culturally and intellectually. And the other is the deep resentment this causes outside of the conurbation. The Netherlands is small but not homogenous and contains diverse cultural identities with high levels of local chauvinism. This was noticeable in policing where there was a clear informal hierarchy of forces that had a deleterious effect on solidarity and coordination within the system. With 165 forces up to the early 1990s, there were major differences in size of forces and quality of chiefs and this fostered arrogance in the larger forces and a resentful response from the smaller forces. This highly fragmented, somewhat incestuous system, with its parochialism and status frictions, was cumbersome and unwieldy and long in need of reform, but the many mayors were reluctant to lose 'their' police. The eventual compression to 25 regional forces and one national unit was an improvement, but old habits eventually resurfaced.

Of those interviewed, nearly all had attended the former Netherlands Police Academy – known as the NPA – for a four-year, residential course or its three-year predecessor, prior to assignment to a force.[4] The one female chief was a lateral entrant, for whom a tailor-made, individual course was devised. It should be explained that, almost perversely, Dutch police training, including leadership training, was traditionally developed and delivered at arm's length from the police organisation through independent institutes financed by national government as specified in law. In terms of selection and education for leadership positions, prospective senior officers used to go almost straight from secondary school to the former Police Academy, following a strict selection process. Only a fraction of those who applied were selected so there was an emphasis on being an elite group and also on 'character development'. The curriculum was based largely on legal technicalities learned by heart, languages and sport. Van der Vijver (2009) recalls that at the earlier course before the NPA opened in 1967, he learned nothing about 'leadership, decision making, policy, care for personnel, organizational theory, communications', and there was no discussion about 'dilemmas in police work, work related ethical issues, about how to cope with deviant behaviour within the organisation or with the emotions of the personnel'. But 40 years later, he could still recite of the Law on Birds (*Vogelwet*) by heart.

During the former NPA course, there were work placement periods spent in the field as constable, sergeant and inspector. There was also a strong informal culture similar to the traditional student societies of Dutch universities; friendships and networks were developed here that lasted throughout careers. Later the curriculum altered considerably, while there was a growing antipathy to the residential element; the courses were increasingly given in module form and the residential programme was abandoned. Completing the course gave graduates direct access to the senior ranks; they would enter a force within the officer caste as inspectors, and promotion was largely through seniority. The lower ranks in that old system who were less educationally qualified than those entering the NPA went to 'police schools' for basic training. As in much of Continental European policing, there was a separate training centre for other ranks who might reach supervisory level but who would normally never reach senior officer rank. When the senior officer started as inspector, he or she had a solidly secure job with good secondary benefits and automatic promotion until the age of 60 with no further formal requirements to fulfil. Those officers would have opportunities to undertake periodic professional training but those who wanted to take a degree had to do it in their own time and at their own expense. Given that many forces were small and the policing relatively undemanding, this could make for a comfortable existence and the prevailing culture was not to exert oneself and not to rock the boat.

This reflected a dominant theme in Dutch society of not needing to excel, and a belief that a moderate performance is sufficient, and that those who put their heads 'above the cornfield' risk losing them (Mak, 2001, p 5). The system was largely characterised by 'sponsored mobility' (Turner, 1960), which was strongly evident in Dutch society. This was very different from the 'contested mobility' that was ostensibly more typical of policing in Anglo-American society, where senior officers started at the bottom of the ladder and had to work their way up. But Caless (2011) makes it clear that a degree of sponsored mobility, lubricated – or hindered – by one's chief, remained prominent in upward mobility in Britain, and this is no doubt also true of the US, where the mayor's preference was and is the determining factor.

In the 1970s, however, a radical group of young Dutch officers calling for renewal were motivated to change that ossified institutional culture and, as some had studied one of the social sciences, also to alter that uninspiring educational programme at the NPA that had little relevance to actual policing practice or developments in society. Since then, there has been substantial change and a major investment in the educational opportunities offered at all levels, with a rich variety of courses at home and abroad. Yet two systemic factors have remained. One is that educational qualifications are a major element in determining who enters the higher ranks, meaning that there is still a stratified system with performance at school as significant in the selection process. The other is that while the senior ranks may take various degree and executive programmes, there is no compulsory course for all who want to reach the top.

All police training has, then, in the past two decades altered considerably, with that separate NPA course being abolished in the early 1990s and subsumed in 1994 into the forerunner of the Dutch Police Academy – the Central Selection and Training Institute for the Police (*Landelijk Selectie en Opleidingsinstituut Politie*, or LSOP) – which functioned until 2004. The standard professional education in policing now reflects the wider move in Dutch higher education towards the Anglo-Saxon model of an undergraduate Bachelor's degree and a postgraduate Master's. Recruits enter through a number of streams for the various ranks and functions in relation to the rank they hope to reach and this is, as before, strongly tied to their prior educational qualifications. The best qualified take a four-year Bachelor's degree interspersed with periods of practice where in the fourth year they select options, one of which indicates the intention to seek a leading position. 'Dual education' was also introduced, whereby theory and 'on the job' practice alternate. Furthermore, all trainees, who function as probationary constables during the courses, have to start work on graduation as a qualified constable as in the Anglo-American system. The system has further moved to build in a higher knowledge component in training, as well as a higher element of practically applicable knowledge.

The School for Police Leadership (SPL) was founded in 2001, offering courses at diverse levels for those moving toward high rank including at the Master's level. For instance, a two-year postgraduate police leadership programme had already started in 1997 that was outsourced to three institutes of higher education. But it was not compulsory and some 'high-flyers' simply bypassed it in favour of other executive programmes or managerial courses abroad. Critics soon argued that the predominant role of academia meant that the programme was too detached from the strategic and practical needs of the police and it was discontinued. In particular, a leading figure in academia whose voice carried weight, Cyrille Fijnaut (1999), expressed strong criticism of the course in that no police chief was involved in designing it while it dealt with every topic except policing. There is also the option of taking a two year Master's in policing at the Dutch Police Academy or at Canterbury Christ Church University. Furthermore, the SPL offers various courses, including a strategic one, with a strong accent on 'personal development', but it was argued that it went too far on individual development. In short, there has been a continuous search for suitable programmes, with much debate about what is most appropriate. But, importantly, there has never been a *compulsory course* for mid-career officers seeking force leadership level.

This uncertain and shifting backcloth to senior leadership training mirrored a much wider concern that, for a raft of reasons, has led to severe criticism of the entire Dutch training system in recent years. This dissatisfaction formed an element in the appointment of the Working Group Police Leadership (see Preface). The formation of the National Police also led to the idea that a new type of leader was needed, and the working group was charged with redesigning police leadership education. We now examine the approach it took and the results that emerged.

Wanted: (new) Dutch police leaders

A system reorganisation of this magnitude presents a clear challenge for leadership and the new head of the National Police expressed his profile for the forthcoming leaders as follows:

> 'They should be able to take on everything. Who understand the policing craft and what is going on. Who can link up the diverse parts. Who have an eye for the interests of administrators, can get into contact with the public and who have to be real professional types.' (The

then prospective First Police Commissioner Bouman, in Holla and Hanrath, 2011, p 12)

This language of 'real professional types' who can take on 'anything' conveys something of a 'back to basics' message with a seemingly robust style of leadership. Yet it almost appears as if the new police leaders are not supposed to think too much for themselves, suggesting also a somewhat deferential relationship. In the documentation leading to the formation of the National Police there also emerged a desired change in leadership style away from 'management' and towards commitment to 'on the ground' results and operational involvement. The term *operational leadership* – described vaguely but obviously related to the 'back to basics' approach – was used (Final Report TOLNP, 2013). This seemed to convey the conventional police understanding of 'operational' as applying primarily to executive policing, but it was given a different interpretation by the Working Group supervising the project on leadership development. The ambitions stated in the founding documentation accompanying the new National Police were threefold (Final Report TOLNP, 2013). The new Dutch police leaders were to produce better results in terms of security; create a unified service; and increase the legitimacy and trust in the police. But, as intimated, that system change raised a host of underlying political, constitutional and cultural issues about the very nature of policing within Dutch society. Rather than simply accepting this, the Working Group's effort became focused on how to reconcile the tension between a more assertive yet value-driven leadership style with the expressed desire for a more 'back to basics', results-oriented approach. To understand the group's efforts it is important to refer to the thoughts of the professionals that predated the political choice for the National Police.

Briefly, there had been an outspoken group of police chiefs in the 1980s and early 1990s but they had been put in their place in the mid-1990s and have now retired. The following generation were necessarily more managerial and somewhat reticent, and they increasingly encountered at the local level force managers who wanted to dominate the regional triangle. However, in the past decade, a fresh generation of chiefs has arrived on the scene. They felt, in the spirit of *A changing police* in 1977, the need to produce a new strategy document. The resulting *Police in evolution* (CCPC, 2005) held a clear choice for mission, vision and strategy. The formulated mission was to stand firmly for the values of a democratic society under the rule of law with the core values defined as freedom, equality and justice. The clear purpose was to position the police as an intrinsically *value-driven* organisation with adequate professional discretion. To a degree, then, the context was of the police arguing for a renewed degree of freedom for police leadership, for the refurbishment of the social paradigm and for a value-driven institution. However, the socio-political climate, as intimated, had become increasingly unreceptive to this. Clearly, the approach taken by the working group represents the ambition to maintain the perspective of *Police in evolution*,[5] while at the same time the pressure 'to produce results' is taken seriously. It is an attempt to manage 'competing values', as is also evident in the leadership model. The foundation of the National Police was accompanied by the adoption of the leadership model of Robert Quinn in terms of 'competing values' (Quinn and Rohrbaugh, 1983). This had been selected a few years before as a conceptual guideline for Dutch policing. Quinn describes two well-known dimensions (leading to four quadrants): flexibility–control, and internal–external. In the police model, the police leader is located at the crossroads of two dimensions and is responsible for 'connecting' different competing values, or, more concretely, for connecting 'people within the organisation leading to results within a context'. This 'connecting leader' is held to be characterised by openness and self-reflection. It could be argued that openness and self-reflection are not always natural ingredients of conventional police culture and the police leadership it has produced (Loftus, 2009). Moreover, the Quinn model points to a leader who can competently handle the competing values, but it does not provide much direction for implementing this in leadership development. In response, the working group set out in two directions. One was to go against the grain of reductionism in the concept of 'operational' leader – and against the assumptions of that resilient occupational culture – to argue for 'reflective' and value-driven leadership. The other was to find out what people within the organisation think about their institution, leadership and training.

The state of leadership and leadership education

In June 2013, the working group presented its preliminary results to the new chief of the National Police based on four activities. First, over a hundred interviews were conducted within the service on existing and preferred police leadership. This drew on the opinions of employees (some in lower leadership positions) about their senior leaders illustrated by examples of good and bad leadership. Second, around 90 group meetings – with more than a thousand participants – were organised within different units of the National Police regarding the development of new leadership; participants discussed value-driven leadership and ways of overcoming obstacles to developing the preferred culture and leadership. Third, the then existing leadership education was evaluated. Various evaluation reports on police education were analysed and additional interviews were undertaken within the police educational system (with teachers, students and alumni). Fourth, the leadership literature was reviewed; comparison was made with developments in the UK; and a study was made into leadership developments in the Dutch military, healthcare and education.

The interviews and group meetings generated a crystal clear message from participants. They maintained that the existing police culture is characterised by a lack of frank professional feedback, widespread insecurity and a fear of making mistakes. The dominant formal hierarchy is an obstacle to change, and the working culture is one of control, not of trust. The classical opposition between street cops and management cops emerged with considerable clarity, and the acceptability of this clearly decreases sharply as one moves down the hierarchy. What constitutes, according to respondents, good leadership? In their opinion, leaders should know from experience 'what the job is like'; should trust their professionals, support them, and give them backing (the so-called 'heat shield'); and should know their team and the interactional dynamics within it. Further, they should know how to motivate and how to facilitate the further development of their employees; be clear and able to explain the rationale behind their choices; dare to take decisions and intervene if necessary, but also know when to leave the decision to others; and be authentic and personal. The integrity of leaders needs to be beyond doubt; their 'moral compass' should be well developed and they should be an example for their personnel. Finally, 'actions speaks louder than words' is the most applicable credo for a leader. The problem, of course, is getting the leaders to display the required behaviour in real-life settings and there was some predictable cynicism on this.

But respondents also expressed a measure of pride regarding police culture and conduct. They saw police as action-prone and result-oriented, but also strongly value-driven – they try to make a difference, contribute to a just world and show compassion to citizens. They valued the family-like culture and related solidarity of the occupational community. Yet there were concerns about management by spreadsheet eroding value-driven conduct, and about policing increasingly becoming – especially for the younger generation – a regular job and less of a 'calling'. Their views on the state of police education were also crystal clear. They reflected the opinion widely held within

Dutch policing about police education being organised at a deleterious distance from the police organisation. They also felt that the attempt at 'dual education' had largely failed because the educators left it to the forces to fill in the practical part without taking a real interest in how things work in practice. The lack of interest was mutual; in the forces, formal education was not seen as very important in learning about how things 'really work'. As a consequence, there was no synergy between theory and practice, just alteration of formal and informal learning. This only strengthened the well-known mechanism that the newcomer in a police agency was supposed to forget everything learned during formal education (Chan, 2003). Many of the critical remarks from respondents derive from the above situation:

> There is a gap between what is needed at the workplace and what is taught in the classroom ... the teachers are out of tune with modern police work ... the students are trained for ideal-type situations markedly different from what happens in reality ... not enough use is made of real life cases and questions in structuring the courses. (van Dijk et al, 2013)

Clearly, the courses do not align with the dominant forms of informal learning; they were seen as non-committal, lacking in challenge and not necessarily related to new behaviour at the workplace. There was too much 'theory' and not enough 'practical' training, for example in communication skills, like providing feedback 'on the job' in difficult circumstances.

At a more fundamental level, the evaluation of leadership education showed that an effective contribution to the acquisition of a so-called 'professional identity' was lacking. This is related to ideas on character development, socialisation and internalisation of professional values and practices. These developmental ideas were, in fact, the explicit basis for the Strategic Leadership Course, but in reality the course became characterised by non-committal personal development only marginally related to day-to-day practices. With little involvement from the police organisation, the educators were more or less providing what suited them rather than what the profession wanted and needed. The consequence of that split between the police organisation and police training came home to roost with an implicit collective agreement that undermined the necessary synergy that should feed continuous debate, evaluation and improvement in the programmes. The resulting approach satisfied no-one. The input from the cluster of four activities by the working group contributed to reflection and debate, which led to a set of design principles for the new leadership education.

Organisational change and demands on leadership

The working group digested the diverse activities and research data to arrive at five necessary transitions for the National Police, strongly related to the demands on leadership:

- from administrative management towards operational involvement;
- from procedure-based towards value-driven behaviour;
- from positional power towards goal-oriented interaction;
- from non-committal reflection towards conscious behaviour;
- from (internal) organisational goals towards societal contribution.

This, in a nutshell, is what the working group has formulated, but the thinking behind it is that the police institution is still largely a hierarchical organisation, where who is directing whom is based on the formal position of the leader. 'Unfreezing' this rigidity requires an organisational development trajectory on the five lines proposed above. For example, the leadership of major incidents/operations – a fundamental component of policing – can only be meaningful if it is related to low-level leaders who learn to perform positively within the hierarchical chain. The hierarchy remains an important factor in operations, but the interaction between the levels in the chain is equally important. Chaleff (2003), for example, shows the importance of lower-level leaders having at a certain stage to become *followers*. The follower is a *leader* at his or her specific level who also learns to shift from leader to follower at the right moment as an operation unfolds; this will especially be the case in an immediate response to an unexpected event whereby those from the lower ranks are the first on the scene. It is equally clear that in emergency response situations at major incidents these relative positions need to be based on the knowledge-skills-attitude nexus rather than on formal positions. Furthermore, the legitimacy of the police – and the subsequent trust of citizens – is based on the contribution to solving societal problems with the emphasis not on 'output' but on 'outcome'. This presupposes a self-assured police, confident in the face of political and societal pressures, combined with a measure of humility, for the police are a *public service* and officers are *public servants*. This plainly very much echoes the Anglo-Saxon consent paradigm. The rationale behind the proposed organisational transitions is described in greater detail in the final report of the working group (Final Report TOLNP, 2013).

However, the key insight was that leadership and leadership education should strengthen the five, sometimes difficult, transitions. This may sound like a statement of the obvious, but leadership and leadership training have not explicitly been linked before to transformational goals. Rather, they have primarily been based on increasing the quality of individual leaders, focused on what is needed 'now', and have been 'conservative' in that respect. In effect, leadership education was not tailored to where the police organisation needs to go in the future and what is needed to accomplish that. In the end, one's formal position in the hierarchy – in that conservative mode reflecting the status quo – is deemed to trump the ability to be an effective leader. And although the importance of the unique and in some ways constant character of policing has been stressed, change is necessary to perform these functions adequately in a shifting socio-political context. Those preferred transitions led to a specific emphasis within the 'competing values' model of Quinn, with development in the direction of so-called 'operational leadership', conceptualised by the working group as a focus on the quadrants 'people' and 'results'. However, it is possible to discern a subsequent shift in emphasis within the working group that led to a rebranding of the term into 'new operational leadership' as shorthand for value-driven leadership, connecting people and results. This can be seen as an attempt to rescue the term from a narrow, 'hands-on' approach with a neglect of essential values. New operational leadership is now viewed as value-driven and characterised by an emphasis on the explicit linking of human resources to societal results, or connecting people and results through values. This focus differs from the narrow emphasis of New Public Management where results tend to take precedence. From an institutional politics perspective, however, the reorganisation of the Dutch police is clearly on the 'control-side' of the diagram: 'controlling' the organisation and 'controlling' results. That would strengthen the managerial perspective and lead to a more instrumental – and perhaps subservient – police service.

In a way, the choice for value-driven leadership with a commitment to people and to societal results is obviously not in tune with that rationale. It can be interpreted as the profession positioning itself as a countervailing power to an all-embracing, and potentially distorting, political control. However, the choice for this alternative type of leadership echoes the general development of public leadership in domains like education and healthcare. It can even be fruitfully combined with the 'back to basics' trend and the revaluation of the 'professional' in the broader sense. Rather than dichotomous thinking, it can lead to strengthening the professional identity, based on having the adequate portfolio of skills, knowledge and attitudes. In the proposals for the new leadership education, for example, developing and strengthening a professional identity, based on the core values of the organisation, takes centre stage. And in the classical combination of skills-knowledge-attitude, attitude is seen as the most important. Attitude is described as the combination of 'to want and to dare', which is intimately related to the value-driven characteristics of operational leadership. 'To dare' refers to having courage, related to both external and internal challenges. Externally, it is about the realisation that decision making in policing is always a form of risk taking. Internally, it is about speaking your mind and making contested choices if needed to further societal results. This is to a large extent taking responsibility – and the willingness to be accountable – in challenging circumstances. It is, furthermore, crucial to bridge the gap between training and education on the one hand, and daily working practices on the other. The proposed leadership education is about leading *people*. However obvious this might seem, the reality is that contemporary leadership has become to a large extent about numbers on a spreadsheet, to the detriment of a focus on people.

In addition, the police are plagued with the traditional hierarchical structure, which easily gives the impression that position equals leadership. An officer may be in a position of authority without qualifying as a formally 'adequate' leader, as argued earlier. Position, moreover, typically equates with authority that is related to the status quo, while the type of leadership the working group has in mind is related more to transformation. In that sense, leadership potentially – and uncomfortably – undermines the self-evident character of authority (Aigner, 2011, pp 36-9). In the proposed form of leadership education, establishing whether or not leaders meet the course standards is not first and foremost based on formal qualifications but on what leaders accomplish in their own position and within their own team. In other words, assessment is based on the extent to which leaders apply their knowledge and experience when managing their own teams. Leadership education is, then, not only about the individual leader as the main focus but is also about the interaction between leaders and followers (Kelley, 1988; Riggio et al, 2008). The 'light-touch' leader, who is not overly dominant, yet is decisive and delegates judiciously, strives to ensure that the members of his or her team become courageous followers; realises that he or she is primarily a 'leader of leaders' who is not afraid to assume greater responsibility if required; and is fully accountable for the choices of their courageous followers if things go wrong. In the proposed leadership education, there has to be, then, a marked shift from 'knowing' towards 'doing', with considerable value attached to experiential learning. Effective programmes are feedback-intensive and integrate assessment, challenge and support (King and Santana, 2010, p 97).

Finally, although the proposals for the new Dutch leadership education may seem at odds with important cultural and organisational traits of conventional policing and the political climate of the mid-2010s, they build on a rich tradition of a value-driven, 'thinking' police in the Netherlands. Above all, the proposals effectively end the relatively privileged and protected position of leading officers. They will place new demands on professionals, on the organisation and on the Police Academy, which will take responsibility for the leadership courses. And this in the demanding context of a wide-ranging reorganisation where many leaders still have to be allocated their positions in the new set-up. This may seem not to be a highly favourable context for a fundamental reform of leadership, but, given that the institution is in a state of flux with an unusual measure of flexibility, it may just prove to be an opportunity that allows or even encourages such a reform.

Leadership development: necessary ingredients

In turning to a number of key elements underpinning both the insights derived from our research and subsequent proposals for leadership development, one must bear in mind that the choices to be made are never simple and are a matter of nuanced balancing. It is evident, moreover, that the specific focus on leadership cannot be seen in isolation from the macro issues of system – and societal – change that form the backdrop to this book. Building on this, the central issue becomes: what sort of leadership is required to cope with the impact of these multiple changes in the wider environment, the criminal justice system and the persistent pressures to produce 'results'? The pragmatic starting point adopted is that policing and the police system require leadership at the system, force and diverse operational levels. To an extent, leadership at the force level in the chief officer team can be defined partly as generic 'managerial' leadership, and in some functions civilians with special expertise have taken responsibility for these roles. But it is of the essence to realise constantly that the police organisation is *unique* in its powers and responsibilities and the range of tasks it has to perform. It is possible to see policing as an 'industry' with 'products' (for example, safety, security, justice) but the complex, diffuse and multi-faceted nature of its work, which in turn relates to a set of diffuse values, makes the parallel with the private business model limited (Manning, 2010). The police service remains a unique institution and even among other public emergency agencies it has unique tasks and exceptional obligations of accountability. One vital, core task is emergency response requiring a double institutional shift – first, in structure, style of operating and leadership roles, and second, in mobilising external contacts and stakeholders. The implication is that there simply has to be a highly developed and tested operational capacity at the chief officer level and, indeed, throughout the organisation. A force that does not have that capacity makes itself vulnerable to mistakes, to failing in its duty of care to the public and to its own personnel, and exposes itself to liability – criminal as well as civil.

We have drawn on the philosophy underpinning the UK model of 'command' and the structure using gold, silver and bronze categories. This implies that officers will be trained and certified for those roles that are based on competency – which needs to be tested – and not rank. There is an issue with lateral entry as to whether or not those entering the profession in this way have had sufficient exposure to operational experience and learning to be able to take the gold role or to appreciate the roles, functions and experiences of silver and bronze. For instance, if officers are recruited laterally to a high rank – which has been a possibility since 2014 – the authors' assumption is that they will have to have a period of years in which they gain patrol experience, undergo a course equivalent to the SCC and take the Gold Commanders Course before being permitted to perform the gold role in operations. From the Dutch data, there were indications about how people lower in the organisation perceived the organisational culture and what they expect from superiors. This is valuable as a template to hold up to senior staff to help them see what others expect from them. The input clearly shows that what the lower ranks, including those at other leadership levels, desire is seniors who are involved, responsive and have an affinity with, or direct experience of, their work and the dilemmas they face (cf Alison and Crego, 2008). Furthermore, the Dutch material touches not only on the issue of leadership but also on 'followership'. This draws attention to the fact that there are leaders at the various levels – who may be low in the hierarchy but who are the first on the scene of an incident – who in turn become 'followers' when a higher-level leader takes over. That interaction and transaction, in pre-planned and spontaneous incidents, needs far more attention and training. An extension of that could be that leaders at the three command levels are seen as a team whose members are geared to working with one another, and that the organisation has a pool of such teams that may be mobilised to fit specific operations, rather like American football with defence and offence teams. One could think of such teams as having a specific expertise in public order, siege management, firearms, large sporting events and so on, alongside their generic ability in command roles.

A great deal of education for leaders is still too heavily classroom-based, sometimes with basic texts that have been around for many decades and are periodically updated (Neyroud Report, 2011). For senior managerial positions as well as for operational leaders, there needs to be far more experiential learning, with skills that can be applied in practice and with follow-up to see how they are applied in operations. In business schools and management institutes in the US and elsewhere, there is a growing focus on leadership and on exploring it through experiential learning. This is also reflected in the simulation exercises and other practices based on research by Crego and colleagues at the Centre for Critical Incident Research in the UK (Alison and Crego, 2008). In debriefing, for instance, officers show themselves to be acutely aware of leadership styles and of the organisational context in which that leadership functions. There are specific characteristics that may be attributed to police organisations and operations and to how officers function within them – sometimes with reticence towards those with high rank, concern about the blame culture and fear of displaying emotions – but according to numerous debriefs it is clear what officers want in a leader (Jonathan Crego, personal communication). For them, a leader is emphatic; plans operations well; displays clarity of role – which is the essence of the gold, silver and bronze model; is visible – but not too visible – and communicates clearly; gives clear direction but is also supportive; and manages the direction of large numbers, say of detectives, during a major investigation. Further, she or he displays a clear understanding of the policing area involved; shows concern for the needs of the officers – rest, refreshments and resources; and pays attention to the stresses and strains of major, intense effort both during operations and, importantly, after them (Alison and Crego, 2008). Moreover, she or he is encouraging throughout operations and delivers praise where due after they have been completed while being ultimately accountable. This clearly indicates a judicious combination of leadership, analytical, decision-making, management/logistical and human resource skills. It also reveals what officers do not appreciate: this is someone who is autocratic, does not understand the specific area he or she is working in, is confused about the command role, is poor at directing the operation and neglects the interests of the personnel. Plainly, the demands are high and it is impossible to perform all of the tasks required in a perfect manner. However, leaders need to be conscious of those demands, clear about their role, and not afraid to take responsibility or to be held accountable for the inevitable mistakes. This is less likely to happen if they are inexperienced and unsure.

Building on that insight, one can see the benefit of encapsulating some of the major incidents, operations and institutional failures and successes of recent years, geared to all facets of policing, as learning cases. These could usefully be structured to follow the decision-making process with use of original visual and other material and with group and individual assignments. A course based on this material could be taken with the members of other emergency services and other agencies (for example, fire and rescue, ambulance, child protection and mental health services). There is, indeed, a treasure trove of cases available in each country where courses often rely on those with first-hand experience of the incident or operation to convey the learning elements. This can be most fruitful, but when the officers in question leave the organisation, that data and those insights are lost; it must be possible, however, to build a portfolio of learning cases across the range of issues that officers are likely to encounter – and for which they have to plan. This could also be linked to constructing an 'institutional memory' in each force, which preserves the lessons learned from historic cases. Unlike management and legal education, the case-teaching method is rarely employed in police education. There are issues of accreditation and ownership of education and development here – think of the Dutch case where training and the police organisation have been quite separate, with deleterious consequences – and the consequences of outsourcing much of police training.

There is also the balance between what is seen as 'useful' knowledge and more abstract, 'academic' knowledge. In the period when part of the SCC was delivered at Cambridge, evaluations indicted that while the academics were endeavouring to be 'practical' some of the officers would have preferred more 'theoretical' and challenging material on crime, security and governance in a changing society. It can be that what the Neanderthals deem 'useless' knowledge is in fact highly 'useful' – on the grounds that there is nothing as practical as a good theory. This suggests a judicious mix of disciplines and approaches with history, philosophy (ethics) and psychology (say, related to major incident management) along with an 'applied criminology', which was the base of the Cambridge programme, and evidence-based material (to the extent that that is available). The selection process and SCC course for senior officers in British policing are seemingly attractive as a model for choosing and grooming senior officers. There is PNAC and HPDS with the selection and sifting of candidates while only those who have successfully taken the SCC can become chief officers. This is sound – certainly compared to systems where officers automatically 'roll up' the hierarchy on seniority and where courses are not assessed on a pass/fail basis – providing all the selection and assessment methods are valid. Moreover, the SCC has a broader function of shaping future members of a national elite who have shared the same training.

But the leadership component of the SCC course is slight. It is highly knowledge-based, which is fine, but the skills/competencies elements are weak. The officers interviewed by Caless say that they would have liked a programme specifically geared to their future role not only as chief officer but also as chief constable. Indeed, in interviews by David Bayley and Philip Stenning with some 40 police chiefs in six countries, nearly all participants said that nothing had equipped them for the top function (personal communication: David Bayley). Perhaps it is not possible to do this fully, but efforts could be made to prepare candidates for the dilemmas, tensions and pitfalls of high office. There will always be a discrepancy, as between a flight simulator and the physical act of landing a Boeing 747 at Heathrow Airport on a busy and blustery night, but that does not prevent continuous improvement of the simulator. This is clearly an area that requires development to help senior officers move into the top position in a force. In general, the material employed in this work points in the direction of taking leadership in policing more seriously, not just locating it at the top of the organisation but throughout, and not just individually but especially within the teams that constitute so much of police work. The uniqueness of the police organisation lies partly in the fact that some of the most important decisions are taken by those lowest in the hierarchy, and partly in the fact that some of the most impressive examples of leadership and courage are shown by ordinary personnel facing exceptional circumstances. And that it is crucial to provide back-up swiftly for front-line leaders as an institutional imperative.

There should be, then, a significant retooling of learning to repair that lacuna. Taking leadership seriously implies that from day one there should be an emphasis on formal and informal leadership roles and on selecting, grooming, testing and evaluating candidates for those roles and on not permitting unqualified and poorly competent officers to take those roles (unless they are willing, and capable, to being 'brought up to speed'). But as well as competent leaders in the operational sense, what is equally important are officers who are value-driven, reflective professionals. Policing is always about values, rights, justice and accountability within a democracy. Without sufficient attention to these elements, the police cannot expect the legitimacy that generates the consent essential to successful policing. A senior officer who neglects this dimension is, in the eyes of the authors, not a true police leader.

One mechanism for giving the senior officer a 'safe space' to reflect and to be challenged on values and decision making is the 'agora' developed in Amsterdam, whereby, outside of the formal structure, the chief weekly consulted and debated with two colleagues who acted as something between devil's advocates and mental coaches (van Dijk et al, 2012; see Appendix). It is an effort to build in confrontational thinking in a positive manner that can aid the chief and keep him or her from making a rash decision and that avoids the pitfalls of group think and other collective distortions (Alison and Crego, 2008). The true leader reflects on the profession of policing and then *leads* the organisation by taking charge, being decisive (which may mean not taking any action), communicating decisions, admitting mistakes, praising achievements, displaying affinity with all ranks and all personnel, motivating and empowering others, making themselves available in a considerate manner and representing the organisation soundly with acumen and presence. And having placed responsibility downwards, *drawing accountability upwards*.

This has to be genuine because police officers are critical and censorious of their leaders – sometimes excessively and even unjustly so – and the chief can never please all of the people all of the time. But if that affinity and commitment is genuine, officers will accept, follow and support the leader. In the Brightlingsea 'animal rights' case, for example, the gold commander went to court to answer to a charge of breaking a local ordinance (banning traffic at certain times), despite legal advice to place the accountability on a lowly constable who had followed instructions to break the ordinance. This was important symbolically in conveying that accountability rose with rank and that the institution did not scapegoat those low in the hierarchy. Insignia of rank – and the accompanying salary – should be symbols of the willingness to embrace accountability and not to hide behind them.

In summary, these demands may combine to make the senior officer role seem impossibly daunting, with its multiple pressures and fluctuation in styles. The view taken here is to accept this as something that goes with the territory and to acknowledge that policing is replete with dilemmas, competing values and conflicting rights, that decisions may never be optimal, and that external evaluation typically focuses on failure and ignores success. In that permanent balancing act, the most to be achieved is probably 'satisficing' through 'good enough' policing that judiciously balances fairness and effectiveness (Bowling, 2008). The authors are also in favour of confrontational thinking, reflexivity and 'thinking outside of the box': but these have to be carefully crafted into the decision-making process in order to be positive, creative and have added value for policies and operations.[6] There are also moments when the diverse ideas and various styles have to crystallise around the decisive leadership that is necessary in operations. This is not to say that 'decisiveness' excludes reflection or that pressure of events should be an excuse for neglecting it, but that it in some dynamic, fast-moving situations it is simply difficult to employ. And for us, rather than settling on one particular style, leadership is best based on a set of skills and competencies that allow different styles to be employed in the appropriate contexts. This patently means that it is of the essence that the leader is confident and competent, aware of the impact of leadership styles, adaptable in style and flexible in command during operations. This makes the senior officer something of a paragon, but a leader should be able to cope if he or is confident and competent. He or she will be confident when they are tried, tested and have achieved competence, and that competence will in turn reinforce confidence. This is not talking of super-human powers, but of solid reliability guaranteed and certified across the service. And while the focus taken here is primarily on senior officers, this process should start early with the 'confident constable' (Gilmour, 2010). This all sounds easy, but it never is. That is why the police institution has to take the responsibility for making this happen: it is an urgent matter both for the individual leader and for the entire organisation as well as for the legitimacy and credibility of policing within our respective societies.

Conclusion

During recent decades, Dutch policing has been characterised by a high investment in 'professionalism' in relation to improving policing practices, investing in people and espousing values (cf *Police in evolution*, CCPC, 2005). In a sense, this process has accelerated precisely in reaction to the system change to the National Police, although it is unclear how precisely the National Police will develop paradigmatically and professionally during the change period of several years. The debate on professionalism in the Netherlands has traditionally been partly tied to the 'emancipation' of the police chief as a professional from political-administrative control. The response to change in the mid-2010s is somehow saying that, even within a new and tighter governance structure, it is vital to remain concerned with professionalism in the sense used in the Dutch debate. And that it is crucial for senior leadership to continue to claim ownership of that process, seeing policing and the leadership within it as value-driven within an accountable democracy. The British police has – variously in the three jurisdictions – also invested heavily in reflecting on both professionalism and police practice for several decades. In recent years, and largely under the Labour Administration (1997-2010) – and with a number of key figures including Sir Hugh Orde (ACPO), Sir Ian Blair (Met), Peter Neyroud (NPIA), Sir Ronnie Flanagan and Denis O'Connor (both of HMIC) – there has been a series of valuable reports, articles and speeches on policing. There was also the impressive BBC Dimbleby Lecture by Blair in 2005 and the publication of the comprehensive and thoughtful Stevens Report (2013). In relation to the particular subject under consideration in this work, the two NPIA reports – Review of police leadership and training' (Neyroud Report, 2011) and *What makes great police leadership* (Campbell and Kodtz, 2011) – are extensive and most valuable. Peter Neyroud in particular, with a number of his colleagues, has played a key role here and has argued for turning policing into a 'real' profession – in terms of formal status, membership, accreditation, ethical standards and governance – with evidence-based knowledge underpinning that professionalism which in turn implies strategic alliances with academia.

As a backcloth, then, there is the changing landscape of contemporary societies and the subsequent shifting architecture of policing systems, and all that has been written on those macro matters by academics, commentators, practitioners and policymakers. Sifting through all that material is beyond the scope of this work, but it has to be kept constantly in mind when considering what sort of leadership that system calls for, as well as what sort of leadership the establishment seems to want. And the key to tackling those questions is to persist in raising the issue 'what matters?'. One might think that this is an issue constantly put to practitioners. But someone with long and intensive contact with British police officers maintains that although this is the primary question he always asks them during simulation exercises and debriefing sessions he holds with police, the typical answer is that no one has ever posed it before. In the complex, demanding and sometimes stressful occupational world they inhabit, pushing the question fruitfully helps to generate rich observations and profound reflections (Jonathan Crego, personal communication). Best thinking drawing on 'what matters?' can, then, greatly enhance best practice.

Notes

[1] Scotland Yard was an early location of the Met and later its current headquarters were named New Scotland Yard. The term is often used to refer to the Met leadership and also to its CID.

[2] In general, UK police websites are excellent and highly informative; Police Scotland's site is available in over 80 languages.

[3] Trenchard had been Chief of the Air Staff and was largely responsible for developing the Royal Air Force in WWI. Later, in 1931, he was appointed Met Commissioner, serving until 1935. He proposed direct recruiting from outside of policing including to an officer's course at the new Hendon Police College, which opened in 1934. This scheme attracted recruits from outside the service as well as from serving officers. However, there was much opposition to it from within and without the police, as it was viewed as too elitist and too close to the military model. It was shelved at the outbreak of WWII and never revived, although it produced a remarkably high proportion of chief officers (Ascoli, 1979).

[4] Occasionally exceptional candidates could rise from the lower ranks and be allowed as an 'external' to take certain courses and graduate from the NPA.

[5] This same tension is visible in the documents leading up to the NP, with *Police in evolution* clearly used as a founding document, but with the importance of better results in terms of crime figures given just as much emphasis.

[6] Paddick (2008, p 324) reports that on the SCC, the group were told that as chief officers they should 'challenge the existing paradigm ... and to literally think outside the perceptual box'. After toeing the line for much of his career, he did precisely that in his last five years and pursued innovative and successful policies, but as these did not suit the populist tabloid press (he was also openly gay) he was labelled 'Britain's most controversial policeman', becoming the target of much hostile publicity and institutional friction.

SIX

Towards a comprehensive paradigm

This book has tackled highly complex issues and has ranged widely. Given their professional backgrounds and working experiences, the authors are well aware of the difficulties of organisational life in general and institutional change in particular, and that policing is by its nature 'accident prone'. Indeed, at times, policing is rather like the religious procession of Echternach in Luxembourg: which was characterised by three steps forward and two steps backwards, except that in policing the number of steps backwards can vary. The preceding chapters have elucidated with a broad brush that the two police systems under consideration – along with others – face challenges emanating from socio-political change, institutional reform, organisational restructuring and constant debate about the direction policing should take. Moreover, police leaders are increasingly confronted with politicians and civilians gaining enhanced control over the police organisation and over the decisions of senior officers. There is near-constant change, involving multiple stakeholders, considerable pressure to achieve improved performance and the need to adjust to more intrusive forms of media scrutiny. Furthermore officers have to learn to cope with new structures of governance.

Beyond cutting crime

The current predicament of policing in the mid–2010s is a matter of some urgency as policing is in rough water. Choices are being made that may determine what policing will look like for the next generation of officers and what policing will mean to people in society, and some of these choices go against a considerable body of knowledge that informs the views of acknowledged experts within academia, policing and criminal justice. The authors have no power to make things happen but come down firmly on the side of an integral paradigm of policing. The distinction made between the 'control' and 'consent' paradigms is simplistic, reductionist and based on a false dichotomy. To argue, for instance, that the only focus for the police is 'control', primarily in the sense of cutting crime, is to do a disservice to the reality of policing and to ignore the accumulated evidence from decades of research. Vacillation between the two paradigms is particularly damaging and a retrograde swing back to control may be destructive of institutional investments and engrained competencies. This would be the case in the Netherlands, which has for three decades specialised in a social-consent model and would have to reskill, or deskill, its workforce in this scenario. It is, moreover, a special conceit of the control paradigm that it is assumed, as a matter of fact, to be a self-sufficient, stand-alone concept. In actual practice, an undue emphasis on control is almost always bought at the cost of the consent paradigm. Behind 'control' is a latent ideology of punitiveness, macho hardness and firmly tackling crime and disorder that decries a softer, 'feminine' touch, perceived as akin to turning police officers into 'social workers'. This ideologically driven rhetoric is a distortion that makes for poor policy. There is no reason why consent cannot be compatible with control and be as 'hard' as necessary when the circumstances demand it, rather than being hard for hardness' sake. In brief, the authors contend that the two paradigms are compatible and complementary, but only when driven largely by the consent paradigm, which generates more options and subtlety in choosing and applying those options. We, therefore, reject control as a dominant, stand-alone concept.

Indeed, referring to Chapter Three on the nature of policing, a credible paradigm will have to do justice to the broad policing function. There is the overwhelming evidence that the police service is not exclusively a law enforcement agency, does not spend most of its time on crime control and only has a limited impact on crime patterns. To impose a blunt 'cut crime' aim on policing is to saddle it with chasing the 'quixotic impossible dream' of reducing crime (Reiner, 2013, p 167). Moreover, crime levels have been dropping for some two decades for a variety of reasons in a range of countries with diverse enforcement strategies and resources, indicating that societal changes rather than police performance have driven the drop. The convincing evidence is that police perform multiple functions and it is not an easy matter to divest those functions. People approach the police for myriad reasons, and it is clearly not the case that officers should respond equally to all these calls for help and advice. But 'problems' do not come with a simple label and issues that the police encounter – say, related to drug use, sex work, mental health, domestic violence or child abuse – all have a potential law enforcement element as well as social welfare and health elements. This brings the police into contact with multiple agencies seeking cooperative solutions (Christie Report, 2011).[1] The philosophy underlying Goldstein's problem-oriented policing was, for example, to tackle problems in cooperation with others in the interest of police not being called to deal repeatedly with the same person with the same problem. But more than self-interest it is a humane and compassionate approach which takes account of the fact that the police as first responders will inevitably be involved with inadequate, disturbed and needy people who are in trouble, (potentially) causing trouble or have been victimised and require help. The dismantling of the welfare state, with cut-backs in provision for such groups, will only exacerbate this demand (O'Hara, 2014). It would be foolhardy to try to dispense with these tasks to concentrate on 'cutting crime' just at the moment when there is a growing awareness of the vulnerability of certain groups – for example, young, disabled and elderly people, and those suffering from mental illness – to exploitation and victimisation (Jones, 2014).

Furthermore, police systems in the UK and in other countries have been transformed in recent years. The 'force' is now a 'service' – one that is much more customer-focused. For example, citizens are encouraged to contact the police via social media, not just in person or by phone, and there is much more of a focus on quality of service through delivery standards that are set in collaboration with stakeholders and measured by periodic surveys. Even though members of the public often have little choice in their dealings with the police, they can still be treated as a certain sort of 'customer' who may expect quality of service. For example, state-of-the-art, open-plan police stations in the Netherlands signify that the 'customer' is welcome and will be treated properly, and much of the work process is also visible. The architecture is designed to convey that the police are there to serve the public and, further, are transparent about what they do (Millie, 2012). Importantly, these new stations are also intelligently designed to be comfortable, well-resourced workplaces. Will these Dutch stations have to be rebuilt, then, if cutting crime becomes the priority? Will the caller to the station, as in some forces in the US, encounter an unwelcoming brick façade with just a small grilled window for contact with a grim-looking police officer? Will the Dutch public be told not to bother the police unless their problem is related to crime – like the formerly crude, unreformed Dutch forces of the past described by Zwart (2004) and van der Vijver (2009)? Will the tag line on the patrol cars be changed to 'National Police: we only cut crime'? And will it return to being known as a 'force' rather than 'service', as happened with the New South Wales (NSW) Police in Australia? The NSW Police had undergone extensive reform, but, in the light of 'panics about public lawlessness', clearly wished to get back to 'business as usual' (Chan and Dixon, 2007). In short, the one-sided, reductionist, 'only cut crime' model is undesirable, if not damaging, and the authors propose an integral, 'comprehensive' paradigm not just out of conviction but largely because it is strongly supported by the body of research evidence. In addition, paradigms are not only intrinsically value-driven but also carry with them an implicit 'contract' between the police as the visible and powerful representatives of the state and the public as to how the public will be policed: and, indeed, between the police organisation and its officers as to what is expected of them and how they will be treated. Driving this thinking is, then, the evidence on the importance of the relationship between the police and the public.

Symbolic value of policing

Every police–public contact is in a sense symbolic of the interaction between the state and its citizens, and is potentially a 'learning moment'. And what citizens want from representatives of the state is to be taken seriously and treated with respect (see the Appendix and the Policing for London Study). They are not exclusively satisfied by favourable outcomes but will accept other outcomes if they receive an explanation about their case while sensing the police have made a serious effort on their behalf (Hough, 2014). Implicit in that is a model of procedural justice and there is evidence that those treated according to such a model are more positive about the police and more willing to cooperate with them. This is of the essence, as consent leading to information, cooperation and compliance is the life-blood of policing (Tyler, 2011). Without them, crimes and other matters are difficult to solve and resolve. Importantly, there is also evidence that if police officers are treated according to procedural justice, they, in turn, are more likely to treat people fairly and with consideration. This is of significance, given that there is evidence in the UK of poor morale and of officers feeling demoralised about the work and organisation, and being pressurised and intimidated in the workplace (*Guardian*, 24 December 2014; Hough, 2014).

Given much of what has been said here, there follows a strong preference for mainstream policing being conducted by full-time warranted officers. Although Police Community Support Officers and 'special' constables (unpaid, volunteer, part-time officers) in Britain – or the civilian volunteers, patrol officers with limited powers (*surveillanten*) and town patrols (*toezichthouders*) in the Netherlands – can be useful in support roles, it remains the case that handling a serious situation requires someone with powers, authority and experience, which means a fully trained professional officer. Bayley (1994) has said, tongue in cheek, that much policing could be done by a boy scout and most detective work by an insurance agent; this is correct up to a point with some routine matters, but it is the situations that are complex, dangerous, unclear in outcome and demand knowledge, judgement and experience that require a warranted officer. Indeed, police are called to intervene in conflict situations because of their power and authority and precisely because they are *not* scouts. We have to be wary of downsizing policing functions (Millie, 2013) and of a 'McDonaldisation' and deskilling of policing that implies that almost anyone can do it; in reality, it forms a unique craft that cannot be 'infantilised' (Sennet, 2008). Police have exceptional powers and vital responsibilities that cannot be viewed lightly and cannot be exercised by someone who is not adequately trained. Brodeur (2010) presents a strong case that this should not be done, and in practice predominantly is not done, by private police.

Reflective practitioners and honest policing

What the authors propose is generating a virtuous circle of an intelligent, reflexive, responsive service that fosters consent from the public, and which, in turn, elicits the crucial factor of compliance. The lubrication for that is trust, which is something that has to be earned continually, and can be lost rapidly following an operation gone wrong or a critical incident that indicates system failure. Indeed, in US policing, trust has become central in President Obama's Task Force on 21st Century Policing (2014). Clearly, the benign-sounding 'broken windows' approach has fostered in the US since the mid-1990s a preoccupation with minor offences, which, allied to crude pressure for results, has led to large numbers of young males from disadvantaged minority communities being arrested, sanctioned and incarcerated (Greenberg, 2014). Moreover, this robust enforcement has been reinforced by increasing use of military resources, weaponry and tactics in the dominant interest of crime suppression, which may lead to the alienation of entire communities (Manning, 2010). The accumulated grievances generated by this have brought about the crisis of trust confronting many police forces in the US that is dividing communities and fostering societal unrest. Given, then, this vital importance of trust – gaining it and restoring it when it is dented or lost – leads to arguing strongly for what (Bayley, 1994) calls 'honest policing'. The essence of this is to lay out openly and with good arguments what the service can do and cannot do. Police leaders have to learn to be clear, consistent and unambivalent. For the police organisation is an institution of the state that can interfere directly in the lives of citizens, deprive them of their freedom and, if necessary, deprive them of their lives. On the one hand, this implies serious attention to human and civil rights; but, on the other hand, it also requires being open and 'honest' with citizens. Hence police chiefs need to be able to spell out unambiguously that policing is a service primarily geared to the needs of the public; that if threatened officers may, as a last resort, use force or even lethal violence; that during public order disturbances officers may use appropriate force and may deprive people of their freedom; and that in relation to crime control it may be necessary for officers to stop and question people who turn out to be perfectly innocent of any offence. Of the essence is to convey that these tasks are part of the policing mandate and will be conducted with professionalism, transparency and accountability.

This is being honest so that the public, and the police themselves, do not confuse the vital social task of the police as being incompatible with essential and necessarily 'hard' control tasks. A great deal of commotion, for instance, is caused when the public is not quickly and fully informed following a controversial incident, such as a fatal shooting of a suspect who turns out to be unarmed. This is particularly the case if disinformation or leaks distort the picture. This happened with the Hillsborough disaster which, with a new inquest in 2014 into the deaths opening 25 years after the disaster, has seriously scarred the reputation of policing because of the fabrication of 'black propaganda'. Honesty is also required in the delicate, intricate and prolonged negotiations that are required to generate community safety programmes. Here senior officers must take care not to raise unduly high expectations among diverse stakeholders; honesty is not a case of promising what you cannot deliver.

Police leaders must also be honest with essential front-line workers engaged in primary service delivery, who make some of the most important decisions in the organisation. This involves acknowledging that the leadership of the organisation recognises the vital work they do in delivering services to the community; and that senior officers identify with those functions and will do all they can to provide adequate resources and training, to ensure continuity of personnel and supervisory staff, to coordinate efforts with specialised units and to grant the autonomy and discretion, within clear guidelines, needed to adapt to local needs and demands. That in turn requires a genuine investment by leaders who personally carry the message with conviction and invest socially and institutionally in the primary processes through sound, sensible management. The experience of developing change and inculcating values in organisations is that this has to be supported from the top and has to 'live' in the organisation; this means it must be resourced, encouraged and rewarded, with the senior personnel leading the way.

Comprehensive paradigm

In essence, this discussion refers to the central significance of integrity, legality, professionalism, transparency and accountability in policing, allied to sound and sensible management. These should be core institutional values that are followed as a matter of course and implemented by leaders as simply the right thing to do, and leaders are vital to fostering and personifying these values. There is evidence from a swathe of organisations that leaders set the tone and that people look upwards for cues as to what sort of values underpin organisational practice and culture (Srivastva, 1988; Walton, 1988; Robinson and Smith, 2014). These core values are, moreover, ones that a force may claim to have but, importantly, has to deliver convincingly at a moment of need. Abiding by these values also builds a form of credit, or insurance policy, that can be of value when trust is at risk and the record can be produced to convince public opinion, and the regulators, that a force abided by those norms and standards. In that sense, it is a form of enlightened self-interest. For when trust is contested or is at risk of being withdrawn, honest policing should be able to convince stakeholders of the forces' and its leaders' good intentions by drawing on a sound record. But it is far better that these values and practices 'run through the bloodstream of the whole body of a police service', as the Patten Report (1999) recommended for accountability in policing.

Patten also argued for policing in Northern Ireland to be embedded in human rights, and Manning (2010) engages in a strong plea, referring to Rawls, for policing to be concerned fundamentally with justice, becoming a force for good while committing as little harm as possible. It can be argued, however, that there is a broad tendency, even in liberal societies, to revert to tougher enforcement policies. Then the danger is that an adversarial relationship between the public and the police develops – where police officers 'kick ass' and are viewed as an army of occupation – and the organisation 'regresses to the mean'. Encouraged and rewarded by an 'only cut crime' regime, police can become the 'lean, mean crime-fighting machine' (Loader, 2014, p 43) beloved of the populist Right and certain hard-line officers. It is clear that that can be considered a serious and dangerous distortion of all that healthy policing should represent as an accountable, socially engaged, rights-respecting service in democratic society.

Drawing on all that has been set out in this book, the authors propose a **comprehensive paradigm** that is built around three main pillars of policing:

- **Crime and security management** in the widest sense: criminal investigations, preparing prosecutions and appearing in court (depending on jurisdiction), crime prevention, forensics and scene of crime work, counter-terrorism, organised crime, transnational policing, internal investigations, and external investigations (for other governments and agencies at home and abroad).
- **Social welfare and community outreach** tasks based on inter-agency cooperation; attention for vulnerable groups with public health risks and open to victimisation: the whole area of community, problem and neighbourhood-oriented policing, family liaison, and community engagement. The police response to calls from the public has a crucial support function for citizens and all police services – such as those concerned with sudden deaths (including cot deaths), road accidents, civil emergencies and disasters, domestic violence – should be driven by service delivery standards that are generated together with the relevant stakeholders and monitored though periodic surveys.
- **Order maintenance** in the widest sense, including public order situations, sport and events management, emergencies and disaster management, large-scale searches, high-level political visits or meetings, and so on.

These should be seen as three essential, equally important and interlinked elements. They should be formally acknowledged and firmly rooted in a comprehensive paradigm that integrates consent with control, but with consent having primacy. The Stevens Report (2013), for example, recommends having the 'social welfare' dimension adopted in law as a central police function. This has nothing to do with being 'soft' on crime, as tackling crime in the widest sense will always remain pivotal. An over-emphasis on crime control and maintaining order, however, runs the risk of destroying trust and alienating segments of the population – think of Brixton in 1981. And undue focus on a single category obscures the unavoidable links between the three pillars of the paradigm. The social cement that unites the pillars and glues the integral paradigm is a rights-respecting, holistic and accountable approach rooted in the philosophy that in a democratic society police can only function effectively and legitimately with the consent, trust

– and *compliance* – of the public. This brings us to Manning's (2014, p 26) assertion that public policing is a service based on trust.

That has been the guiding theme throughout this work and has led to an emphasis on the complexity and intricacy of the police agency's tasks and responsibilities. These are not served by a regression to a servile and subservient relationship with the authorities, a narrowing of the mandate or with increasing 'Taylorisation' of the lower ranks. Here, then, the police organisation is viewed as a complex service agency that delivers a bevy of services based around ensuring safety, promoting tranquillity, combating disorder, supporting citizens at times of need and coping with and preventing crime. In order to achieve this, it has to have legitimacy and credibility, which means abiding by the democratic rule of law, due process, impartiality, integrity and accountability, and by negotiating 'policing by consent', which generates the essential ingredient of trust (Tyler, 2007).

Conclusion

The path to earning and retaining trust is honest, solid, nuanced policing founded on delivering the promise of the comprehensive paradigm with its three constituent pillars in a highly professional manner 'without fear or favour' and driven by a values-based philosophy of policing. Throughout this work, the authors have combatted simplistic and reductionist views of policing by emphasising the complexity of the tasks that face police, the need for the organisation and its leaders – at all levels – to be prepared to shift instantly from devolved to central 'command and control' mode and the exceptional powers and unique mandate that bring with them constant scrutiny and a permanent requirement to be held accountable. There remains our deep concern about police being pushed to take too many steps backwards so that the organisation 'regresses to the mean', making the steps forwards near unattainable. In all, leadership – at every level – is essential and at the higher levels needs to be soundly rooted in competent and confident professionalism with an ability to reflect on the nature and dilemmas of policing. In that complex and demanding arena, the strongest asset for an embattled but self-respecting profession is a sound and convincing comprehensive paradigm founded on 'what matters in policing?'.

Notes

[1] The topic of law enforcement and public health has been promoted by Professor Nick Crofts at the Centre for Law Enforcement and Public Health, University of

Melbourne, with conferences in Melbourne (2012) and Amsterdam (2014); see www.cleph.com.au. The latter was partly sponsored by the Amsterdam Unit of the National Police and the Amsterdam Public Health Service, with the Free University (Talma Institute) as co-convenor.

Appendix

This Appendix is divided into two parts. Part One comprises two case studies – one from the UK and one from the US – illustrating how difficult it is to deliver service under the community policing label, hereafter referred to as 'COP', and how this reveals deep ambivalences within policing. Part Two contains an outline of 'agora', a safe haven for confrontational thinking, in Amsterdam.[1] Police employ concepts that are vague and infinitely elastic but that promise to take the public seriously and to accommodate their needs. As the case study from the UK shows, the structure and functioning of the Met undermines the institution's espoused goals and its implicit contract with the people of London, and, importantly, it demonstrates what Londoners want from their police. In Seattle we can see that the promise to implement COP is highly dependent on what is meant by 'community' and the nature of the community being policed. We also learn that while COP is marketed in the US as the defining concept in American policing of recent decades, it is hardly ever wholeheartedly supported throughout the organisation and is rarely adequately evaluated. Manning (2010) portrays this at length. Hence policing runs the danger of constantly promising what it cannot deliver, and if it does make a serious effort – as in Chicago (Skogan, 2004) – a change of wind in the administration can thwart or reverse that effort. To a considerable extent, that reversal is evident in the UK and the Netherlands. The rhetoric remains the same, but the reality is that in several societies less effort than before is being put into COP-related activities.

Agora in the Netherlands moves attention to a different level within the organisation. It was mentioned in Chapter Five that some police leaders feel they were not adequately prepared for senior positions; and that senior officers in England and Wales feel they needed to be better prepared for the chief officer level and chief constable function (Caless, 2011). Taking this into consideration, agora is a means of supporting the chief individually in decision making by offering thinking space and 'breathing space'. It does, however, require the chief to display courage in entering a dialogue that he or she may not be comfortable with but that – if operated properly, and there are delicate balances to be made – can aid in improving the quality of decision making for the chief and for her or his institution. All three cases have various implications for reform, paradigms, implementation of change and leadership.

Part One: Two cases of why COP falls short of its promise: London and Seattle

UK: Policing for London Study

The Metropolitan Police Service of London (MPS) is the largest force in the UK with about 33,000 officers for around 7.5 million inhabitants. Policing the capital brings with it unusual problems. Its size and the complexity of the tasks involved makes it unlike most other police forces in the country. Yet millions of people, from very diverse origins, live and work in London and have to be policed as ordinary citizens with local, everyday problems related to the very diverse areas they live in. What do Londoners think about their police, what do they want them to do and what do the police think about their work? These questions were answered by Fitzgerald and colleagues (2002) in their Policing for London Study (PFLS). Their data can be compared with a survey from 20 years previously, but both pieces of research have to be put into context.

For in 1981 heavy-handed policing in the racially mixed area of Brixton sparked severe rioting. In his report on the disturbances, Lord Scarman (1981) argued for a stronger emphasis on policing by the consent of the public and by involvement in the community. This became the orthodoxy for policing during the 1980s. In the wake of his report, the Policy Studies Institute (PSI) (Smith and Gray, 1985) conducted a survey of the public and the police. At the time, this caused a lot of consternation, as there were reports of racism, sexism, poor supervision and rule bending among officers while a substantial minority of the population voiced serious allegations of misconduct against the police (for example, using undue violence and manipulating evidence). There can be little doubt that some officers were racist in opinion and behaviour. Since then, there has been an effort to reduce discrimination, to recruit more police from minorities and to be more aware of policing a 'diverse' population. Then in 1993 a black youth, Stephen Lawrence, was murdered in London in an unprovoked attack by a group of young white men. As mentioned in Chapter One, various failures led to a public inquiry that accused the MPS of 'institutional racism' (Macpherson, 1999). Effectively since then the MPS has been trying to gear its policing to working with a diverse population in a 'professional' manner, free of prejudice.

The PFLS looks at opinions about policing London as well as comparing that data with the original PSI findings. The PFLS data were based on a representative sample of the adult London population, weighted to contain more black and Asian respondents, case studies of three 'boroughs' (police and local government districts), focus groups and interviews, and some statistical material (including the London sub-sample of the 2000 British Crime Survey). We present the main finding below.

- *Fear of crime had not substantially risen in 20 years.* But anxiety was high in poor areas and Londoners of minority ethnic origin expressed more concern than other Londoners given the high crime rates and fear of racial attacks prevalent in their neighbourhoods. What had increased was concern with 'incivilities' – street drug dealing and the accompanying litter of used needles, disorderly teenagers, graffiti, vandalism and accumulated rubbish. Respondents wanted the police to reassure them about protection from the threat of crime and disorder.
- In particular, respondents wanted *a more visible and responsive police agency that was engaged with the local community.* There were differences related to age and ethnic origin; young people and those from minorities were understandably less keen on foot patrol than others as they were more likely to be stopped. Yet the vast majority believed that the police should have powers to stop and search suspects. Stop and search tactics have been widely criticised as it is held that minorities tend to be prime targets for control; indeed, resistance to them sparked the Brixton disturbances in 1981. The respondents did, however, argue for stops that were soundly based on grounds of reasonable suspicion as well as for more scrutiny of others from outside their territory. It was also noticeable that black respondents were more resentful than others of being stopped. This wide support for stop and search sounds surprising until one appreciates that many respondents in poor areas are themselves likely to be victims of crime.
- *Respondents want more police but a different police*, in other words officers who engage with the local community and with whom they can interact in a non-confrontational way.
- *Over a third of Londoners sought some sort of help from the police in the period 1999-2000.* More than half of those who sought help did so in relation to a crime but almost the same percentage had other reasons, such as reporting noise or disturbances. Victims of crime were generally satisfied with the police response, but the percentages for 'most satisfied' had fallen, and for 'dissatisfied' had risen in the 20 years. Dissatisfaction arose from feelings that the police displayed a lack of interest or too little effort; the 'result' was not as important as

having police who showed interest and kept complainants informed about their case.

- *A quarter of Londoners were approached by the police.* Generally this was when the person stopped was in a car or on foot. Many young men under 35 had experience of being stopped by the police and this was especially true for young black males. The best demographic predictor of being stopped was young, black, single and working class. Fewer people were stopped than in the early 1980s, but more Asians were subject to control. The majority of respondents were happy with police behaviour during controls but those who were young or lived in poor areas, or were from minority ethnic backgrounds, were more likely to be dissatisfied than others. A third of the sample of respondents stated that they or someone they knew were really annoyed by police conduct; the best predictor for this was being black, young, middle class and owning a car (owning a car increased the likelihood of being subject to control and being middle class meant the individual affected was more likely to resent being selected for police attention).

- *Confidence in the police had fallen in 20 years.* Fewer respondents felt that the police did a 'very good job' and more considered that they did a bad job; but this decline has been witnessed more widely in British police forces and not just in London. In focus groups there were strong feelings among young people, of all ethnic origins and in various areas, that police activity was biased against them. About a third of the sample thought the police treated ethnic minorities unfairly and this had risen since 1983; but most people thinking this were white (minority views were fairly stable). There had been a rise in willingness to help the police, and more people from minorities were prepared to consider joining the police.

- Police views of their relationship with the public tended to be based on a perception of areas where residents were willing to cooperate with them. Those living in deprived, high-crime areas were seen as negative in their response to the police and this was compounded by the fact that calls for assistance in those areas were often confrontational. *Many officers were frustrated at their inability to respond to people's needs and to provide the quality of service they expected.*

- Within the police organisation there was pressure, they lamented, to meet targets that were not very relevant to most of the local calls they answered, there was too much paper work and teams were short-staffed. They were also often critical of management. They felt they were in a no-win situation, with different sections of the local community who *saw them as biased in favour of other ethnic groups.*

There was a high chance that encounters with residents from ethnic minority communities would result in claims of discrimination so there was even a tendency to avoid contact with these groups. Officers were often moved around London and found it difficult to adjust to the new groups they encountered in different boroughs (there had been a rise in the number of immigrants from countries in the Middle East during the previous years). Senior officers were caught between central demands and the needs of local residents; often they had little chance to get to know their personnel and to keep up morale and performance.

The broad thrust of the PFLS findings is that in 2000 Londoners found their police less responsive, less visible, less accessible and less engaged with the community than they would like. In essence, nearly everyone wants more police, but with a different style; and officers would like to adjust to the needs and demands of the public. So why isn't that happening? There are various reasons for this.

- *Crime has been falling* since the mid-1990s (except for street robberies, often recently of mobile phones). In some ways, then, the workload had not become heavier except perhaps in terms of involvement in multi-agency cooperation.
- *The public's expectations had doubtless risen* as a result of the police positioning itself more as a service organisation, and of the rise in public sector consumerism.
- *Police resources had dwindled* and the MPS had lost many experienced officers to outside forces where the work is less hazardous and housing is cheaper.
- *Relentless government pressure* to abide by centrally set performance measures, with an emphasis on crime fighting, had limited the capacity of the local police to react to community needs.
- *The MPS is a highly centralised organisation* that restricts local commanders' discretion in policing their own boroughs; furthermore, the crime-fighting focus and the reaction to many forms of crime had led to the establishment of *specialised units*, which has drawn experienced personnel away from the uniformed branch.
- Officers in focus groups were *cynical about 'management'* because the emphasis on centralisation and quantitative targets disempowered middle managers and demoralised their staff (although it must be said that such cynicism is almost universal in police culture).
- *Training was held to be inadequate* for the situations encountered on the streets of London; there was much *turnover of senior staff* who

were often moved after short periods in a borough resulting in a lack of continuity and leadership.

All these factors accumulated to foster a large measure of dissatisfaction among officers; they felt unsupported by their senior managers, under-rewarded and under-resourced. This is a sombre picture, but we suspect it is true of many large, urban forces. Policing has becoming increasingly complex in many ways and especially in relation to the diversity in communities. While many commentators would argue that the police should be investing in the COP paradigm with serious and professional attention to local needs, successive governments (first under the Conservatives from the 1980s but just as firmly under Labour from 1997 to 2010 and even more so under the Conservative-Liberal Democrat coalition since 2010) have chosen a crime-fighting focus. This, coupled with an emphasis on quantitative performance measures, represents an alternative, centrally imposed paradigm that limits local police discretion and undermines efforts to implement COP in the various districts.

What do the authors propose as a solution? They argue for improved local consultation; focusing particularly on the 'incivilities' that disturb people; a more visible and accessible police presence on the streets but with a clear sense of purpose and not just as symbolic 'reassurance'; reinforcing the capacity of officers to respond to calls with better integration of specialist and generalist work; giving local managers more autonomy with increased flexibility to respond to local needs; and more commitment to multi-agency partnerships.

It could be said that there is nothing new here. The PFLS project has two main conclusions. First, there is *a legacy of discrimination and over-policing* that overshadows relations with black people but this is related to the cycle of poverty, deprivation and high-crime rates in areas where minorities tend to live; as the police focus disproportionately on the young they often get locked into adversarial and confrontational contacts with minority youth (black but also Asian). It is crystal clear that *the police in isolation cannot achieve better relations with minorities* and this has to be a concerted effort by many agencies. Second, *the police cannot be effective in tackling crime unless they re-engage with the public.* The use of quantitative performance measures geared to a narrow range of targets imposes short-term thinking while ignoring the interconnection between crime, disorder and incivilities; it also draws resources away from activities that win the trust of local people. Yet the police depend on that trust if they are to be well informed about local patterns of crime and disorder. And they can only effectively tackle crime and disorder when local people are willing to play an active role in the identification and prosecution of those involved.

Although London is an exceptional city, many police officers and others will recognise the dilemmas facing the police there as mirroring in some ways the problems they encounter in other towns and regions. Here are some general reflections on the material presented by PFLS. What strikes one immediately is how the police organisation is wrestling with dilemmas and solutions that have been circulating for at least 20 years. The underlying ideas of COP, and POP (problem-oriented policing), have been familiar since the work of Goldstein (1977, 1979) and others, and seem to be periodically rediscovered, reinvented and regurgitated. So one has to be wary of double-speak. COP is, then, infinitely elastic and may be misused to fit all sizes (Brogden, 2005). For over 20 years, research has been telling us that people in communities want a visible, approachable responsive, 'local' police; and many police chiefs and politicians have been promising to deliver that 'new-style' policing. What, then, hampers implementation? The two major hurdles are politicians and police management.

Politicians are increasingly fixated on crime and crime reduction and make demands on the police that the police cannot deliver. Every first-year undergraduate lecture on crime control informs the students that the police alone can do very little to reduce crime; but politicians continue to ignore the overwhelming evidence for this. Neoliberal thinking with a focus on targets, ranking and quantification has amplified this one-sided governmental thrust and distorted policing. Police managers are caught between the crime control model and the community involvement model. In theory, these should not be incompatible; indeed, the PFLS report, along with much other material, maintains that they are interlinked and complementary. But there are two factors that make it difficult to deliver both adequately. One is that the police organisation itself is obsessed with crime control; its culture is primarily geared to 'catching crooks' and even to denigrating other policing efforts as 'soft' and as marginal to the 'core business'. And the other is that police managers are often not very good at the balancing act. In London, you have a population that wants more and better policing and officers who want to deliver that, but the organisation and management are the stumbling blocks: too centralised, too specialised, too many changes, not enough resources, senior managers who are too distant and middle managers with too little power. All this may be related to the size of the organisation and the complexity of the tasks but there is also an element of top management simply not being able to solve these glaring dilemmas.

US: Seattle

The US study by Herbert (2006) is on a much smaller scale than the PFLS. It uses observation and interviews to examine closely one particular part of Seattle. In essence, Herbert conveys that the promise of COP cannot readily be delivered. It may be the case that COP has become the essential buzzword for US policing in the past few decades, with the Federal Government investing billions of dollars in it, but Herbert looks at what COP actually means to citizens and to police officers. In a nutshell, he makes the following observations about the delivery of COP in a mixed part of Seattle with an affluent settlement, a less affluent segment and a fairly poor area.

- Respondents tended to have a traditional, nostalgic view of a harmonious 'community' which in fact no longer exists alongside increasing individualism.
- The more affluent citizens saw the notion of community largely in terms of home ownership, taking care of their property, knowing their neighbours and their neighbours' children through shared schools and a sense of security arising from stability and a willingness to help one another.
- This perception was less prevalent in the less affluent area, where many residents rented property and where there was a high turnover of population, and even less so for the third area with much public housing and an accumulation of 'social problems' including street crime and many calls for police assistance. Both of the less affluent areas were seen as 'transient', with the latter one having a reputation for being disreputable and unsafe.
- Even in the affluent area the depth of 'community' interaction and cohesion was not high: people talked about community but apart from ritual occasions they largely valued their privacy and kept to themselves.
- Those residents most likely to engage with COP comprised a small handful of active, citizens who were white, middle-class and educated, and owned their own homes. The more problem-ridden the area, the less likely were its citizens to contribute, sometimes because of fear of retaliation from notorious troublemakers who appeared successfully to evade retribution.
- Attendance at COP meetings was low and it was nearly always the same people who turned up. The more educated and articulate the citizens were the more likely they could get something done, yet their area had the least problems.

- They typically came to the meetings with fairly mundane issues related to safety and a sense of security in their specific locality.
- The attending officer would come in full uniform and the accompanying equipment, would be sympathetic but often try to explain why external forces (the mayor, other local government agencies, budgets, and so on) prevented him or her from tackling many of their problems.
- The interaction tended to be that the officer deflected any real interference that impinged on his own professional authority and that of the police department while the citizens routinely deferred to this stance. In body language and communication he was effectively refuting the conception that in some way he and the police were *subservient* to their needs.
- In interviews, citizens explained that it took a great deal of time and effort to effect any positive change in their communities. This was tiring and frustrating, but generally accepted, given the low level of engagement among residents in general. There was little evidence of 'co-production' and 'partnership'.
- In short, Herbert is saying that nowhere – even in the most likely area – was the reality of 'community' strong enough to mobilise a solid, consistent and challenging agenda to present to the police. Equally, the police force was not fully committed to COP.
- COP was but one segment within the uniformed branch. It was almost universally looked down upon by other officers, who saw their COP colleagues as a 'soft', office hours, coffee-drinking, meeting-oriented group that had lost touch with 'real' policing; community officers were derided as 'social workers' and as such 'feminised'. In one US force, neighbourhood-oriented policing' (NOP), was referred to as 'No-one On Patrol'.
- Most other officers were geared to the traditional police culture based on danger, suspicion, solidarity, excitement and a masculine stance of authority and social distance from citizens. They looked for non-conforming behaviour in predictable hot-spots, precisely where most of the social problems were located – problems which COP was ostensibly helping to ameliorate – and they welcomed the chase and the arrest of a suspect. They were often abrasive and authoritarian and their occasional excesses, conveyed by the media, damaged the reputation of the force and undermined the credit built up by the COP officers. Their attitude sometimes rubbed off on COP officers, who attempted to create the impression that they too were geared for action and looking to make arrests, doubtless

to prove to themselves and others that they were still 'real' police officers.

- For many officers, the COP assignment was likely to be temporary, and they would expect to return to mainstream policing. If there was some notion that COP personnel would stay around and somehow become embedded in the community then the reality was that they soon moved on ("They change them officers like you change underwear", according to one respondent).

- Observations revealed that the police organisation was not finely tuned to coherent and consistent policies and practices, but was more like a poorly integrated network of loosely coupled systems. There was much room for individual autonomy so a lot depended on the motivation and skill of an individual officer as to how he or she fulfilled their tasks. There was an evident lack of coordination between COP and the rest of the organisation that was never resolved, and a sense of 'organisational disarray' leading to an 'intractable problem' that was never dealt with: 'The community is thus demoted to a mere "information provider", as the "eyes and ears of the police".... When the police employ this narrative of crime control and its possible eradication, they downplay the robust role for citizen involvement that community policing represents' (Herbert, 2006, p 108).

Effectively, Herbert concludes that there is not enough 'community' to generate serious citizen involvement in COP and not enough genuine institutional investment in COP from the police department to deliver its promise adequately. He states that 'urban neighbourhoods cannot bear the weight of responsibility that programmes like community policing are meant to place upon them' and 'various internal dynamics limit the capacity of the police to engage in genuine partnerships with community organizations', while 'the police's social world ... underwrites a robust resistance to community policing' (Herbert, 2006, pp 13-14).

Although COP has been called the 'most important development in policing in the last quarter of a century' (Skogan and Roth, 2004), it has rarely been properly implemented. There have been serious efforts in certain societies and forces at certain times, but if we take Manning's concept of landing the police with the intractable problem of tackling crime, COP faces a twin intractable problem in the difficulty of delivering COP to citizens, partly because 'community' is rarely there and partly because the police organisation, and especially its political environment, remain deeply ambivalent about it.

Part Two: Netherlands, Amsterdam: agora, safe haven for confrontational thinking

Police organisations in Western societies are facing multiple challenges that leave little room for reflection on current issues or anticipate future developments. The risk is that police leaders will overlook important matters and inadvertently land in trouble. Reflecting on these complex developments, the Amsterdam Police (then a regional force) decided in 2006 to create a strategically positioned 'safe haven' where thinking – and contradicting – could flourish (van Dijk et al, 2011, 2012). Everyone concerned was aware of the pitfalls of decision making in organisations and was conscious that such a scheme would be difficult to implement. The initiative was called Agora Police and Security, an *agora* being the central spot in ancient Greek cities for debate and civic activities. Here it signified a 'marketplace of ideas'. In practice, the agora consists of two advisers to the Chief Commissioner (*hoofdcommissaris*). The experiment has brought forth some do's and don'ts related to encouraging contradicting in a police organisation. The authors will sketch the agora concept and the experiences of the first five years during which its functioning began to draw on the critical 'best thinking' ideas of Cartwright and Shearing (2013) as illustrated in *Where's the chicken?*. The cornerstone of agora was scheduled weekly sessions with the police chief (*korpschef*) (then Bernard Welten) and the two strategic advisers (Auke van Dijk and Frank Hoogewoning). Anything could be discussed, the initiative could lie with the chief or with the advisers, and there was no fixed agenda. Above all, thoughts and opinions were expressed freely, which required considerable mutual trust. The essence was to 'break open' day-to-day operations and reflect on how things were going and where they were – or should be – heading. Without an agenda the meetings often became 'personal' as they were also about the drives of various stakeholders, obstacles to decision making and performance, loose thinking, comprehending societal developments, matters of personal conscience and public ethics and teasing vague concerns to the surface.

During these meetings, there were three principles at work. First, the emphasis was on analysing how things work and why, as a basis for developing and enhancing strategic goals. Agora was an unashamedly *analytical* arena. Second, there was a premium on contradicting and on advocating opposing views. The style was *confrontational*. Third, the discussion was *value-driven*, which meant that practice and operations were evaluated with close regard to the philosophy and principles of the rule of law. These choices could heat up the debate because it was not only operational or intellectual capabilities at stake but also moral standards. The meetings sometimes felt like a weekly performance interview, for the advisers and the chief, and at times sleep was lost over matters that were raised. The weekly sessions were also the basis for extra meetings, mostly exchanging thoughts on urgent matters with strategic implications. The frequent interaction was the basis for agora's influence, which was curiously enhanced by it not having any formal power. It was crucial that the advisers were in a so-called 'free role' so they could pick up on activities deemed necessary or interesting. These agora meetings were anchored in a 'critical thinking architecture' with three main pillars.

First, the agora was positioned as an 'intellectual playground' with academics as advisers, signalling that reflection was highly valued within the organisation. The Amsterdam Police and City of Amsterdam had together funded a chair with a related research group on 'security and citizenship' at the Free University of Amsterdam, which fostered an easy exchange of ideas and insights between academia and police. The group's research was 'independent and relevant', provocative research was stimulated and two police officers were part of the research group for one-year periods. The agora was positioned as a pivotal node in this development, which conveyed an important message in an institution with an underlying DNA based on 'doing' always trumps 'thinking'. Second, there was an open relationship within the organisation. The agora worked as a focal point for strategic projects and other initiatives with labels like 'academic', 'creative' and 'independent'. On many occasions, the advisers to agora were marginally involved in projects and were an important bridge between 'content' and 'management'. A central method was 'strategic explorations' that combined professional knowledge, academic insights and high-level support and became an important instrument in linking up with operational policing. What a strategic exploration exactly *is* and *how* it is organised varies, but the process of getting there was more important. Depending on the subject, external stakeholders were included, research was done, high potentials in the service were appointed as responsible, teams were formed and concrete action taken. So, as opposed to what was normally done – start with a concrete goal and define a position and structure – there was nothing more than a vague notion followed by a process of inspiring people to begin shaping the answer. Interestingly enough, the definitional process took up most of the time and probably was the most important yield of the exploration, as it was one of intense interaction with many people and drawing in many spheres of knowledge and experience. Third, the agora actively sought the outsider perspective. This meant fostering curiosity and a feeling for weak signals, encouraging transparency and actively engaging in diverse arenas. In 2007, for instance, the Amsterdam Police set up the *Juxta* project (from juxtaposition), whereby 12 promising academics from diverse disciplines were allowed to study whatever they wanted to for 18 months, providing it challenged the organisation's assumptions. *Juxta* has had an important impact on the organisation and on how the organisation is viewed externally.

The thinking behind agora was that thought, reflection, diversity and engagement with adversarial argument actually enhances operational performance. Based on the Amsterdam experience, the following design principles for an agora as a safe haven for thinking and contradicting may be identified.

- Within agora, content was the central element. Organisational power was absent; it was the strength of argument that tipped the balance. Furthermore, the activities did not directly affect the existing division of responsibilities in the organisation.
- The agora was and has to be protected space in which bureaucratic interests play no part. There was always a constant danger that it would be sucked into the mainstream organisation, where it simply would have become a regular strategy department.
- Agora was independent. In the Amsterdam experiment, the employees were encouraged to be forceful and critical professionals and this was directly related to the chief, who was deeply committed to it.
- Agora was positioned close to the top of the organisation, but the advisers were not part of the management team; this required a permanent balancing act about roles and functions.

Creating and maintaining a safe haven for thinking and contradicting in a complex, executive organisation with diverse tasks and multiple stakeholders may at times feel hazardous. An agora generates friction, and independent thinking can easily be perceived as a threat to the current power structure and stereotypical thinking. But given the complexity and dynamics of current societies, not to organise critical thinking within an executive, emergency organisation that is by the nature of its work 'accident prone', seems unduly risky if not irresponsible. In short, the Amsterdam experiment is based on the philosophy that best thinking precedes best practice and that leaders should be reflective practitioners. The authors are convinced that an agora is also a mechanism that can help any police chief out of getting into troubled waters, professionally as well as personally, by institutionalising an adversarial arena for best thinking.

Note

[1] The first piece is adapted from Punch (2004); the second is also by Punch, but is unpublished; and the third is a revised version of van Dijk et al (2012).

References

ACPO (Association of Chief Police Officers) (2009) *Guidance on command and control*, London: NPIA.

ACPO (2010) *Risk principles*, London: NPIA.

Adeney, M. and Lloyd, J. (1986) *The miners' strike*, London: Routledge and Kegan Paul.

Adlam, R. and Villiers, P. (2003) *Police leadership in the 21st century*, Winchester: Waterside Press.

Aigner, G. (2011) *Leadership beyond good intentions. What it takes to really make a difference*, Crow's Nest: Allen & Unwin.

Alderson, J. (1979) *Policing freedom*, Plymouth: Macdonald & Evans.

Alison, L. and Crego, J. (eds) (2008) *Policing critical incidents*, Cullompton: Willan.

Allason, R. (1983) *The branch*, London: Secker and Warburg.

Allum, F. and Gilmour, S. (eds) (2012) *Routledge handbook of transnational organized crime*, Abingdon/New York, NY: Routledge.

Anckar, C. (2008) 'On the applicability of the most similar systems design and the most different systems design in comparative research', *International Journal of Social Research Methodology*, vol 11, no 5, pp 389-40.

Andersen, T. (2014) 'William Evans to be named Boston police commissioner', *Boston Globe*, 7 January.

Andreas, P. and Nadelmann, E. (2006) *Policing the globe*, New York, NY/Oxford: Oxford University Press.

Appelbaum, A. (2012) *Iron curtain: The crushing of Eastern Europe 1944-1956*, London: Allen Lane.

Argyris, C. and Schön, D. (1974) *Theory in practice: Increasing professional effectiveness*, San Francisco, CA: Jossey Bass.

Ascoli, D. (1979) *The Queen's peace*, London: Hamish Hamilton.

Asher, M. (2008) *The regiment: The real story of the SAS*, London: Penguin Books.

Bailey, V. (ed) (1981) *Policing and punishment in nineteenth century Britain*, London: Croom Helm.

Bangma, K. (2014) 'Sturing versus professionele ruimte', *Symposium veranderingen in het openbaar bestuur*, University of Groningen, 25 February.

Banton, M. (1964) *The policeman in the community*, London: Tavistock.

Barham, D. (2010) 'Multi-point of direct entry', *Police Review*, 20 August.

Barker, A. (2004) *Shadows: Inside Northern Ireland's special branch*, Edinburgh/London: Mainstream.

Bayley, D.H. (1994) *Police for the future*, New York, NY/Oxford: Oxford University Press.

Bayley, D.H. (2006a) *Changing the guard: Developing democratic police abroad*, New York, NY: Oxford University Press.

Bayley, D.H. (2006b) 'Police reform: who done it?', Paper presented at *Police Reform from the Bottom Up*, Conference, University of California, Berkeley, CA, October.

Bayley, D.H. and Nixon, C. (2010) 'The changing environment for policing 1985-2008', *New perspectives in policing: Harvard executive session on policing and public safety*, Cambridge, MA: Harvard Kennedy School/NIJ.

Bayley, D.H. and Perito, R.M. (2010) *The police in war*, Boulder, CO/London: Lynne Rienner.

Bayley, D.H. and Shearing, C. (2001) *The new structure of policing*, Washington, DC: NIJ.

BBC Radio (2009) 'The reunion: Iranian Embassy siege', 6 September.

Beevor, A. (2009) *D-Day: The battle for Normandy*, London: Viking.

Belur, J. (2010) *Permission to shoot: Police use of deadly force in democracies*, London: Springer.

Bennis, W. (2003) *On becoming a leader*, New York, NY: Basic Books.

Bennis, W. and Nanus, B. (2003) *Leaders: Strategies for taking change*, New York, NY: HarperCollins.

Bennis, W., Parich, J. and Lessem, R. (1997) *Beyond leadership*, New York, NY: Wiley.

Bianchi, H. (1975) 'Social control and deviance in the Netherlands', in H. Bianchi, M. Simondi and I. Taylor (eds) *Deviance and control in Europe: Papers from the European Group for the Study of Deviance and Social Control*, London: Wiley, pp 1-11.

Bichard Report (2004) *The Bichard inquiry report*, London: House of Commons.

Bittner, E. (1967) 'The police on skid row: a study of peace-keeping', *American Sociological Review*, vol 32, no 5, pp 699-715.

Bittner, E. (1970) *The functions of the police in modern society*, Chevy Chase, MA: NIMH.

Bittner, E. (1974) 'Florence Nightingale in pursuit of Willie Sutton: a theory of the police', in H. Jacob (ed) *The potential of reform for criminal justice*, Beverly Hills, CA: Sage, pp 17-44.

Blair, I. (2003) 'Leading towards the future', Speech at *Future of Policing Conference*, LSE, London.

Blair, I. (2005) *Richard Dimbleby Lecture*, BBC, London.

Blair, I. (2009) *Policing controversy*, London: Profile Books.

Boin, R.A., van der Torre, E.J. and 't Hart, P. (2003) *Blauwe bazen: Het leiderschap van korpschefs*, Zeist: Kerckebosch.

Bootsma, P. (2001) *De Molukse acties*, Amsterdam: Boom.

Bowling, B. (1999) 'The rise and fall of New York murder', *British Journal of Criminology*, vol 39, no 4, pp 531-54.

Bowling, B. (2006) 'Quantity and quality in police research: making the case for case studies', unpublished paper presented at *Cambridge Symposium on Research Methods*, March.

Bowling, B. (2008) 'Fair and effective policing methods: towards "good-enough" policing', *Journal of Scandinavian Studies in Criminology and Crime Prevention*, vol 8, no 1, pp 17-32.

Bowling, B. and Phillips, C. (2003) 'Policing ethnic minority communities', in T. Newburn (ed) *Handbook of policing*, Cullompton: Willan, pp 528-54.

Bowling, B. and Ross, J. (2006) 'The Serious Organised Crime Agency: should we be afraid?', *Criminal Law Review* , 12, pp 1019-34.

Bowling, B. and Sheptycki, J. (2012) *Transnational policing*, London: Sage Publications.

Brants, C. (1999) 'The fine art of regulated tolerance: prostitution in Amsterdam', *Journal of Law and Society*, vol 25, no 4, pp 621-6.

Bratton, W. and Knobler, P. (1998) *Turnaround: How America's top cop reversed the crime epidemic*, York: Random House.

Brodeur, J.-P. (1981) 'Legitimizing police deviance', in C. Shearing (ed) *Organizational police deviance*, Toronto: Butterworths, pp 127-60.

Brodeur, J.-P. (1983) 'High and low policing. Remarks about the policing of political activities', *Social Problems*, vol 30, no 5, pp 507-20.

Brodeur, J.-P. (2010) *The policing web*, New York, NY/Oxford: Oxford University Press.

Brogden, M. (2005) 'Horses for courses and "thin blue lines": community policing in transitional society', *Police Quarterly*, vol 8, no 1, pp 64-98.

Browaeys, M.-J. and Price, R. (2008) *Understanding cross-cultural management*, Harlow: Pearson.

Brown, J.M. (ed) (2014) *The future of policing*, Abingdon and New York, NY: Palgrave.

Brown, J.M. and Heidensohn, F. (2012) 'From Juliet to Jane: women police in tv cop shows, reality, rank and careers', in T. Newburn and J. Peay (eds) *Policing: Politics, culture and control*, Oxford/Portland, OR: Hart, pp 111-34.

Brunger, M. (2013) 'Counterblast: policing in the blues: Was 2012 policing's *annus horribilis?*', *Howard Journal of Criminal Justice*, vol 52, no 3, pp 336–41.

Buruma, I. (2006) *Murder in Amsterdam*, London: Atlantic Books.

Caless, B. (2011) *Policing at the top: The roles, values and attitudes of chief police officers*, Bristol: Policy Press.

Campbell, I. and Kodz, J. (2011) *What makes great police leadership?*, London: NPIA.

Cartwright, J. and Shearing, C. (2012) *Where's the chicken? Making South Africa safe*, Kenilworth: Mercury.

CCPC (Council of Chief Police Commissioners) (2005) *Police in evolution. Vision on policing*. The Hague: NPI (English version of: Raad van Hoofdcommissarissen (2005) *Politie in ontwikkeling. Visie op de politiefunctie*, Den Haag: NPI).

Chaleff, I. (2003) *The courageous follower: Standing up to and for our leader* (3rd edn), San Francisco, CA: Berrett-Koehler.

Chan, J. (2003) *Fair cop: Learning the art of policing*, Toronto: University of Toronto Press.

Chan, J. and Dixon, D. (2007) 'The politics of police reform', *Criminology and Criminal Justice*, vol 7, no 4, pp 443-68.

Christie Report (2011) *Commission on the future delivery of public services*, London: Public Services Commission.

Cochrane, A. (2014) 'Scotland's police must do more to ease public concerns', *The Telegraph*, 30 July.

Cohen Commission (2013) *Twee werelden*, Main report, Commission Project X: Gemeente Haren.

College of Policing (2013) *College of Policing: The professional body for policing. Our strategic intent*, Coventry: College of Policing Ltd.

Conway, V. (2014) *Policing twentieth century Ireland*, London/New York, NY: Routledge.

Cook, K. (ed) (2001) *Trust in society*, New York, NY: Russell-Sage Foundation.

Cornelisse, L. (2013) *Naar één nationale politie*, Zeist: Kerckebosch.

Cramphorn, C. and Punch, M. (2007) 'The murder of Theo van Gogh', *Journal of Policing, Intelligence and Counter Terrorism*, vol 2, no 1, pp 34-53.

Crank, J.P. (1998) *Understanding police culture*, Cincinnati, OH: Anderson.

Crawford, A. and Lister, S. (2005) *Plural policing*, Cambridge: Polity Press.

Crawshaw, R., Cullen, S. and Holmström, L. (2006) *Essential cases on human rights for the police*, Leiden/Boston, MA: Martinus Nijhoff.

Crawshaw, R., Cullen, S. and Williamson, T. (2007) *Human rights and policing*, Leiden/Boston, MA: Martinus Nijhoff.

Critchley, T.A. (1978) *A history of police in England and Wales*, London: Constable.

Cumming, E., Cumming, I. and Edell, L. (1965) 'Policeman as philosopher, guide and friend', *Social Problems*, 12, pp 276-86.

Dalton, M. (1959) *Men who manage*, New York, NY: Wiley.

Dekker, V. (1994) *Going down, going down*, Amsterdam/Antwerp: Veen.

de Koning, B. (2012) 'De veiligheidsmythe', *Vrij Nederland*, 22 September.

de Rooy, P. (ed) (2011) *Waakzaam in Amsterdam. Hoofdstad en politie vanaf 1275*, Amsterdam: Boom.

Dixon, N.F. (1979) *On the psychology of military incompetence*, London: Futura Publications.

Dixon, D. (ed) (1999) *A culture of corruption*, Sydney: Hawkins Press.

Downes, D. (1988) *Contrasts in tolerance*, Oxford: Clarendon Press.

Edwards, B. (2014) *The rise of the American corporate security state*, San Francisco, CA: Berrett-Koehler.

Ellis, S. (1988) 'The historical significance of South Africa's third force', *Journal of South African Studies*, vol 24, no 2, pp 261-99.

Ellison Report (2014) *Stephen Lawrence independent review*, London: House of Commons.

Emsley, C. (1996) *The English police: A political and social history*, London: Longman.

Emsley, C. (2009) *The great British bobby*, London: Quercus.

Ericson, R.V. and Haggerty, K.D. (1997) *Policing the risk society*, Oxford: Oxford University Press.

Ermann, M.D. and Lundman, R.J. (eds) (1996) *Corporate and governmental deviance* (3rd edn), New York, NY/Oxford: Oxford University Press.

Eterno, J. and Silverman, E. (2012) *The crime numbers game: Management by manipulation*, Boca Raton, FL: CRC Press.

Fijnaut, C. (1999) 'De top van de Nederlandse politie verdient beter', *Het Tijdschrift voor de Politie*, 10, October.

Fijnaut, C. (2007) *De Geschiedenis van de Nederlandse politie*, Amsterdam: Boom.

Final Report TOLNP (2013) *Traject operationeel leiderschap Nationale Politie: Eindrapport van de werkgroep Welten*, Apeldoorn: Police Academy.

Firman, R. and Pearson, W. (2011) *Go! Go! Go!*, London: Phoenix.

Fitzgerald, M., Hough, M., Joseph, I. and Qureshi, T. (2002) *Policing for London*, Cullompton: Willan.

Flanagan, R. (2008) *Flanagan review of policing*, London: HMIC.

Flin, R. (1996) *Sitting in the hot seat*, New York, NY: Wiley.

Fyfe, N.R. (2014) 'A different and divergent trajectory: reforming the structure, governance and narrative of policing in Scotland,' in J.M. Brown (ed) *The future of policing*, Abingdon and New York, NY: Palgrave, pp 493-505.

Fyfe, N.R., Terpstra, J. and Tops, P. (eds) (2013) *Centralizing forces? Comparative perspectives on contemporary police reform in Northern and Western Europe*, The Hague: Eleven.

Garland, D. (2001) *The culture of control: Crime and social order in contemporary society*, New York, NY/Oxford: Oxford University Press.

Geraghty, T. (2000) *The Irish war*, London: Harper Collins.

Gilmour, S. (2006) *Why we trussed the police: An examination of police governance through the lens of trust*, Oxford: University of Oxford, Institute of Criminology.

Gilmour, S. (2010) 'The confident constable: a search for the intense simplicity of trust', *Policing*, vol 4, no 3, pp 218-24.

Goldsmith, A. (2010) 'Policing's new visibility', *British Journal of Criminology*, vol 50, no 5, pp 914-34.

Goldsmith, A. (2013) 'Disgracebook policing: social media and the rise of police indiscretion', *Policing and Society*, vol 23, no 4, pp 1-19.

Goldstein, H. (1977) *Policing a free society*, Cambridge, MA: Ballinger.

Goldstein, H. (1979) 'Improving policing: a problem oriented approach', *Crime and Delinquency*, April, pp 236-58.

Greenberg, M. (2014) '"Broken windows" and the New York police', *New York Review of Books*, 6 November.

Guardian, The (2000) 'Skyjack cost put at £3.6m', 17 February.

Guardian, The (2014) 'Met police taking time off work with stress-related illnesses', 24 December.

Hales, G., May, T., Belur, J. and Hough, M. (2015) *Chief officer misconduct in policing: An exploratory study*, Ryton-on-Dunsmore: College of Policing.

Halstrom, L. (2013) 'Scandinavian police reforms: can you have your cake and eat it, too?', *Police Practice and Research*, vol 15, no 6, pp 447-60.

Hastings, M. (2011) *All hell let loose*, London: HarperPress.

Henry, A. and Smith, D.J. (2007) *Transformations of policing*, Aldershot: Ashgate.

Herbert, S. (2006) *Citizens, cops and power*, Chicago, IL: University of Chicago Press.

Hillsborough Report (2012) *Report of the Hillsborough Independent Panel*, London: House of Commons.

Hinton, M.S. (2006) *The state on the streets*, Boulder, CO/London: Lynne Rienner.

Hinton, M.S. and Newburn, T. (eds) (2009) *Policing developing democracies*, Abingdon/New York, NY: Routledge.

HMIC (Her Majesty's Inspectorate of Constabulary) (2008) *Policing London: Winning consent*, London: HMIC.

HMIC (2009) *Adapting to protest: Nurturing the British model of policing*, London: HMIC.

HMIC (2011) *Policing public order*, London: HMIC.

HMIC (2014) *Policing in austerity*, London: HMIC.

Holdaway, S. (ed) (1979) *The British police*, London: Edward Arnold.

Holdaway, S. (1983) *Inside the British police*, Oxford: Basil Blackwell.

Holla, P. and Hanrath, M. (2011) 'Interview Gerard Bouman: De politie heeft zich laten wegspelen', www.websitevoordepolitie.nl, 12 May.

Holmes, P. (ed) (2014) *Police corruption: Essential readings*, Cheltenham: Edward Elgar.

Hoogenboom, B. (2010) *Governance of policing and security*, Basingstoke: Palgrave Macmillan.

Hoogenboom, B. and Punch, M. (2012) 'Developments in police research', in T. Newburn and J. Peay (eds) *Policing: Politics, culture and control*, Oxford/Portland, OR: Hart, pp 69-98.

Hoogenboom, B. and Vlek, F. (eds) (2002) *Gedoogbeleid: tolerantie en poldermodel: tellen we, onze zegeningen nog?*, Zeist: Kerkebosch.

Hoogewoning, F.C. (1993) *Van driehoeksoverleg tot wijkagent. De politie in overleg over sociale veiligheid in Amsterdam, Rotterdam en Den Haag*, PhD thesis, Amsterdam: University of Amsterdam/Arnhem: Gouda Quint.

Hopkins-Burke, R. (ed) (2004) *Hard cop, soft cop: Dilemmas and debates in contemporary policing*, Cullompton: Willan.

Hornberger, J. (2007) 'Don't push this constitution down my throat: human rights in everyday practice. An ethnography of police transformation in Johannesburg, South Africa', Unpublished PhD thesis, University of Utrecht.

Hough, M. (2014) 'Procedural justice and professional policing in times of austerity', *Criminology and Criminal Justice*, vol 13, no 2, pp 181-97.

House of Commons (2013) *Leadership and standards in the police service: Oral evidence, Home Affairs Committee*, London: House of Commons.

Huggins, M.K. (ed) (1991) *Vigilantism and the state in modern Latin America: Essays on extralegal violence*, New York, NY: Praeger.

Hurd, D. (2007) *Robert Peel: A biography*, London: Phoenix.

Independent, The (2013) 'More than 160 arrested at EDL Tower Hamlets march', 8 September.

IPCC (Independent Police Complaints Commission) (2004), *Highmoor Cross Report*, London: IPCC.

IPCC (2007) *Stockwell one: Investigation into the shooting of Jean Charles de Menezes at Stockwell underground station on 22 July 2005*, London: IPCC.

Janis, E.L. (1972) *Victims of groupthink*, Boston, MA: Houghton Mifflin.

Johnson, S. (1998) *Who moved my cheese?*, New York, NY: Penguin.

Jones, R. (2014) *The story of baby P*, Bristol: Policy Press.

Jones, T. and Newburn, T. (2007) *Policy transfer and criminal justice*, Maidenhead: Open University Press.

Karmen, A. (2001) *New York murder mystery: The true story behind the crime crash of the 1990s*, New York, NY: New York University Press.

Keegan, J. (1978) *The mask of command*, London: Jonathan Cape.

Kelley, R.E. (1988) 'Rethinking followership', in R.E. Riggio, I. Chaleff and J. Lipman-Blumen (eds) *The art of followership: How great followers create great leaders and organizations*, San Francisco, CA: Jossey-Bass, pp 5-15.

Kellerman, B. (2012) *The end of leadership*, San Francisco, CA: Berrett-Koehler.

Kelling, G.L. and Coles, C.M. (1996) *Fixing broken windows*, New York, NY: Free Press.

Kets de Vries, M. (1995) *Life and death in the fast lane*, San Francisco, CA: Jossey Bass.

Kets de Vries, M. and Miller, D. (1984) *The neurotic organization*, San Francisco, CA: Jossey Bass.

King, S.N. and Santana, L.C (2010) 'Feedback-intensive programs', in E. van Velsor, C.D. McCauley and M.N. Ruderman (eds) *Handbook of leadership development* (3rd edn), San Francisco, CA: Jossey Bass, pp 97-125.

Kleinig, J. (1996) *The ethics of policing*, Cambridge: Cambridge University Press.

Klinger, D. (2004) *Into the kill zone*, San Francisco, CA: Jossey Bass.

Klockars, C.B. (1985) *The idea of police*, Beverly Hills, CA: Sage Publications.

Knights, D. and McCabe, D. (2003) *Guru schemes and American dreams*, Maidenhead: Open University Press.

Kotter, J. (2012) *Leading change* (revised edn), Cambridge, MA: Harvard Business Review Press.

Kraska, P. (ed) (2001) *Militarising the American criminal justice system*, New York, NY: New York University Press.

Kraska, P. (2007) 'Militarization and policing – its relevance to 21st-century police', *Policing*, vol 1, no 4, pp 505-13.

Lee, M. and Punch, M. (2006) *Policing by degrees*, Groningen: Hondsrug Pers.

Leishman, F., Savage, S. and Loveday, B. (eds) (2000) *Core issues in policing* (2nd edn), London: Longman.

Lerner, M.J. (1980) *The belief in a just world*, New York, NY/London: Plenum Press.

Leveson Report (2012) *An inquiry into the culture, practices and ethics of the press* (volume 1), November, London: The Stationery Office.

Levitt, L. (2009) *NYPD confidential*, New York, NY: St Martin's Press.

Lewis, M. (2010) *The big short*, London: Allen Lane.

Lipsky, M. (1980) *Street level bureaucrats*, New York, NY: Russell Sage Foundation.

Loader, I. (2004) 'Policing, securitization and democratisation in Europe', in T. Newburn and R. Sparks (eds) *Criminal justice and political cultures*, Cullompton: Willan, pp 47-9.

Loader, I. (2014) 'Why do the police matter?', in J.M. Brown (ed) *The future of policing*, Abingdon/New York, NY: Palgrave, pp 40-51.

Loader, I. and Walker, N. (2007) *Civilizing security*, Cambridge: Cambridge University Press.

Loftus, B. (2009) *Police culture in a changing world*, Oxford: Clarendon.

LSE (London School of Economics and Political Science) (2011) *Reading the riots*, London: LSE/*The Guardian*.

Lustgarten, L. (1986) *The governance of the police*, London: Sweet and Maxwell.

Maas, P. (1974) *Serpico*, London: Collins.

Macpherson, Sir William of Cluny (1999) *The Stephen Lawrence inquiry: Report of an inquiry by Sir William Macpherson of Cluny*, London: HMSO.

Maguire, M., Morgan, R. and Reiner, R. (eds) (2012) *The Oxford handbook of criminology* (5th edn) Oxford: Oxford University Press.

Mak, G. (2001) *Amsterdam: A brief life of the city*, London: Harvill Press.

Manning, P.K. (1977) *Police work*, Cambridge, MA: MIT Press.

Manning, P.K. (1997) *Police work* (2nd edn), Prospect Heights, IL: Waveland Press.

Manning, P.K. (2003) *Policing contingencies*, Chicago, IL: University of Chicago Press.

Manning, P.K. (2008) *The technology of policing*, New York, NY: New York University Press.

Manning, P.K. (2010) *Democratic policing in a changing world*, Boulder, CO: Paradigm.

Manning, P.K. (2014) 'Policing: privatizing and changes in the policing web', in J.M. Brown (ed) *The future of policing*, Abingdon/New York, NY: Palgrave, pp 23-39.

Marenin, O. (1982) 'Parking tickets and class repression: the concept of policing in critical theories of criminal justice', *Contemporary Crises*, 6, pp 241-66.

Mark, R. (1978) *In the office of constable*, London: Collins.

Markham, G. (1999) 'A risky decision: law breaker or public guardian?', *Risk Management*, vol 1, no 1, pp 63-5.

Markham, G. and Punch, M. (2004) 'Animal rights, public order and police accountability', *Policing: International Journal of Police Science and Management*, vol 6, no 2, pp 84-96.

Markham, G. and Punch, M. (2007a) 'Embracing accountability: the way forward – Part one', *Policing: Journal of Research and Practice*, vol 1, no 3, pp 1-9.

Markham, G. and Punch, M. (2007b) 'Embracing accountability: the way forward – Part two', *Policing: Journal of Research and Practice*, vol 1, no 4, pp 485-94.

Marks, M. (2005) *Transforming the robocops*, Scottsville: University of KwaZulu-Natal Press.

Marshall, G. (1978) 'Police accountability revisited', in D. Butler and A.H. Halsey (eds) *Policy and politics*, London: Macmillan, pp 51-65.

Marx, G.T. (1988) *Undercover: Police surveillance in America*, Berkeley, CA: University of California Press.

Mawby, R.I. (ed) (1999) *Policing across the world*, London: University College London Press.

McDonald, L. (2009) *A colossal failure of common sense*, London: Ebury Press.

McGarry, F. (2007) *Eoinn O'Duffy: A self-made hero*, Oxford/New York, NY: Oxford University Press.

McLaughlin, E. (2005) 'From reel to ideal: the blue lamp and the popular construction of the English "bobby"', *Crime Media Culture*, vol 1, no 1, pp 11-30.

McNee, D. (1983) *McNee's law*, London: Collins.

Meershoek, A.J.J. (2004) 'Hoofdcommissaris van politie in Amsterdam', in H. Kapsenberg et al (eds) *Rust'loos wakend*, Alphen aan den Rijn: Kluwer, pp 7-80.

Meershoek, A.J.J. (2011) *De Groep IJzerman*, Amsterdam: Boom.

Miller, W. (1977) *Cops and bobbies*, Chicago, IL: University of Chicago Press.

Millie, A. (2012) 'Police stations, architecture and public reassurance', *British Journal of Criminology*, vol 52, no 6, pp 1092-112.

Millie, A. (2013) 'The policing task and the expansion and contraction of British policing', *Criminology and Criminal Justice*, voln13, no 2, pp 143-60.

Mintzberg, H. (1973) *The nature of managerial work*, New York, NY: Harper and Row.

Mintzberg, H. (1989) *Mintzberg on management*, New York, NY: Free Press.

Moskos, P. (2008) *Cop in the hood*, Princeton, NJ: Princeton University Press.

Morgan, G. (1986) *Images of organization*, Beverly Hills, CA: Sage Publications.

Muir, W.K. (1977) *Police: Streetcorner politicians*, Chicago, IL: University of Chicago Press.

Muller, E.R., Rosenthal, U., Zannoni, M., Ferwerda, H. and Schaap, S.D. (2009) *Strandrellen in Hoek van Holland*, The Hague: COT.

Nadelmann E. (1993) *Cops across borders: The internationalisation of US law enforcement*, University Park, PA: Pennsylvania State University Press.

Naeyé, J. (1995) *Het politieel vooronderzoek in strafzaken*, Arnhem: Gouda Quint.

Newburn, T. (1999) *Understanding and preventing police corruption: Lessons from the literature*, London: Home Office.

Newburn, T. (ed) (2003) *Handbook of policing*, Cullompton: Willan.

Newburn, T. (ed) (2005) *Policing: Key readings*, Cullompton: Willan.

Newburn, T. (2015) 'The 2011 England riots in recent historical perspective', *British Journal of Criminology*, vol 55, no 1, pp 39-64.

Newburn, T. and Peay, J. (eds) (2012) *Policing: Politics, culture and control*, Oxford/Portland, OR: Hart.

Newburn, T. and Sparks, R. (eds) (2004) *Criminal justice and political cultures*, Cullompton: Willan.

Newsinger, J. (2006) *The blood never dried*, London: Bookmarks.

New York Times (2012) 'Indians outraged by account of gang rape on a bus', 30 December.

Neyroud Report (2011) *Review of police leadership and training*, London: NPIA.

Neyroud, P. (2011) 'Leading policing in the 21st century', *Public Money and Management*, vol 31, no 5, pp 347-54.

Neyroud, P. (ed) (2013) *Policing UK: Priorities and pressures: A year of transition,* London: Home Office.

Neyroud, P. and Beckley, P. (2001) *Policing, ethics and human rights*, Cullompton: Willan.

Nordholt, E. and Straver, R. (1983) 'The changing police', in M. Punch (ed) *Control in the police organisation*, Cambridge, MA: MIT Press.

North, M. (2000) *Dunblane: Never forget*, Edinburgh/London: Mainstream.

O'Connor, D. (2003) 'Policing by consent', Paper presented at *Future of Policing Conference*, London School of Economics and Political Science, London.

O'Connor, D. (2005) *Closing the gap*, London: HMIC.

O'Donnell, E. (2007) 'Why police are so hard to recruit: the bosses can make life miserable', *The Inquirer*, 7 March (http://articles.philly.com).

O'Hara, M. (2014) *Austerity bites*, Bristol: Policy Press.

O'Hara, P. (2005) *Why law enforcement agencies fail*, Durham, NC: Carolina Academic Press.

O'Neill, M., Marks, M. and Singh, A.-M. (eds) (2007) *Police occupational culture*, Oxford/Amsterdam: JAI Press.

O'Toole, F. (2010) *Ship of fools*, London: Faber and Faber.

Paddick, B. (2008) *Line of fire*, London: Simon and Schuster.

Pakes, F. (2004) 'The politics of discontent: the emergence of a new criminal justice discourse', *The Howard Journal*, vol 43, no 3, pp 284-98.

Parker Report (2014) *Independent review of ACPO*, London: APCC.

Patten Report (1999) *A new beginning: Policing in Northern Ireland. Report of the Commission on Policing for Northern Ireland*, London: Home Office.

Peay, J. (2010) *Mental health and crime*, London: Routledge.

Porter, B. (1987) *The origins of the vigilant state*, London: Weidenfeld and Nicolson.

POS (*Projectgroep Organisatie Structuren*) (1977) *Politie in verandering*, The Hague: Staatsuitgeverij.

Priest, D. and Arkin, W. (2012) *Top secret America: The rise of the new security state*, New York, NY: Little Brown.

Punch, M. (1979a) *Policing the inner city*, London: Macmillan.

Punch, M. (1979b) 'The secret social service', in S. Holdaway (ed) *The British police,* London: Edward Arnold, pp 102-17.

Punch, M. (ed) (1983) *Control in the police organisation*, Cambridge, MA: MIT Press.

Punch, M. (1985) *Conduct unbecoming: The social construction of police deviance and control*, London: Tavistock.

Punch, M. (1989) 'Researching police deviance', *British Journal of Sociology*, vol 40, no 2, pp 177-204.

Punch, M. (1996) *Dirty business*, London: Sage Publications.

Punch, M. (2003) 'Rotten orchards, "pestilence", police misconduct and system failure', *Policing and Society*, vol 13, no 2, pp 171-96.

Punch, M. (2004) '"Eerlijk" politiewerk in Londen', *Het Tijdschrift voor de Politie*, vol 66, no 10, pp 27-31.

Punch, M. (2005) 'The Belgian disease: Dutroux, scandal and system failure in Belgium', in R. Sarre, D. Das and H.J. Albrecht (eds) *Policing corruption: International perspectives*, Langham, MD: Lexington Books, pp 367-81.

Punch, M. (2007) *Zero tolerance policing*, Bristol: Policy Press.

Punch, M. (2009) *Police corruption*, Cullompton: Willan.

Punch, M. (2011) *Shoot to kill: Police, firearms and fatal force*, Bristol: Policy Press.

Punch, M. (2012) *State violence, collusion and the Troubles: Counter insurgency, government deviance and Northern Ireland*, London: Pluto.

Punch, M. and Markham, G. (2000) 'Policing disasters: the British experience', *Policing: International Journal of Police Science and Management*, vol 3, no 1, pp 40-54.

Punch, M. and Naylor, T. (1973) 'The police: a social service', *New Society*, vol 24, no 554, pp 358-61.

Punch, M., Hoogenboom, B. and van der Vijver, K. (2008) 'Community policing in the Netherlands: four generations of redefinition', in T. Williamson (ed) *The handbook of knowledge-based policing*, Chichester: Wiley, pp 59-78.

Punch, M., Hoogenboom, B. and Williamson, T. (2005) 'Paradigm lost: the Dutch dilemma', *The Australian and New Zealand Journal of Criminology*, vol 38, no 2, pp 68-281.

Punch, M., van der Vijver, K. and van Dijk, N. (1998) *Searching for a future* (translation of SMVP *Toekomst Gezocht*), Dordrecht: SMVP.

Punch, M., van der Vijver, K. and Zoomer, O. (2002) 'Dutch "COP": developing community policing in the Netherlands', *Policing*, vol 25, no 1, pp 60-79.

Quinn, R. and Rohrbaugh, J. (1983) 'A spatial model of effectiveness criteria: towards a competing values approach to organizational analysis', *Management Science*, 29, March, pp 363-77.

Rawlinson, P. (2010) *From fear to fraternity: A Russian tale of crime, economy and modernity*, London: Pluto Press.

Reiner, R. (1978) *The blue-coated worker*, Cambridge: Cambridge University Press.

Reiner, R. (1991) *Chief constables: Bobbies, bosses or bureaucrats?*, Oxford: Oxford University Press.

Reiner, R. (1997) 'Policing and the police', in M. Maguire, R. Morgan and R. Reiner (eds) *Oxford handbook of criminology* (2nd edn), Oxford: Oxford University Press, pp 997-1049.

Reiner, R. (1998) 'Copping a plea', in S. Holdaway and P. Rock (eds) *Thinking about criminology*, London/New York, NY: Routledge.

Reiner, R. (2007) *Law and order*, Cambridge: Polity Press.

Reiner, R. (2010) *The politics of the police* (4th edn), Oxford: Oxford University Press.

Reiner, R. (2013) 'Who governs? Democracy, plutocracy, science and prophecy in policing', *Criminology and Criminal Justice*, vol 13, no 2, pp 161-80.

Reisman, D. (1979) *Folded lies*, New York, NY: Free Press.

Reiss, A.J. Jr (1971) *The police and the public*, New Haven, CT: Yale University Press.

Reuss-Ianni, E.R. (1983) *Two cultures of policing*, New Brunswick, NJ: Transaction Books.

Reith, C. (1956) *A new study of police history*, London: Oliver & Boyd.

Rietbergen, P.J. (2011) *A short history of the Netherlands* (9th edn), Amersfoort: Bekking & Blitz.

Riggio, R.E., Chaleff, I. and Lipman-Blumen, J. (eds) (2008) *The art of followership: How great followers create great leaders and organizations*, San Francisco, CA: Jossey-Bass.

Robinson, S. and Smith, J. (2014) *Co-charismatic leadership*, Oxford: Peter Lang.

Rosenthal, U. (1989a) 'Managing terrorism: the South Moluccan hostage takings', in U. Rosenthal, M. Charles and P. 't Hart (eds) *Coping with crises*, Springfield, IL: Thomas, pp 225-54.

Rosenthal, U. (1989b) 'A compulsive crisis: the inauguration of Queen Beatrix', in in U. Rosenthal, M. Charles and P. 't Hart (eds) *Coping with crises*, Springfield, IL: Thomas, pp 367-96.

Rowson, J. and Lindley, E. (2012) *Reflexive coppers*, London: RSA.

Rubinstein, J. (1973) *City police*, New York, NY: Ballantine.

Savage, S. (2007a) *Police reform*, Oxford: Oxford University Press.

Savage, S. (2007b) 'Neighbourhood policing and the re-invention of the constable', *Policing*, vol 1, no 2, pp 202-13.

Savage, S., Charman, S. and Cope, S. (2000) *Policing and the power of persuasion*, London: Blackstone.

Scarman Report (1981) *The Brixton Disorders 10-12 April 1981*. Harmondsworth: Penguin.

Schein, E. (1985) *Organizational culture and leadership*, San Francisco, CA: Jossey Bass.

Schön, D. (1983) *The reflective practitioner*, London: Temple Smith.

Scraton, P. (1999) *Hillsborough: The truth*, London/Edinburgh: Mainstream.

Sennett, R. (2008) *The craftsman*, New Haven, CT: Yale University Press.

Shalev, S. (2009) *Super Max*, Cullompton: Willan.

Shearing, C. (ed) (1981) *Organizational police deviance*, Toronto: Butterworths.

Shearing, C. (2007) 'Policing our future', in A. Henry and D. Smith (eds) *Transformations of policing*, Aldershot: Ashgate, pp 249-72.

Shearing, C. and Johnston, L. (2003) *Governing security*, London: Routledge.

Sheptycki, J. (ed) (2000) *Issues in transnational policing*, London/New York, NY: Routledge.

Sherman, L. (1978) *Scandal and reform*, Berkeley, CA: University of California Press.

Sherman, L. (2013) 'The rise of evidence-based policing: targeting, testing and tracking', *Crime and Justice*, 42, pp 377-431.

Silverman, E. (1999) *NYPD battles crime: Innovative strategies in policing*, Boston, MA: Northeastern University Press.

Skogan, W. (ed) (2004) *Community policing: Can it work?* Boston, MA: Cengage.

Skogan, W. (2008) 'Why reforms fail', *Policing & Society*, vol 18, no 1, pp 23-34.

Skogan, W. and Frydl, K. (2004) *Fairness and effectiveness in policing: The evidence*, Washington, DC: National Academies Press.

Skogan, W. and Roth, J.A. (2004) 'Introduction', in W. Skogan (ed) *Community policing: Can it work?*, Boston, MA: Cengage, pp xvii-xxxiv.

Skolnick, J.H. (1966) *Justice without trial*, New York, NY: Wiley.

Smith, D.J. and Gray, J. (1985) *Police and people in London: The PSI report*, London: Policy Studies Institute.

SMVP (*Stichting Maatschappij, Veiligheid en Politie*) (1995) *Toekomst gezocht*, Dordrecht: SMVP.

Srivastva, S. (1988) *Executive integrity*, San Francisco, CA/London: Jossey Bass.

Steinberg, J. (2008) *Thin blue*, Johannesburg/Cape Town: Jonathan Ball.

Stenning, P. (1989) 'Police and government: *The governance of the police*, by Laurence Lustgarten', *Osgoode Hall Law Journal*, vol 27, no 1, pp 211-18.

Stenning, P. (2000) 'Powers and accountability of private police', *Crime and Justice*, vol 8, no 3, pp 325-52.

Stenning, P. (2015) 'Review: *Policing at the top* by Caless', *Police Practice and Research*, vol 16, no 1, pp 94-6.

Sterling, T. (2012) 'Robert M. paedophilia conviction: "Monster of Riga" sentenced to 18 years', *The Huffington Post*, 21 May.

Stevens Report (2013) *Policing for a better Britain: Report of the Independent Police Commission*, Essex: Anton.

Storm, S. and Naastepad, R. (2003) 'The Dutch distress', *New Left Review*, 20, March-April, pp 131-51.

Summers, A. (2011) *The secret life of J. Edgar Hoover*, London: Ebury Press.

't Hart, P. and Pijnenburg, B. (1989) 'The Heizel Stadium tragedy', in U. Rosenthal, M. Charles and P. 't Hart (eds) *Coping with crises*, Springfield, IL: Thomas, pp 197-225.

Taylor Report (1989) *Hillsborough Stadium disaster inquiry*, London: House of Commons.

Telegraph, The (2006), 'Daddy Cameron knows best', 5 January.

Telegraph, The (2012) 'Two female officers shot dead as man arrested', 18 August.

Telegraph, The (2014) 'Scrap Human Rights Act and limit European migration, says Prime Minister', 1 October.

Terpstra, J. and Fyfe, N.R. (2014) 'Policy processes and police reform: examining similarities between Scotland and the Netherlands', *International Journal of Law, Crime and Justice*, vol 42, no 4, pp 366-83.

Terpstra, J. and Fyfe, N.R. (2015) 'Mind the implementation gap? Police reform and local policing in the Netherlands and Scotland', *Criminology and Criminal Justice*, published online 19 February.

Tilley, N. (2003) 'Community policing, problem-oriented policing and intelligence-led policing', in T. Newburn (ed) *Handbook of policing*, Cullompton: Willan, pp 311-39.

Tonry, M. (2004) *Punishment and politics*, Cullompton: Willan.

Turner, R.H. (1960) 'Sponsored and contest mobility and the school system', *American Sociological Review*, vol 25, no 6, pp 855-62.

Tyler, T. (ed) (2007) *Legitimacy and criminal justice*, New York, NY: Russell Sage Foundation.

Tyler, T. (2011) *Why people cooperate*, Princeton, NJ: Princeton University Press.

Tyler, T. and Huo, Y.J. (2002) *Trust in the law*, New York, NY: Russell Sage Foundation.

Useem, M. (1998) *The leadership moment*, New York, NY: Ransom House.

Useem, M. (2011) *The leader's checklist*, The Wharton School; Wharton Digital Press.

van der Vijver, C.D. (2004) 'De functie en gezag van de politie', *Rust'loos Wakend*, Amsterdam: Regiopolitie Amsterdam-Amstelland.

van der Vijver, C.D. (2009) 'Doolhof of kaleidoscoop', farewell oration, University of Twente.

van Dijk, A., Hoogenboom, B., Hoogewoning, F., Punch, M. and van der Vijver, K. (2010) *De kogel moet door de kerk: Pamflet over de toekomst van de politie*, Dordrecht: SMVP.

van Dijk, A.J. and Hoogewoning, F.C. (2014a) 'Visieontwikkeling binnen de politieprofessie', in E.R. Muller, E. van der Torre, A.B. Hoogenboom and N. Klop (eds) *Politie. Studies over haar werking en organisatie* (3rd edn), The Hague: Wolters Kluwer, pp 501-28.

van Dijk, A.J. and Hoogewoning, F. (2014b) 'Vergezichten naderbij: maatschappelijke ontwikkelingen en hun praktische betekenis voor de politie', *Cahiers Politiestudies*, 33, pp 83-96.

van Dijk, A., Hoogewoning, F. and Punch, M. (2012) 'Best thinking, best practice', *Policing Today*, vol 18, no 4, pp 17-18.

van Dijk, A., Hoogewoning, F. and Punch, M. (2013) 'Reflections on policing and leadership development: work in progress, the Netherlands', Paper presented at the *Fourth Annual Conference of the Higher Education Forum for Learning and Development in Policing*, Canterbury Christ Church University.

van Dijk, A., Hoogewoning, F. and Welten, B.(2011) *Dienstbaar aan de rechtsstaat: Biografie van een agora*, Amsterdam: Boom.

van Iersel, S. (2010) *Spoedassistentie: Hoek van Holland*, Rotterdam: Politie Rotterdam-Rijnmond.

Van Maanen, J. (1978) 'The asshole', in P.K. Manning and J. Van Maanen (eds) *Policing: A view from the street*, Santa Monica, CA: Goodyear, pp 273-317.

Van Maanen, J. (1983) 'The boss: first-line supervision in an American police agency', in M. Punch (ed) *Control in the police organisation*, Cambridge, MA: MIT Press, pp 221-37.

van Swaaningen, R. (2000) 'Tolerance or zero tolerance: that is the question', Paper presented at *American Society of Criminology Conference*, San Francisco, CA.

van Swaaningen, R. (2004) 'Public safety and management of fear', Paper presented at *European Society of Criminology Conference*, Amsterdam.

van Traa Commission (1996) *Inzake opsporing: Enquête-commissie opsporingsmethoden*, The Hague: Sdu.

Verbij, A. (2005) *Tien rode jaren*, Amsterdam: Ambo.

Vlek, F., Bangma, K., Loef, K. and Muller, E. (eds) (2004) *Uit balans: politie en bestel in de knel*, Zeist: Kerkebosch.

Vinzant, J.C. and Crothers, L. (1998) *Street-level leadership*, Washington, DC: Georgetown University Press.

Vuyk, S. (2010) *De vuurwerkramp*, Utrecht: Fontein.

Waddington, P.A.J. (1991) *The strong arm of the law*, Oxford: Oxford University Press.

Waddington, P.A.J. (1994) *Liberty and order*, London: UCL Press.

Waddington, P.A.J. (1999) *Policing citizens*, London: UCL Press.

Waddington, P.A.J. (2007) *Policing public disorder*, Cullompton: Willan.

Walker, C. and Starmer, K. (1999) *Miscarriages of justice: A review of justice in error*, London: Blackstone.

Walker, S. (2005) *The new world of police accountability*, Thousand Oaks, CA: Sage Publications.

Wall, D. (1998) *The chief constables of England and Wales*, Aldershot: Dartmouth.

Walton, C. (1988) *The moral manager*, New York, NY: Ballinger.

Wansink, H. (2004) *De erfenis van Fortuyn*, Amsterdam: Meulenhoff.

Watson, T. (1994) *In search of management*, London: Routledge.

Weick, K. (1990) 'The vulnerable system: An analysis of the Tenerife air disaster', *Journal of Management*, vol 16, no 3, pp 571-93.

Weitzer, R. (2010) *Sex for sale: Prostitution, pornography and the sex industry* (2nd edn), New York, NY: New York University Press.

Weitzer, R. (2012) *Legalizing prostitution: From illicit vice to lawful business*, New York, NY: New York University Press.

Williamson, T. (ed) (2008) *The handbook of knowledge based policing*, Chichester: Wiley.

Wilson, J.Q. (1968) *Varieties of police behavior*, Cambridge, MA: Harvard University Press.

Wilson, J.Q. (1975) *Thinking about crime*, New York, NY: Basic Books.

Winsor Report (2014) *Annual report, HMIC*, London: HMIC.

Winsor Review (2013) *Police pay: Winsor review*, London: HMIC.

Wolfgang, B. (2014) 'Obama plays top cop, forms task force on police conduct post-Ferguson', *The Washington Times*, 18 December.

Wood, J. and Shearing, C. (2007) *Imagining security*, Cullompton: Willan.

Young, M. (1991) *An inside job: Policing and police culture in Britain*, Oxford: Clarendon.

Zimring, F. (2007) *The great American crime decline*, New York, NY: Oxford University Press.

Zwart, C. (2004) *Over het wezen van de Nederlandse politie*, Leiderdorp: Elsevier/Politie Hollands Midden.

Index

Page references for notes are followed by n

A

Abilene paradox 143
accountability 22, 23, 87–91, 92, 95,
  183
  high policing 33
  leadership 3, 148, 173
  UK 2, 42
  US 17
agora 173, 187, 197–200
Alderson, John 61
Alison, L. 133
Alkmaar norm 65
Alphen aan den Rijn 105
Amelisweerd 113
Amsterdam
  1966 riots 52, 114
  agora 173, 187, 197–200
  cruise missile demonstrations 113
  El Al plane crash 115, 116, 131n
  inauguration riots 110–11
  Indonesian Consulate siege 97
  Jordaan disturbances 36
  Juxta 199
  Nieuwmarkt riots 110
  police numbers 52
  red-light district 56
  vice case 102–3
Anglo-Saxon model 5, 6, 30, 66
  consent paradigm 40–5
animal rights activists 112–13, 173
Apeldoorn 141–2
Appelbaum, A. 31
Argyris, C. 136
armed response vehicle (ARV) 121
Asian Tsunami 79, 131n
Assange, Julian 73
Association of Chief Police Officers
  (ACPO) vii, 123, 125, 128, 156
Association of Chief Police Officers
  Scotland (ACPOS) vii
Australia 30, 79, 179
autonomy 42, 44, 46–7, 49–50, 151

B

Baflo 104
Balcombe Street siege 105
Baltimore 48
Barham, D. 95
Bayley, David 172, 180–1
Beatrix, Queen 110–11
Belgium 30, 143
Bennis, Warren 136
Birmingham 100

Bittner, E. 20, 73
Blair, Sir Ian 48, 155, 175
Bloody Sunday 130n
blue wall 80
Blunkett, David 68n
Boin, R.A. 17–18, 156–7
Border Agency 14
Boston marathon 111
Bouman, Gerard 160–1
Bovensmilde 97, 98
BP oil spill 141
Bramshill Police Staff College 9, 116,
  123, 128–9, 152, 154
Brants, C. 55
Bratton, Bill 43, 47, 49, 62, 68n, 137
Brazil 92n
Breivik, Anders 64, 104–5
Brightlingsea 112–13, 173
Brighton bombing 100
British policing model vii, 5, 40–51, 66
Brixton riots 37, 46, 114, 184, 188, 189
Brodeur, J.-P. 29, 32–8, 44, 66, 102, 181
broken windows approach 57, 62, 181
bronze commanders 121, 122, 124
Buenos Aires 72

C

Caless, B. 135, 151–2, 154, 155, 156,
  159, 172
Cambridge University 153, 154, 171
Cambridgeshire Police 103–4
Cameron, David 23, 120
Campbell, I. 175
Canada
  criminal investigations 102
  high policing 34–5
  police reform 2, 25n
  police system 30
  recruitment 13
Canterbury Christ Church University
  160
Carbine Brigades 36
Cartwright, J. 25, 197
CCTV 90
centralisation 11–12, 14, 64–6, 127
Centre for Critical Incident Research
  170
Chaleff, I. 165
change 1–2
  drivers of 10–16
  inhibitions to 16–19
  Netherlands 5, 6–8

UK 5, 9–10
changing police, A (POS) 53, 59, 161
Charman, S. 135
Chemipack explosion 115
Chicago 48, 187
Chief 149
child sex exploitation xi, 102–3
Chilean mine rescue 138
civil emergencies 72–3, 114–20
  see also emergency response
civilians 15–16
COBRA (Cabinet Office Briefing
  Room A) 99
cognitive dissonance 143
College of Policing (England and Wales)
  5, 9, 45, 128–9, 153
colonial policing vii, 9, 30–1
command and control 128–9
  Netherlands 125–8
  UK 121–5, 169
Commander, The 149
Commission for Home Affairs 90
community outreach 184
community policing (COP) 65–6, 187,
  196
  Netherlands 53, 55, 62–3, 66
  New York 47, 48, 61–2
  Policing for London Study 18, 187,
    188–93
  Seattle 18, 187, 194–6
  UK 17, 60, 62–3
  US 18
Compagnies républicaines de sécurité (CRS)
  35
competence 148
concern leadership 21, 150
confidence 148
confrontational thinking 173, 187,
  197–200
consent paradigm 5, 38, 40–5, 60–4,
  66–7, 177
  accountability 88–9
  Netherlands 55
  paradigm shift 45–51
conservatism 82
Conservative Party
  crime reduction 192
  NPM 12
Conservative-Liberal Democrat
  government 10, 151
  crime reduction 46–7, 61, 192
  NPM 13
  Police and Crime Commissioners
    13–14
contested mobility 158–9
control paradigm 38, 39–40, 46–7,
  60–4, 66–7, 177–8
Cope, S. 135
corruption 75, 84–7, 92n, 93n
Council of Chief Officers (England and
  Wales) vii

see also National Police Chiefs Council
Council of Chief Police Commissioners
  (CCPC) (Netherlands) 59, 161–2,
  176n
counter-terrorism 14, 23, 62–3
Crego, Jonathan 133, 156, 170
crime xi, 1, 2, 4, 5, 8, 11, 14–6, 23, 33,
  38, 40, 43-4, 46-9, 52, 54, 60, 64–5,
  70–5, 81–7, 90–1, 102–3, 105, 117,
  137, 171, 176n, 178-85
  London 189, 191
  New York 137
  Netherlands 54–9, 60
crime control 1, 2, 49, 50, 70–2, 81, 82,
  91, 184, 192, 193
  beyond 178–80
crime reduction 1, 2, 10, 47, 177–80,
  193
criminal investigations 102–4
Crofts, Nick 185–6n
culture 79–83, 92
cynicism 80

D
Dalton, M. 135
danger 80–1, 105–6, 110, 112, 118, 121,
  181, 195
de Menezes, Jean Charles 107
democratic policing 67
demonstrations 111–13
Denmark 64, 66
Denning, Lord 42, 50
deviance 32, 38, 67, 84, 86–7, 90, 92
dichotomous thinking 82
Disaster Victim Identification Team 96,
  116, 131n
disasters 72–3, 114–20
discretion 20, 45, 49, 55, 59, 70, 77,
  162, 182, 191–2
discrimination 75, 192
Dixon, N.F. 134
Dixon of Dock Green 45
domestic violence xi, 74
Downes, D. 54–5
drugs
  IRT affair 56
  New York 62
ducking and diving 82
Duisburg 111
Dumfries and Galloway police 101
Dunblane 104
Dutch Police Academy (DPA) xiii, xiv,
  160
Dutroux scandal 143

E
easing behaviour 81, 93n
Eastern Europe 2, 31–2
economies of scale 13
El Al plane crash 115, 116, 131n
emergency response 72–3, 74–5, 114–20

see also major incidents
enemy within 84
England and Wales
 leadership development 150, 151–6, 169, 171–2
 loss of trust 23–4
 police system vii–viii, xi, 2, 5, 9, 13
 see also United Kingdom
English Defence League (EDL) 111
Enschede fireworks depot explosion 115–16
environmental activists 112
espoused paradigm 39, 45, 61
Essex Police 98, 130n
European Convention on Human Rights 23
Evans, Bill 111
evidence-based policing 3, 24, 51
excitement 82

F
Facebook Party 126–8
FBI 34
Ferguson, Missouri 107
Fielding, N.G. 63
Fijnaut, Cyrille 160
firearms and shootings 104–8, 121, 130n, 132n
fireworks depot explosion 115–16
Fitzgerald, M. 18, 187, 188–93
Flanagan, Sir Ronnie 175
flooding 115
followership 165, 169
foot-and-mouth disease 115
force managers 12, 57, 127, 128, 161
forensic accountancy 15
Fortuyn, Pim 57–8
Foundation for Police and Society (SMP) 54
France
 control paradigm 39
 haute police 33
 militarised policing 35
 police system 29–30
Free University of Amsterdam 198
French-Continental model 5, 6, 29–30, 36, 41, 51, 66
 control paradigm 39–40
Frydl, K. 70
Full Metal Jacket 139
Fyfe, N.R. 66

G
G20 131n
Gaddafi, President 130n
Garda Síochána 31
gedogen 55, 56
gemeentepolitie 6, 7, 51
Gendarmerie (*Marechaussee*) 6, 7, 26n, 36, 51
Genoa 108

Germany
 environmental activists 112
 Love Parade 111
 policing 30, 31
globalisation 23
gold commanders 119, 121–2, 123, 124, 125, 169
Goldstein, H. 178, 193
Gothenburg 108
governance
 autonomy 47–8
 Netherlands 12, 51, 125
 UK 2, 11–12, 50, 90, 151
 see also mayors; Police and Crime Commissioners
grass eating 85
Gray, J. 188
group think 143-4, 173
Guiliani, Rudy 47

H
The Hague
 cruise missile demonstrations 113
 Hofstad group siege 105
 IRA shooting 130n
 Nuclear Security Summit 108
 railway station shooting 106
Halstrom, L. 66
Haren 126–8
hate crime 75
haute police 33
hedonism 81
Heizel Stadium 79, 93n
Her Majesty's Inspectorate of Constabulary (HMIC) 128, 151, 156
Herald of Free Enterprise 116, 117
Herbert, S. 18, 194–6
high policing 32, 33–5, 73, 101–2
High Potential Development Scheme (HPDS) 152, 155, 172
Hillsborough Stadium disaster 90, 116, 118–20, 131n, 182
Hinton, M.S. 72
Hirsi Ali, Ayaan 58
Hofstad group 105
Home Office 12, 42, 50, 61, 151, 154
Home Secretary 50, 90, 98, 154
 Metropolitan Police 42, 48, 154
 NCA 15
 see also May, Theresa; Peel, Sir Robert
Homeland Security (US) 14
honest policing 181–3
Hook of Holland 109–10
Hornberger, J. 17
human relations management 145–6
human rights 23, 75, 183
Human Rights Act 23
Hungerford massacre 104, 121, 142

I

ICT (information and communication technology) 15
incident leadership 21, 22, 150
Independent Police Complaints Commission (IPCC) 88, 107, 120
India 72
industrial disputes 113–14
  miners' strike 63, 68n, 113–14, 131n
Innes, M. 63
institutional leadership 21, 150
integrity 75, 163, 183
Inter-Regional Crime Squad 56
IRA (Irish Republican Army) 26n, 34, 100, 101, 105, 121, 130n
Iranian Embassy siege 98–9
Ireland
  Garda Síochána 31
  Royal Irish Constabulary 30, 41
  unarmed police 104
IRT affair 56
Italy 30

J

Janis, E.L. 143
Japanese Red Army 129n
Johnson, Boris 48–9
Johnson, S. 136
Jordaan disturbances 36
just deserts 82
Juxta 199

K

Karabijnbrigades 36
Kelling, G.L. 61–2
Kelly, Ray 47
Kent Police 117
Kets de Vries, Manfred 133, 144
Kodz, J. 175
Kok, Wim 59
Korps Landelijke Politiediensten (KLPD) xiii, 57
Korps Politietroepen 35–6

L

Labour Party
  crime reduction 46, 192
  Hillsborough 119
  NPM 12–13
  policing 175
  Stevens Report 10
Landelijk Selectie en Opleidingsinstituut Politie (LSOP) ix, 159
lateral entry 13, 27n, 49, 152, 157
Lawrence, Stephen 10, 26n, 75, 90, 188
leadership 4, 19–22, 24, 133–44, 174–5, 185
  command and control 121–8
  major incidents 97–120, 129
  occupational culture 82
  pathology 134

US 129
leadership development 133
  agora 173, 187, 197–200
  England and Wales 151–6
  necessary ingredients 168–74
  Netherlands 156–68
  police 144–50
Libya 101, 130n
List Pim Fortuyn (LPF) 58
Loader, I. 46–7
Lockerbie 101, 130n
Loftus, B. 81
loggists 123–4
London
  2011 riots 37, 107, 114
  Balcombe Street siege 105
  Brixton riots 37, 46, 114, 184, 188, 189
  de Menezes shooting 107
  EDL demonstration 111
  G20 131n
  Iranian Embassy siege 98–9
  Mayor 48–9, 90
  Olympic Games 108
  Policing for London Study 18, 187, 188–93
  7/7 23, 62, 100–1, 107, 141
  table leg shooting 130n
  Troubles 100
  see also Metropolitan Police
Love Parade 111
low policing 32, 34–5

M

machismo 81
MACP (military aid to the civil power) 98–9
Madrid bombings 105–6
major incidents 95–7, 128–9
  command and control 121–9
  criminal investigations 102–4
  disasters/civil emergencies 114–20
  firearms and shootings 104–8
  leadership 141
  police organisation 78–9
  public order/security 108–14
  sieges 97–100
  terrorism 100–2
management cops 149, 163
Management of Disasters and Civil Emergencies course 116, 123
managerial accountability 88
Manchester 100, 104
Manning, Bradley (Chelsea) 73
Manning, P.K. 63–4, 183, 185, 196
Maple, Jack 62
Marechaussee 6, 7, 26n, 36, 51
Mark, Sir Robert 76, 136
May, Theresa 1, 4, 9, 12, 50–1, 151
Mayne, Sir Richard 41
mayors

disasters/civil emergencies 116
London 48–9, 90
Netherlands 7, 8, 12, 39, 51, 65, 90,
116, 125–7, 157
US 47–8
see also force managers
meat eating 85
media 16
accountability 88, 90
corruption 86
depictions of police chiefs 148–9
Hillsborough 119, 120
occupational culture 83
unconventional police chiefs 46, 176n
see also social media
mental health 73–4
Metropolitan Police Service (MPS, Met)
vii, 6, 13
accountability 42, 90
appointments 154–5
Asian tsunami 79
corruption 86
Emerging Leaders Scheme 155
founding 30, 40
Mayor 48–9
Menezes shooting 107
occupational culture 82, 136
police functions 72
Policing for London Study 18, 187,
188–93
Scotland Yard 176n
Special Patrol Group 37
Stephen Lawrence case 10, 26n, 75,
188
undercover officers 10
see also London
MH17 95–6, 131
militarised policing 30–1, 32, 35–8, 63
military 14
aid to the civil power 98–100
gendarmerie 30, 39
group think 143, 144
leadership 83, 134, 138–40
Marechaussee 6, 7, 26n, 36, 51
public order 40, 108, 140
Miller, D. 144
miners' strike 63, 68n, 113–14, 131n
Ministry of Defence (Netherlands) 26n,
51
Ministry of Security and Justice
(Netherlands) 8, 26n, 51, 57, 60,
127–8
Ministry of the Interior (Netherlands)
26n, 51, 53, 57, 60
Mintzberg, H. 135
Mobiele Eenheid (ME) ix, 36, 67n
MODACE course 116, 123
Morgan, G. 136
Moskos, P. 70, 92n
Murdoch, Rupert 86
Muslims 58

N
National Crime Agency (UK) 14, 15
National Police (*Nationale Politie*) xiii, 8,
18, 26n, 60, 61, 66, 90
Intelligence Departments 33
leadership xiii, 160–1, 162–8
professionalism 174–5
National Police Chiefs Council (NPCC)
(England and Wales) vii
National Police Improvement Agency
(NPIA) (England and Wales) 156,
175
National Police Internal Investigation
Department (Netherlands) 88
National Police Scotland vii, xi, 2, 5,
9, 176n
National Police Services Agency
(Netherlands) xiii, 57
neighbourhood policing (NOP) 60,
61, 62–3
neoliberalism 146–7, 193
Netherlands
accountability 88, 89, 90
agora 173, 187, 197–200
Amsterdam vice case 102–3
centralisation 12, 64, 65
command and control 125–8
community policing 187
corruption 86
criminal justice 54–5
disasters/civil emergencies 115–16
firearms and shootings 104, 105, 106
flooding 115
French-Continental model 66
high policing 33
leadership development 147, 156–68,
169
ME 67n
MH17 95–6
militarised policing 35–6
NPM 13
paradigms 39–40, 51–61, 178
police chiefs 47, 135–6, 173
police organisation 78
police stations 179
police system viii–ix, xi, xiii, 2, 5, 6–8,
13, 18, 26n, 30
political system 58–9
professionalism 174–5
public order/security 108–11, 113
Queen's birthday incident 141–2
reform fatigue 17
sieges 97–8
support roles 180
terrorism 100, 130n
women police officers 15, 27n
zero tolerance policing 11
Netherlands Police Academy (NPA)
157–8, 159
New Public Management (NPM)
12–13, 14, 69, 88, 146, 166

New Scotland Yard 9
New South Wales (NSW) Police 179
New York 43, 71, 85, 137
  mayor 47
  street cops and management cops 149
  zero tolerance policing 11, 57, 61–2,
  137
New Zealand 2, 25n, 30, 43, 104
News Corp 86
Neyroud, Peter xi, xii, 175
9/11 14, 23, 62, 96, 100, 138, 141
noble cause corruption 85, 86
Nordholt, E. 53
Northern Ireland
  accountability 88, 89
  armed police 104
  militarised policing 37
  Patten Report 9, 87, 89, 91, 183
  police system vii–viii, 2, 5, 9
  Special Branch 34
  Troubles 9, 26n, 37, 100, 130n
Norway
  Breivik 64, 104–5
  centralisation 64, 66
  unarmed police 104
Nuclear Security Summit (NSS) 108

O

Obama, President 2, 108, 181
occupational culture 79–83, 92
O'Connor, Denis 63, 175
O'Donnell, E. 92n
Olympic Games 108
operational leadership 161, 166
operations *see* major incidents
Orde, Sir Hugh 10, 175
order maintenance 25n, 40, 45, 184
organised crime xi, 11, 14–5, 23, 56 64,
  85, 102, 150, 184

P

Paddick, B. 15, 123, 154, 176n
para-military 37–8
paradigm 38–9, 177, 183–5
  beyond crime control 177–80
  British policing 45–51
  consent paradigm 40–5
  contested paradigms and fuzzy rhetoric
  60–4
  control paradigm 39–40, 177–8
  espoused paradigm 39, 45, 61
  Netherlands 51–60
  paradigm in use 45–6
Paris 107, 114
Patten Report 9, 87, 89, 91, 183
peace-keeping tasks *see* social tasks
Peel, Sir Robert 37, 40–1, 43, 49
Peel's Principles 5, 42–4
Police and Crime Commissioners
  (PCCs) 2, 9, 13–14, 48–9, 50, 90,
  151

police chiefs 76
  media representations 148–9
  Netherlands ix, 7, 8, 27n, 47, 55, 57,
  156–7, 161–2, 173, 174
  research on 135–6
  UK vii, 12, 42, 47, 48–9, 50, 68n,
  135, 136
  US 47–8
  see also leadership; leadership
  development
Police Community Support Officers 180
Police in evolution (CCPC) 59, 161–2,
  176n
Police Federation 9
Police National Assessment Centre
  (PNAC) 150, 153, 155, 172
Police Ombudsman for Northern Ireland
  88
police organisation 76–9, 91–2
police stations 179
policing 1–4, 25n
  accountability 87–91
  beyond cutting crime 177–80
  command and control 121–9
  deviance, corruption and enemy within
  84–7
  drivers of change 10–16
  honest policing 181–3
  leadership 4, 19–22, 24, 133, 137,
  140–4
  leadership development 144–50,
  151–74
  low and high policing, militarised
  policing 32–8
  major incidents 97–120
  matters of concern 23–5
  nature of 69–76
  in the Netherlands 6–8, 51–60
  occupational culture 79–83, 92
  paradigms 38–67, 183–5
  symbolic value 180–1
  system change 5
  in UK 9–10, 45–51
Policing for a better Britain (Stevens
  Report) 5, 10, 13, 14, 61, 175, 184
Policing for London Study (PFLS) 18,
  187, 188–93
Policy Studies Institute (PSI) 188
political intelligence 33, 34, 73
Politie Academie xiii, xiv, 160
Politie in Verandering (POS) 53, 59, 161
Portugal 30, 31
pragmatism 81
Prime Suspect 149
problem-oriented policing (POP) 17,
  53, 55, 60, 62, 63, 178–9, 193
procedural justice 180
professionalism 174–5, 182, 183, 185
Project X 126–8
Projectgroep Organisatie Structuren (POS)
  53, 59, 161

Provo movement 52
proximity policing 63, 66
  see also community policing
public order 108–14
public prosecutors 8, 39–40, 51, 56, 99, 125–6

Q
Quebec 34
Quinn, Robert 162, 166

R
Randstad 157
Reagan, Ronald 146
reassurance policing 63
recruitment 13, 49–50, 176n
  lateral entry 13, 27n, 49, 152, 157
Red Army Fraction 100
reflective practitioners 144, 147, 181–3
reform fatigue 17
Reiner, R. 50, 68n, 135
repressive policing 31
Reuss-Ianni, E.R. 149
Rijkspolitie 6, 7, 26n, 51
Rijksrecherche 88
riots 108
  2011 37, 107, 114
  Amsterdam 36, 52, 110–11, 114
  Brixton 37, 46, 114, 184, 188, 189
Robert M. case 102–3
Roermond 130n
Roth, J.A. 196
rough justice 82
Rowan, Sir Charles 41
Royal Canadian Mounted Police (RCMP) 13, 30
Royal Irish Constabulary (RIC) 30, 41
Royal Ulster Constabulary (RUC) 9, 34, 37
rule of silence 80

S
sacrifice 80
SAS (Special Air Services Regiment) 98–9, 140
Savage, S. 135
scandals 84–7
Scandinavia 2
Scarman Report 46, 188
SCC (Strategic Command Course) 155, 169, 171–2, 176n
Schön, Donald 136, 144
School for Police Leadership (SPL) xiii, 160
scientific management 145–6
Scotland
  crime 71
  police system vii–viii, xi, 2, 5, 9, 13, 64–5
Scotland Yard 176n
Scraton, P. 119

Seattle 18, 108, 187, 194–6
security 108–14, 184
security services 14, 33–5
sense of mission 80
Serious Organised Crime Agency (SOCA) 14–15
Serpico, Frank 92n
service delivery standards 14
7/7 23, 62, 100–1, 107, 141
Shearing, C. 25, 197
shootings 104–8, 130n, 132n
sieges 97–100, 105, 129n
silver commanders 118–19, 121, 122, 123–4
Skogan, W. 47–8, 70, 196
skyjackings 98, 130n
Smith, D.J. 188
Snowden, Edward 73
social isolation 81
social media 14, 16, 90–1, 126–8
social tasks 2–3, 4, 70, 73–4, 178–9
social welfare 184
Soham 103–4
solidarity 80
South Africa 31, 32, 37–8
South Malaccans 97–8, 100
South Yorkshire Police 118, 120
Soviet Union 31
Spain 30, 31, 105–6
Special Branch 33, 34
sponsored mobility 158–9
sport 48, 67n
Stansted Airport 98, 130n
Stasi 31
Steinberg, J. 32
Stenning, Philip 151, 172
Stevens Report 5, 10, 13, 14, 61, 175, 184
stop and search xi, 189, 190
Strategic Command Course (SCC) 152–3, 155, 169, 171–2, 176n
strategy cops 149
Strathclydification 65
Straver, R. 53
Straw, Jack 50
street cops 149
Submission 58
super-predatory behaviour 85
suspicion 81–2
Sussex Police 106–7
Sweden 64

T
Taylor, Frederick 145
Taylorisation 145, 185
Tenerife air disaster 142
Terpstra, J. 66
terrorism 14, 23, 100–2
Thames Valley Police 132n, 142
Thatcher, Margaret 68n, 98–9, 100, 131n, 134, 146

Thorbecke, Johan Rudolph 7
total policing 49
Townsend-Thorensen 117
train sieges 97–8
transitional model 31–2
transparency 50, 75, 87–8, 91, 149, 179, 182, 183
Trenchard Scheme 152, 176n
Troubles 9, 26n, 37, 100, 130n
trust 1, 17, 24, 71–2, 91, 181, 183, 184–5, 192
tunnel vision 143
Turkish Airlines crash 115
Twenty20 cricket 48, 67n

U

Ukraine 95–6
United Kingdom
  accountability 88–9, 90, 91
  armed police 104
  British policing model vii, 5, 40–51, 66
  centralisation 11–12
  civilians 15–16
  command and control 121–5, 128–9
  community policing 63
  corruption 86
  disasters/civil emergencies 72–3, 114–15, 116–20
  firearms and shootings 104, 106–7, 130n, 132n, 142
  flooding 115
  high policing 33, 34
  militarised policing 37, 63
  miners' strike 113–14
  National Crime Agency 14, 15
  New Public Management 12–13
  occupational culture 81
  paradigms 40–51, 60–1
  police chiefs vii, 12, 42, 47, 48–9, 50, 68n, 135, 136
  Police Community Support Officers 180
  police organisation 76, 77
  police systems vii–viii, xi, 5, 9–10, 13
  Policing for London Study 187, 188–93
  professionalism 175
  public order/security 108, 111–13
  punitive model 11
  reform fatigue 17
  Serious Organised Crime Agency 14–15
  sieges 98–9
  Soham 103–4
  terrorism 14, 23, 62, 100–2
  see also England and Wales; Northern Ireland; Scotland
United States
  Boston marathon 111
  change 2, 16–17, 25–6n

command and control 128–9
community policing 18, 53, 54, 187, 194–6
corruption 86, 92n, 93n
counter-terrorism 14, 23
criminal justice 5, 11
firearms and shootings 106
high policing 34
Homeland Security 14
leadership development 159, 170
militarised policing 35, 38
9/11 14, 23, 62, 96, 100, 138, 141
police chiefs 47–8, 136
police functions 72, 92n
police organisation 76
police research 4–5
police stations 179
trust 181
zero tolerance policing 11, 57, 60, 61–2, 137, 181
Useem, Michael 136, 138

V

values 3, 4, 13, 21-3, 43, 55, 63, 69, 79, 89, 91-2, 96, 129, 147, 161-169, 172-6, 180, 182-5
  agora 197
  leadership 3, 20, 129, 138, 161-9, 183, 185
  MH17 96
van der Vijver, C.D. 158
van Gogh, Theo 58, 62, 63
Volendam fire 115
Vollmer, August 5

W

Waco 143
Wales see England and Wales
Walker, S. 17
Wall, D. 135
Warwick University 151
Wassenaar 97
Weick, K. 142
Welten, Bernard xiii, 59, 131n, 197
West Midlands Police (WMP) 119
Wharton School 138–9
what works approach 3, 24–5
Wiarda, Jan 53
Wilson, O.W. 5
Wire, The 149
women 15, 27n, 151
  corruption 85–6
work avoidance 81, 93n
Working Group Police Leadership xiii, 160, 161, 162–4, 165–6

Z

Zeebrugge 116, 117
zero tolerance policing 11, 48, 57, 60, 61–2, 137, 181